Contents

To h

Worldly Leadership

Worldly Leadership

Alternative Wisdoms for a Complex World

Edited by

Sharon Turnbull

Peter Case

Gareth Edwards

Doris Schedlitzki

and

Peter Simpson

palgrave
macmillan

First published 2012 by
PALGRAVE MACMILLAN

Palgrave Macmillan in the UK is an imprint of Macmillan Publishers Limited, registered in England, company number 785998, of Houndmills, Basingstoke, Hampshire RG21 6XS.

Palgrave Macmillan in the US is a division of St Martin's Press LLC, 175 Fifth Avenue, New York, NY 10010.

Palgrave Macmillan is the global academic imprint of the above companies and has companies and representatives throughout the world.

Palgrave® and Macmillan® are registered trademarks in the United States, the United Kingdom, Europe and other countries.

ISBN 978–0–230–28470–8

This book is printed on paper suitable for recycling and made from fully managed and sustained forest sources. Logging, pulping and manufacturing processes are expected to conform to the environmental regulations of the country of origin.

A catalogue record for this book is available from the British Library.

A catalog record for this book is available from the Library of Congress.

10 9 8 7 6 5 4 3 2 1
21 20 19 18 17 16 15 14 13 12

Printed and bound in Great Britain by
CPI Antony Rowe, Chippenham and Eastbourne

To Susan, Anastacia and Lindsey (from Peter)
To Edwin and to my parents, Reg and Audrey (from Sharon)

Tables and Figures

Tables

Figures

Acknowledgements

We would like to thank The Leadership Trust in Ross-on-Wye, UK for hosting and supporting the Symposium that led to this book. Academics and practitioners from all over the world attended this event, and its legacy has been a worldwide interest in the continuation of Worldly Leadership research.

We are also very much indebted to the Bristol Centre for Leadership and Organizational Ethics at the University of West of England, as co-conveners and partners in the Worldly Leadership Symposium.

Without the organizational capabilities of Linda Keirby-Smith, this project might never have got off the ground. We are grateful for her tireless coordination.

Finally to the one hundred attendees of the Symposium who stimulated this book, and for their ongoing support and interest, we send our gratitude, and hope that they will find the result worth waiting for.

Foreword

There is a delicious paradox in the concept of worldly leadership: to be of any use at all, leadership must be properly indigenous, rooted in a particular time and place. Can such leadership also be generalized to the world at large? I suggest that the answer is yes, because the practice of leadership in a 'worldly' manner educes or draws out universally recognizable ideals of unity, truth, beauty and goodness, even while it is clothed in power, politics and petty instrumentalism. These ideals are ever present in worldly leadership; in fact, idealistic *otherworldliness* may be crucial for fully being in the world. If so, this book will be about manifesting worldly ideals: a proper manifesto.

Worldliness is, as much as anything else, a mindset, a turn of mind or way of thinking about the world 'out there', and about oneself and one's relations to it. Worldliness evokes the all-embracing sense of 'the whole world', and there is a subtle difference to 'global', which implies something more uniform. While 'globalization' speaks to the convergence of cultures and economies, worldliness refers to the tremendous multiplicity of ways of living, of meanings, priorities and choices; of cultural trajectories that hail from different histories and create different contexts in the present. A worldly person is experienced in life, in the affairs of the world, sophisticated, practical, temporal and earthly.

The world is one and many. Conceptually it is impossible to consider anything without a prior assumption of unity, the singleness of 'it', the object of thought. When we think of a world it is as a unity; if we conceive it as synonymous with a planet, we must immediately think of the many other planets, and thus a multiplicity of worlds united in Cosmos. A planet or globe is a singleness of shared space and time, in which a multitude of species and forms of consciousness exist, inextricably interdependent, yet each distinct.

From a human perspective, the world as 'one' emphasizes our common humanity, and makes possible concepts such as 'human nature'; the world as 'many' points to the multiplicity of locales, cultures, species, ecosystems, values.

This book is a celebration of this paradox, and exploration of its twists and turns, and most importantly, it expresses the most longed for quality of leadership: wisdom.

Jonathan Gosling

Contributors

Cigdem Asarkaya is a doctoral candidate in Management and Organization Studies, Management Department, Bogazici University, Turkey under the supervision of Dr Hayat Kabasakal. Asarkaya is a research assistant, lecturer and a project advisor at the MBA section of the Management Department, Istanbul Bilgi University, Turkey. She has a Masters from Otto-von-Guericke University, Magdeburg, Germany. Her research interests centre on organizational behaviour, with a focus on leadership, and employee attitudes and performance in organizations. She has published in a national journal, and has presented her research at a national conference and an international summit.

Roya Ayman is Professor and Head of the Industrial and Organizational Psychology division of the College of Psychology, Illinois Institute of Technology. She is an associate editor of *Journal of Management and Organization* and has served on editorial boards of several peer-reviewed journals such as *Leadership Quarterly, Applied Psychology: An International Review*, and *International Journal of Cross Cultural Management*. Her areas of research are leadership as it relates to culture, gender and diversity as well as work–family interface. In addition to her book *Leadership Theory and Research*, she has published more than 40 articles and chapters including an article on leadership: 'Why Gender and Culture Matter' in *American Psychologist* (2010).

Saba Ayman-Nolley is Professor and Chair of the Psychology Department at Northeastern Illinois University. Her PhD in Psychology is from the University of Chicago with a dual focus on Developmental and Educational Psychology. Her research has explored areas of non-verbal communication and creativity as they relate to Children's understanding of social concepts and roles. She has been a board member of the Jean Piaget Society and is currently its Vice-President of communications. In addition, she has over 40 presentations in the last decade. Some of her publications include a chapter on Children's Implicit Theory of Leadership, and articles including 'Socialization and Leadership Development in Children', 'A Piagetian Perspective on the Dialectic Process of Creativity', and 'Vygotsky's Perspective on the Development of Imagination and Creativity'.

Afshin Bassari lives in Tehran and has an MBA from The Bahai Institute of Higher Education (BIHE) in Iran. This chapter is based on his Masters thesis (2009). He was a teacher in BIHE (sociology department) for five years, and a business entrepreneur in Tehran, Iran.

Richard Bolden is Senior Lecturer in Leadership Studies at the University of Exeter Business School. He teaches on a range of undergraduate, postgraduate and executive programmes and his research explores topics including: distributed/shared leadership, leadership in higher education, cross-cultural leadership and leadership education for sustainability. He is on the editorial board of the journals *Leadership* and *Business Leadership Review* and has an extensive publication history, including numerous journal articles, book chapters, conference papers and research reports. He has recently co-authored the book *Exploring Leadership: Individual, Organization* (2011).

Tricia Calway is a practicing business consultant who runs Knowledgelink, a Northwest leadership and management consultancy. The practice specializes in strategic management, culture change, executive coaching and performance management. Tricia works with and through people to initiate change and is a keen exponent of innovation and people development. In 2000 she was appointed an Entrepreneurial Fellow by Lancaster University Management School and undertook five years research on SME learning. The research legacy has provided the basis of many Lancaster University entrepreneurial business programmes. She was one of the original 22 DTI's non-executive directors and has been a non-executive on several public and private sector boards in the Northwest. Her private sector boards centre on manufacturers and her passion for engineering and overseas development.

Peter Case is professor of management and organization studies at James Cook University (Townsville, North Queensland, Australia) and acting director of the Bristol Centre for Leadership and Organizational Ethics, University of the West of England. He served as general editor of *Culture & Organization* (2007–10) and is currently a member of the editorial boards of *Leadership, Leadership &Organizational Development Journal, Business & Society Review* and the *Journal of Management, Spirituality and Religion*. His research interests encompass the ethics of leadership, corporate social and environmental responsibility and organization theory. His books include *The Speed of Organization* (with S. Lilley and T. Owens, 2006) and *John Adair: The Fundamentals of Leadership* (with J. Gosling and M. Witzel, 2007). *Belief and Organization* (with H. Hopfl & H. Letiche) is due to appear later this year.

Gareth Edwards is Senior Lecturer in Organization Studies at Bristol Business School, University of the West of England. His current interests are in the application of ideas on aesthetics and leadership, community and dispersed theories of leadership. Before entering academia Gareth spent twelve years working for The Leadership Trust Foundation, a leadership and executive development company. He is a chartered psychologist and holds a PhD from the University of Strathclyde. Gareth has published in the *International Journal of Management Reviews, Organizations and People, Advances in Developing Human Resources, Journal of Sports Science and Medicine* and *Leadership and Organization Development Journal.*

Jialin Huang is a graduate student in Psychology at the Illinois Institute of Technology. Her research interests include psychometrics, statistics and research methodology and cultural differences. She has been involved in several projects involving measurement equivalence (ME), differential item functioning (DIF), structural equation modeling (SEM), emotional intelligence (EQ) and personality testing. In 2009, she received her Masters in Developmental and Educational Psychology from South China Normal University, Guangzhou, China.

Vanessa Iwowo teaches at the Centre for Leadership Studies, Exeter University. She obtained a Masters in Human Resource Development & Consulting with an emphasis on Management Learning & Leadership from Lancaster University, UK. Presently, she is working towards a PhD in Leadership Development, and her current research is centred on the Critical Evaluation of an ongoing Leadership Development Intervention within a Global Organization.

Hayat Kabasakal is Professor of Management and Organization Studies, Management Department, Bogazici University, Istanbul, Turkey. She served as the editor of Bogazici Journal: *Review of Social, Economic and Administrative Studies* and on the editorial boards of several international and national journals focusing on management and organization studies. Her research interests centre on organizational behaviour, with a focus on leadership, culture, and gender in organizations. Some of her research has been published in the *Journal of Strategic Management, Journal of Applied Psychology: An International Journal, Journal of World Business, International Journal of Social Economics and International Journal of Human Resource Management.*

Gaye Karacay-Aydin is a doctoral candidate and a research assistant at Management and Organization Studies, Management Department, Bogazici University, Turkey under the supervision of Dr Hayat Kabasakal. Karacay-Aydin has an MBA from London Business School. Her research area is organizational behaviour concentrated on leadership and gender in organizations. She has publications in some of the international journals and has presented her research at various international conferences.

Abdul Shakoor Khakwani is Assistant Professor at Bahauddin Zakariya University, Multan Pakistan. He holds Masters in Applied Social Research, Business Administration as well as in Strategic Studies. He has considerable international teaching and research experience in leadership, Asian and cross-cultural management. Shakoor Khakwani has been awarded various international fellowships. Since September 2007, as a post-graduate teaching assistant, he has been pursuing doctoral studies at the Department of Business and Management, Bristol Business School, University of West of England. His research centres on a comparative study of leadership and organizational culture in MNCs, public sector organizations and large family-owned businesses in Pakistan.

Philip Kirk is a leadership consultant with Operation Mercy, working in Tajikistan on community development in cross-cultural contexts with leaders from many parts of the world, including Central Asia. He was a Principal Lecturer in Organization Studies, Bristol Business School, University of the West of England until he retired in 2007. His interest is in the discovery and passionate exercise of leadership in life's roles. Publications include 'Leadership', in R. Greenwood and C. Pascoe (eds.) *Local Ministry: Story, Process and Meaning* (2006); 'Theatre and Masks' (with Robert French, 2008), in M. Broussine (ed.) *Creative Methods in Organizational Research;* 'African Leadership: Surfacing New Understandings through Leadership Development' (with Richard Bolden, 2009), *International Journal of Cross Cultural Studies* 9(1):69–86.

Liwen Liu is a doctoral student in Industrial–Organizational Psychology at the University of Illinois, Urbana-Champaign. She received her Masters in Personnel and Human Resource Development from Illinois Institute of Technology, where she worked with Professor Roya Ayman on cross-cultural leadership. Her research interests include psychological and educational measurement issues, leadership, and assessment centers. She has interned in several organizations, including the American Red Cross, the State Universities Civil Service System and the College Board.

Susan R. Madsen is the Orin R. Woodbury Professor of Leadership and Ethics in the Woodbury School of Business at Utah Valley University.

She is also an independent leadership and change consultant. She has been heavily involved for many years in researching the lifetime development of prominent women leaders. She has personally interviewed a host of women university presidents, US governors and international leaders and has had two books published on her results. Madsen has also published more than 55 articles in scholarly journals and presents often in local, national and international settings. She recently presented in sessions at the United Nations in New York and Geneva on women, leadership and education. Susan has received numerous awards for her teaching, research and service. Her research has focused on leadership, change, ethics and work–life integration.

Alan D. Mead is Assistant Professor in the College of Psychology at the Illinois Institute of Technology, where he teaches individual differences, psychometrics, structural equations modeling, meta-analysis, research methods and statistical analysis. He is also Scientific Advisor to IIT's Center for Research and Service, helping IIT's students with assessment-related projects such as surveying, testing, analysing jobs and validating selection tests. He sits on the 16PF research advisory panel for OPP Ltd and the editorial board for *Journal of Business and Psychology*. Since 1989, he has published 60 peer-reviewed articles, book chapters and conference presentations. Prior to joining the faculty at IIT, he spent several years as a consultant, research scientist and psychometrician. Alan received his PhD in Psychology from University of Illinois-Urbana in 2000 with a concentration on I/O psychology and a minor concentration on quantitative psychology.

Lynda L. Moore is Professor of Management and Senior Scholar for Global Gender and Inclusive Leadership at Simmons School of Management in Boston, MA, USA. Moore teaches undergraduate, graduate and executive courses in Cross-Cultural Management and Culturally Intelligent Leadership, Gender, Diversity and Leadership, Globalization and Diversity, and Cross-Cultural Comparative Analysis of Women Leaders. She also teaches at the Indian School of Business in Hyderabad. Moore's research and numerous publications focus on women in global leadership, gender, diversity and leadership across cultures and the development of culturally sensitive leadership models. She has conducted research on women leaders in the UAE and India and remains interested in studies of women leaders in the Middle East and Southeast Asia regions. Moore is a faculty Affiliate of the Center for Gender in Organizations at Simmons, recipient of a Fulbright fellowship to the UAE and was appointed a Fellow of the Leadership Trust foundation, UK.

Behice Ertenu Saracer is currently teaching Management at the Management Department, Bogazici University, Istanbul Turkey. She earned her PhD in Organizational Behaviour from Marmara University, Istanbul, Turkey; her BA in Management, Masters in European Studies from Bogazici University. Her topics of interest are leadership and creativity, with a focus on corporate culture and learning organizations. Parallel to her academic studies in these areas, she is involved in consultancy services in organizational development and design to major corporations based in Turkey and in the Middle East.

Doris Schedlitzki is Senior Lecturer in Organization Studies at Bristol Business School. She holds a Masters and DPhil in Management Studies from the Said Business School, University of Oxford. Her research focuses on organizational leadership with specific interest in leadership identities, leadership discourse and leadership construction, taking a comparative, cultural perspective. Doris has published on the topic of leadership in journals such as *Leadership, Scandinavian Journal of Management* and *Leadership and Organization Development Journal*.

K. R. Sekhar is Vice President – Procurement, for Bayer Group of Companies in India, which includes Bayer Cropscience, Bayer Bioscience, Bayer Health Care and Bayer Material Science. He also heads the Logistics and Distribution function at Bayer CropScience Ltd responsible for the Demand fulfillment, warehousing, transportation and C&F operations. Leadership and Sustainability issues are his passion, and he is working on several plans for contributing to leadership development and sustainability aspects in India.

Dr. Peter Simpson is Reader in Organisation Studies at Bristol Business School, University of the West of England. He is Director of MBA and Executive Education and Deputy Director of the Bristol Centre for Leadership and Organisational Ethics. His current areas of interest are spirituality, psychodynamics and complexity applied to issues of organisational leadership and strategic change.

Vasilisa Takoeva is a PhD candidate at the School of Business, Management Department, University of Birmingham, under the supervision of Professor Steve Kempster. Previously, she attained her Masters at Lancaster University Management School in Human Resource Development and Consulting and completed an internship at the Centre for Applied Leadership Research, The Leadership Trust Foundation.

Sharon Turnbull is an independent academic and Visiting Professor at the University of Gloucestershire Business School and the University of

Worcester Business School; she is also Senior Research Fellow at Lancaster University Management School. Sharon was Director of the Centre for Applied Leadership Research at The Leadership Trust Foundation in Ross-on-Wye, UK until January 2011. She has published two books: *Your MBA with Distinction – A Systematic Approach to Success in your Business Degree* (with C. Gatrell, 2002) by and *Critical Thinking in Human Resource Development*, (edited with C. Elliott). Her current research interests are global and worldly leadership, responsible leadership and leadership development.

Onyekachi Wambu was educated at the universities of Essex and Cambridge. He worked as a print and television journalist, editing *The Voice Newspaper*, and working as a senior producer/director at the BBC. He also worked as head of Information and Communications at the charity, African Foundation for Development. African leadership and the challenges around it has been at the centre of much of his journalism and charity work. His publications include *Under the Tree of Talking: Leadership for Change in Africa* (ed., 2007), and *Empire Windrush: 50 Years of Writing about Black Britain* (1998, edited with Victor Gollancz). He will soon undertake a doctorate study into the leadership style of Bernie Grant, arguably the most important black British politician of the last 50 years.

David Weir is Head of the School of Business, Leadership and Enterprise at University Campus Suffolk and Affiliate Professor at ESC Rennes and a Visiting Professor at Lancaster University Management School and the Bristol Centre for Leadership and Organizational Ethics. He has worked for many years in the fields of intercultural management, with especial concerns in the Arab Middle East. His most recent books are *Critique to Action*, a collection of essays on ethical issues in business and management, and *The Gulf States After Oil*, both co-edited with Nabil Sultan of Liverpool Hope University.

Part I
Worldly Leadership Frames

1
Introduction: The Emerging Case for Worldly Leadership

Peter Case, Sharon Turnbull and Shakoor Khakwani

This book is the first of its kind to bring together non-western, indigenous and eastern perspectives on leadership. Leadership theory has for too long been the exclusive domain of western academics developing leadership theories from the perspective of western institutions. Often these theories remain detached from practical action. We know that much leadership wisdom lies outside this dominant Western academy, but that this wisdom is rarely profiled or published. We believe that this must change. *Worldly leadership* calls for a pooling of the combined leadership wisdoms from all parts of the globe – whether these are contemporary or ancient wisdoms. We fear that as the world becomes increasingly homogenous as a result of the 'flattening' impact of the internet and advancing global communication technology, the existing dominant voices may drive out the leadership wisdoms of minority, indigenous and ancient wisdoms. It does not have to be so. With these new technologies, an opportunity now presents itself for leaders across the world to share and combine the leadership knowledge and practice that exist in many corners of the world: wisdoms that would otherwise remain unknown outside their community. Ancient philosophies can enable us to reframe and rethink the enormous challenges of responsible, ethical and sustainable leadership of the world. The majority of leaders across the globe today have been conditioned in some way by western and US-centric leadership theories and methodologies. This thinking has been driven through our global business schools and business cultures, often to the exclusion of non-western traditions and cultures and the valuable insights and wisdom these may have to offer.

Together with colleagues from around the world, we launched a leadership research project which seeks to deepen understanding of leadership wisdom from different cultures and societies around the world.

This leadership wisdom lies hidden in ancient, indigenous societies and cultures and is a highly dispersed body of knowledge, which, we argue, has hitherto been under-researched. We believe that a 'worldly leader' today needs more than western / US-centric leadership theories, and have set out to uncover these alternative wisdoms. This book profiles non-western leadership wisdoms, and draws from papers presented at the first Worldly Leadership Symposium held at The Leadership Trust in Ross-on-Wye in 2009.

What is meant by 'global leadership'? To what kind of practices might this concept refer and what are the implications of such practices? Scholars and practitioners who believe in the 'globality' of management and leadership relate global leadership to multiple organizational themes such as change, culture, performance, values, globalization, environment, vision and strategy. What concerns us in this book is how leadership is *practised* in contemporary organizations and whether it is meaningful to speak of 'global leadership' at all.

In common parlance global leadership may mean looking for a standardized 'one best way' to lead or expedite authority which is applicable across organizations, industries, sectors, nations and cultures. However, we question whether it is possible or desirable to search for such a panacea. The very idea of global leadership seems to have an overbearing positive and normative intention. Its discourse seldom addresses the shadow side of globalization or the problems, paradoxes and grey areas associated with leading complex organizations. For us, there is an inefficacy to the concept of global leadership as, in practice, it is difficult to restrict the degree of diversity associated with leadership or contain it within a universal normative programme (Alvesson & Deetz, 2000).

'Global leadership' is of course a label that has been attached to numerous differing concepts for as long as economic globalization has been on the world agenda. It is a contested term. Not only is *leadership* a word with countless definitions and interpretations, but globalization has a multitude of meanings as well. Mendenhall et al. (2008) traces global leadership back to the emergence of international business as a separate field of study in the 1950s and 1960s. The 1970s then saw an increase in studies of expatriate managers working in cultures different from their own. It was not however, he suggests, until the 1990s that the term globalization came to mean more than this, and to focus on the increased complexity, difference, interdependence and ambiguity that managers were starting to face as a result of these shifts on the world economic stage.

A plethora of books and articles have been published on the subject, seeking to identify what this means for both research and practice, along with a range of offerings for how to develop these individual and organizational competences. Indeed, in March 2008 an internet discussion on the Network of Leadership Scholars discussion site took up the question, 'Is there such a thing as global leadership?', prompting animated debate over a period of a few days, and demonstrating the lack of clarity and diversity of views that this term engenders. Some of the respondents felt that global leadership is about universally endorsed leader attributes. For others, global leadership represents a sub-field of leadership differing from traditional leadership due to the demands of globalization.

Nevertheless, the vast majority of research studies conducted in the field of global leadership have been seeking to define a set of global leadership competencies, and there are many such studies. Jokinen (2005) set out to draw together these studies to establish a more integrative framework, suggesting that 'increasing understanding of different aspects of globalization and interrelationships of various factors and their changes will help organisations to meet the new challenges brought about by globalization, whether their primary operation environment is domestic, international or global'. However, she concludes that there is little agreement among researchers on what constitutes these global competencies, or about what competencies are vital for global leadership, because the definition of global leadership is so unclear. She also points out that much of the early research was focussed solely on expatriates, a much narrower perspective than the one adopted by many researchers today.

The quest for an understanding of the term often seems circular in nature with Moran and Riesenberger (1994), for example, suggesting that for globalization, one of the competencies that managers should have is 'a global mindset' which sounds like a tautology. Indeed, many of the competencies identified for global leaders do not sound dissimilar to the competencies required by domestic leaders. For example, 'global literacies' are defined by Rosen et al. (2000) as 'personal, social, business and cultural literacy'. Another study (Bueno & Tubbs, 2004) has proposed (1) communication (2) motivation to learn (3) flexibility (4) open-mindedness (5) respect for others and (6) sensitivity as the key global leadership competencies. Kets de Vries and Florent-Treacy (2002) take the perspective that global leadership competencies are indeed the same as domestic leadership competencies, but suggest that global leaders are ones who 'retain these capabilities even in completely unfamiliar situations' and they label this ability: 'emotional global intelligence'. Many of the studies that have been conducted to date, however, are limited by being primarily based on a narrow conception of global leader as expatriate leader, or are based on a homogenous sample of data from one country.

Osland's (2008) comprehensive survey of the global leadership literature identified 56 global leadership competencies (a list too long to be useful, as she herself notes). She has distilled these into six core categories of (1) cross cultural relationship skills (2) traits (3) global business expertise (4) global organizing expertise (5) cognitive orientation and (6) visioning. She recognizes that few leaders live up to these ideals, however, and points to the need for further research, specifically into how these competencies are best developed in leaders.

Clearly the term global leader is highly contested, and the competencies required are either too diverse or too broad to assist in shaping a curriculum for global leadership development. Given this confusion, this book seeks to go beyond the competency debate to uncover alternative ways to conceptualize global leadership, and then to reflect on the implications for leadership development. Moving away from the psychological and behavioural perspectives, and adopting alternative lenses from organizational theory, the idea of 'worldly leadership' is explored as an alternative way of thinking about this phenomenon.

The worldly leadership proposition

We propose that 'worldly leadership', based on the 'worldly mind-set' advanced by Gosling and Mintzberg (2003) may be a more fruitful way of conceptualizing international leadership processes. As they have noted, worldliness contrasts with the rapidly growing globalization discourse which 'sees the world from a distance that encourages homogenization of behaviour … A closer look, however, reveals something quite different: This globe is made up of all kinds of worlds' (Mintzberg, 2004, p. 304). The worldly mindset, therefore, is not globalization repackaged, but something quite different that results in the emergence of a different conception of the leadership process.

Worldly leadership can be analysed in terms of three dimensions as follows: (1) the assessment of leadership development processes pervasive in today's corporate world; (2) the evaluation of global leadership from a critical management perspective; and, (3) an appreciation of non-western or indigenous leadership constructs and narratives.

Leadership development

How is global leadership preached and practised in organizations? By 'preaching' we refer to leadership as represented in mainstream academic textbooks and in professional development events organized by management trainers and consultants. Our argument here is that although global leadership may form part of a discourse for education and training, this rendition bears little resemblance to actual practices. Our concern is to demonstrate that even if leadership is commonly construed in global terms, its practice is invariably culturally specific, situation bound and, by nature, emergent. We draw inspiration for our critique of leadership training from observation and a firsthand account of an international training programme on global leadership organized by South Asian International Conference (SAICON) 2008.

The training programme in question was more than five hours long and deliberately incorporated within a three-day international conference on globalization entitled as 'Globalization and Change: Issues, Concerns and Impact' held in Pakistan. This event was hosted jointly by the Association of Global Business Advancement (AGBA), the Higher Education Commission Pakistan and COMSATS University, Islamabad. It was attended mostly by senior executives working in multinationals and prestigious large public and private sector organizations in Pakistan. A few academics who were there to attend the conference also participated in the training session. There were three lead trainers facilitating the event: one academic-turned-trainer (of Pakistani origin) from George Washington University and two professional business consultants, one of Indian origin and other of East Asian descent. One of the authors, Khakwani, attended this session with a view to learning more about the dynamics of corporate training and leadership development in the Pakistani context. Though the sole focus of all three lead trainers was to promote and preach the globality of leadership, looking beneath the surface somewhat revealed a different set of phenomena. It appeared that the success of this type of training programme depended not so much on grand or abstract concepts such as those of 'global' or 'cultural leadership' as on how effectively trainers were able to contextualize and make participants realize, feel and interpret the programme contents in relation to their own *practices*.

Global leadership – a transcendental rhetoric

Here we would like to highlight some participant observations made during the training workshop. First, the concept of global leadership development as promoted in this training was more of a superficial rhetoric than an informing ideology. For instance, leadership was promoted as a panacea for all organizational ills, and is considered as the 'magic wand'. The wordiness of the following claim, used in the slides by the academic-turned-trainer in the leadership programme, is illustrative in this respect, 'Leadership is about shaping a new way of life. To do that you must take risks and accept responsibility for making change happen'. In today's corporate world, leaders are typically lauded for their abilities to manage change, resolve conflict and innovate in shaping organizational life. Hence, the dominant language or discourse is making things or change happen. For instance, 'A leader has to be able to change an organization that is dreamless and visionless ... someone's got to make a wake up call.' The crucial assumption in the above extracts is the leaders' ability to make change happen in a very decisive and assertive way, thereby leading to some kind of predictable, deterministic or, indeed, formulaic way. This kind of discourse is also reflected in some of the academic literature. Trompenaars and Hampden-Turner, for example, claim that 'What increasingly happens is that leaders manage culture by fine tuning values and dilemmas and then that culture runs the organization' (2001, p. 2).

To develop such abilities or competencies among trainees, trainers in this field make use of popular and archetypal analytical frameworks which can be located in two categories: (1) leadership theory, and (2) cross-cultural analysis. Within the first category the most commonly observed frameworks are Michigan School-inspired 'people' versus 'task' orientation of leaders of the 2 by 2 matrix form, producing four 'leadership styles' (e.g. Blake and Mouton's managerial grid consisting of Country Club, Authoritarian, Impoverished and Team leader). Another popular framework, though not mentioned in this particular training session but generally used as the source of leadership development curriculum, is the concept of situational leadership (e.g. Hersey & Blanchard, 1988). This approach focuses on behavioural modification, and rests again on four leadership styles: Telling, Selling, Participating and Delegating. Within the same category of analysis, the recent focus of corporate trainers has shifted towards transaction and transformational leadership frameworks. The imperative here is to make participants aware of, or learn attributes associated with, team leadership, participating and delegating and transformational leadership. So, whatever the framework used, the intention of trainers is to make participants realize that there are universal 'best practices' or 'ideal' modes of leadership which, moreover, can be learnt. During the session attended, participants were given further exercises or case studies through which they could diagnose, assess and score themselves and then make comparisons with others.

The second form of analysis employed was that of cross-cultural frameworks. Until recently the Hofstede (1991) analytical framework has been relied on in corporate training to sensitize leaders to differences and distinctions within or across nations. However, it is the House (2005) framework which is increasingly being considered as state of the art by trainers and used as a comprehensive tool for cross-cultural analyses. Both approaches assume that successful leadership is something global and universal in nature. Once leaders are aware and mindful of a finite number of variations in leadership styles they can readily adjust or adapt to any cross-cultural scenario. In this respect, House's eight ideal types can be viewed as an extension of Hofstede's four or five types. According to these approaches, global leadership entails equipping a global mindset with conceptual tools and frameworks to deal with all possible admixtures of international culture. In the training programme we observed, the first speaker was an academic of Pakistani origin trained in Anglo-US academic settings who proceeded to introduce conceptual aspects of global leadership. This was followed by a speaker of Indian origin who, the audience was told, worked with 'leading multinational firms' and another speaker from East Asia. Interesting to note was that all three were focusing and preaching knowledge and practices which were more Western than Asian in perspective. The two speakers were interested in raising fundamental questions: how do you profile your self, your organization, your city, state or nation? Fascinating to observe was the scope of the training remit – overarching, all inclusive and exhaustive – a phenomenon referred to by Jacob (2005) as that of an 'extensive global sweep'.

Having introduced House's ideal types of leader the trainers moved on to the acquisition of leadership skills. They claimed that only 10 per cent of leaders are born, so the rest have to rely on an MBA education in order to acquire and develop appropriate skill sets. While profiling leading multinationals like IBM, SONY and GE, the trainers made simplistic comparisons between leadership styles and brand images of these organizations. It was rather shocking to find individuals, organizations (like Sony, IBM and GE), countries (like USA, China, Pakistan, India and Singapore) and even cities (Islamabad, Karachi, Dubai and New York) analysed using this single instrument.

Such cultural profiles of organizations are flawed in many respects. For example, they make naïve assumptions with respect to the predictability of human conduct and interaction, reduce leadership skills to stereotypes and promote static models of what are extremely complex processes. Another significant theme of the training throughout was the imperative to search for universal leadership styles that were globally valid. This phenomenon seems consistent with what Alvesson and Sveningsson (2003a, p. 1435) refer to as 'the extra-ordinarization of the mundane'. For example, participants in this training responded enthusiastically to the eight ideal types in part because the typology was dressed in a language that at once took it out of the quotidian yet remained entirely accessible to a non-academic audience. Though conceptually flawed and shallow, the intelligent and sophisticated *presentation* of these materials generated participant engagement.

Based on informal (unstructured) conversations with participants after the event, the training was 'a success' from their perspective. There are several reasons, we conjecture, why the training was viewed this way. First, the fact that all three trainers were of Asiatic origin meant that they had greater ability to locate the training programme contents in more meaningful cultural contexts. Although dealing ostensibly with global 'leadership', the impressive skill of the trainers lay in their ability to make the contents appear to work in an Asian milieu. The trainers made selective use of the conditional 'if' and adjunct 'but' to consciously and judiciously shift position, if required to do so, and hence move with the ebb and flow of participants' sentiments and reactions to the material.

Second, the trainers were enriching the programme and description of 'ideal' leaders by telling 'real life' stories relating to specific individuals, events and corporations. Third, the trainers coined terms and made extensive use of metaphors and analogies. For instance the eight ideal types, it appeared, were a condensation of 21 types of leadership styles or behaviour which were relatively mundane and easy for the lay person to understand. The eight-leader typology was sufficiently open ended and ambiguous so as to combine maximum coverage of leadership behaviour with the possibility of multiple interpretations. The use of examples from 'real life' corporations, for instance, freely talking and analysing the successes of organizations like Google, IBM and Sony operating globally in countries like the United States, China, Pakistan, India and Singapore, also lent practitioner credibility to the training event. Hence the success of professional leadership development trainers, based on this anecdotal experience, would seem to lie in their communication strategy; that is, their ability to contextualize, subjectivize and develop an art of conversation which entailed relating ideal typical models in a selective but general way while allowing participants to see and interpret them in their own *particular* way.

A Critical Management Studies perspective

The knowledge generated by corporate trainers and consultants is most of the time embedded within a mainstream functionalist perspective within the leadership field. This disposition leads us to examine the concept of global leadership from a critical management studies (CMS) perspective and to question the 'totalizing' or 'hegemonic' aspirations of functionalist accounts. A weakness of mainstream leadership studies is that it characterizes leaders as change agents (charismatic, transformational, visionary) or as possessing unique communication expertise, which emphasis tends to downplay issues of power, conflict and politics. CMS scholars tend to approach leadership phenomena from a more skeptical stance, understanding it to be inherently *political* and involving a dynamic interchange of values (Zoller & Fairhurst, 2007).

The position taken by the mainstream normative researchers seems quite paradoxical as, on the one hand, they take note of increasing challenges faced by leaders in today's corporate world – complex organizations are becoming more virtual, global and diverse in their outreach and performance (De Vries, 2009), for instance – while, on the other hand, they infer from this complexity that it is imperative to search for leadership styles which are universally valid across organizations, cultures and countries. For instance, De Vries, Professor of Leadership Development at INSEAD, in commenting on the leader/follower relationship recently claimed, 'Leaders get the best out of followers and followers get the best out of leaders' (2009). Scholars and researchers might therefore ask or search for what this best is? And in their search for the best they take any one dimension of leadership and laud it for its perceived global pervasiveness thus overriding matters of diversity and local and cross-cultural differences. De Vries' proposition contains a lofty aspiration insofar as it implies an ideal state of affairs for both leader and follower. It is as if an ideal leader and ideal follower can do no wrong. Such a position is, we suggest, based on a fallacious ontology as it denies varying cultural versions of leadership which reflect local praxis. Moreover, this also tends to deny outright the efficacy of the concept of equifinality whereby similar results may be achieved from different initial conditions and in many different ways (a view that is widely accepted even by advocates of functionalism and systems theory).

Similarly, one can also observe two opposing swings from research on identity literature differentiating leader and manager, as prompted by Sveningsson and Alvesson's (2003, p. 1188) observation that the manager's identity has become a negative or 'anti-identity' or a 'not-me position' (see also Sveningsson & Larsson, 2006) while the rhetoric of leadership and leadership development processes presents the leader's identity as predominantly idealized, grandiose, rhetorical and elusive (Alvesson & Sveningsson, 2003b; Barker, 2001).

In the same way, for Heifetz and Laurie (1997) there is an important distinction to be drawn between technical work (known problems with known solutions) and adaptive work (unknown or uncertain problems that require a process of creative solutions or problem solving). The former comes within the purview of management while the latter within that of leadership. In other words management is to look for technical, routinized or formalized aspects of organizational processes while leadership forms more of a flexibly creative and non-formal basis of organizational processes. This makes organizational leadership processes inherently fluid, dynamic, immanent and emergent while, by contradistinction, management is relatively deterministic, planned and static in its orientation. Our point is that it is important to look at organization and its constitutive nature (i.e. its *context* – culture, technology, industry, size and stage of development, etc.) from the point of view of leadership or managerial choices. If we accept that today's environment is predicated and characterized by chaos, uncertainty, diversity and complexity it follows that we should look to understand leadership (or leadership development) processes as emergent, practice-based and driven by immanent concerns.

Our argument is further supported by the distinction that Gibbons et al. (1994) make between 'Mode 1' and 'Mode 2' forms of knowledge production. Mode 1 derives largely from academic and investigator-led inquiry whereas Mode 2 knowledge is more context-driven and emergent from practice. Leadership *discourse* is often perceived by the business community to lack relevance and is accused of being overly abstract and esoteric (Knights, 2008, p. 537), hence conforming predominantly to the Mode 1 form. For example, Knights claims that:

> The rhetoric in business and management education and research has been raised to such a level that it tends to lose its relevance for practicality and pedagogical significance even in today's world where business communities are driven by knowledge and information oriented society. (2008, p. 537)

In contrast to Mode 1, Mode 2 approaches are seen to generate knowledge that is *worldlier* and closely linked to the context of application and practice. Leadership entails working with limited understanding and hence, arguably, should not be viewed or treated in overly heroic terms or imbued with romantic attributes (Sveningsson & Larson 2006). However, in the opinion of Monin and Bathurst (2008) leadership literature is replete with 'best of best' attributes and makes frequent recourse to what Burke (1980) refers to as 'god-terms'. A worldly approach to the field would attempt to reclaim leadership from the stratospheric realm it is imagined to inhabit.

As we have attempted to argue thus far, contemporary academic concepts, models and theories in leadership research and those deployed in the development field by trainers and consulting practitioners are implicitly guided by transcendental ideals. To a large extent such abstracting tendencies are a legacy of the Western intellectual tradition (Hadot, 2006; Jullien, 2004). By contrast, our intention in this book is to tease out alternative ways of approaching leadership that are, in an important sense, *worldlier*. In our search for such a perspective we look towards ideas and evidence that derive from non-western traditions.

Ideas and evidence from non-western research

There is already an emerging appreciation of the fact that leadership studies might be enhanced by considering approaches, modes of understanding and enactment that find their origins in communities and societies that differ from those of the west. Traditional Western perspectives on leadership are, at the margins, thus being complemented by insights derived from wider anthropological (Jones, 2005, 2006), postcolonial (Banerjee, 2004; Banerjee & Linstead, 2001,) and non-western studies of leadership phenomena (Case, 2004; Case & Gosling, 2007; Chia, 2003; Jullien, 2004; Senge et al., 2007; Warner & Grint, 2006). Case (2004), for instance, examines the relevance of Buddhist philosophy to contemporary organizational theory, suggesting that 'wholeness of vision' and 'detachment from partial knowledge' may have an important part to play in the conceptualization of organizational processes. Similarly, Senge et al. (2007, p. 195) refer to 'unbroken wholeness' as presenting a challenge to cornerstone doctrine of western science.

The structure of this book

In Part 1, chapters 1 to 6 introduce a range of worldly leadership 'frames'. Schedlitzki discusses the importance of language and linguistic differences in understanding how different cultures view leadership. Bolden and Kirk focus on identity and collective sense-making in leadership development programmes, and discuss how leadership development can act as a catalyst for wider social change. Iwowo picks up a similar theme, contrasting the internationalization of leadership development with a more considered project of 'worldly leadership development'. Madsen applies a worldly leadership lens to bring new thinking to the development of women leaders. Edwards applies constructs of community using a worldly leadership lens.

In Part 2, we include a number of chapters which apply a range of methodologies to worldly leadership research across different parts of the globe, including many fast developing but very different economies such as China, the Middle East, Pakistan, Nigeria, India and Russia. Liu, Ayman and Ayman-Nolley use implicit leadership theory (ILT) to explore perceptions of gender and grade in leadership from the perspective of Chinese children. Ayman et al. apply a similar methodology to examine ILT in Iranian people. Weir discusses leadership in the Arab Middle East, proposing that there is much to learn from traditions beyond the dominant western paradigm. Moore continues our discussion of leadership in the Middle Eastern context drawing on a case study of women business leaders in the UAE. Khakwani and Case demonstrate the limitations of the global leadership paradigm through their study of indigenous Pakistani leadership processes. Saracer et al. report on research into the meaning of 'authentic leadership' in five Middle Eastern countries while Wambu's chapter offers a different perspective on leadership, a close-up study of leadership within the Igbo people of southern Nigeria. These studies are contrasted with Turnbull et al.'s study of the different faces of Indian leadership based on interviews with a number of entrepreneurs representing different identities and generations. The final chapter, by Takoeva and Turnbull, reports on a similar qualitative study conducted in Russia which focuses on the multiple and overlapping leadership identities of Russian leaders across a number of sectors.

Through the chapters in this book, we seek to demonstrate that the construct of 'worldly leadership' challenges most definitions of global leadership and the normative frameworks usually adopted. The research discussed in this book goes beyond the mainstream focus on individual competencies to include leadership as networked processes of interconnectedness and boundary-spanning activities. It goes beyond the emphasis on top leaders to include notions of shared leadership and the importance of giving a voice to the disenfranchised or marginalized.

This book has significant implications for leadership development. The experience of the contributors to this book suggests that to develop a worldly leadership mindset requires deep immersion and encounters at close proximity in new and 'alien' settings, and with leaders who themselves exemplify and embody local wisdoms and leadership traditions. These experiences, based on shared reflective sense-making within culturally rich and diverse groups, combine to produce transformational learning at many levels and serve as exemplars of new forms of leadership practice.

References

Alvesson, M. and Deetz, S. 2000. *Doing Critical Management Research*. London: Sage.

Alvesson, M. and Sveningsson, S. 2003a. Managers Doing Leadership: The Extra-Ordinarization of the Mundane, *Human Relations* 56(12): 1435–59.

Alvesson, M. and Sveningsson, S. 2003b. The Great Disappearing Act: Difficulties in Doing 'Leadership', *The Leadership Quarterly* 14: 359–81.

Banerjee, S. B. 2004. Reinventing Colonialism: Exploring the Myth of Sustainable Development, *Situation Analysis* 4 (Autumn): 95–110.

Banerjee, S. B. and Linstead, S. 2001. Globalization, Multiculturalism and Other Fictions: Colonialism for the New Millennium?, *Organization* 8(4): 711–50.

Barker, R. 2001. The Nature of Leadership, *Human Relations* 54(4): 469–94.

Bueno, C. M. and Tubbs, S. L. 2004. Identifying Global Leadership Competencies: An Exploratory Study, *Journal of American Academy of Business* 5(1/2): 80–7.

Burke, K. 1980. *The Rhetoric of Religion*. London: University of California Press.

Case, P. 2004. The Blind People and the Elephant. In Y. Gabriel (ed.) *Myths, Stories, and Organizations: Premodern Narratives for Our Times*. Oxford: Oxford University Press, pp. 49–65.

Case, P. and Gosling, J. 2007. Wisdom of the Moment: Pre-modern Perspectives on Organizational Action, *Social Epistemology* 21(2): 87–111.

Chia, R. 2003. From Knowledge-Creation to Perfecting Action: Tao, Basho and Pure Experience as the Ultimate Ground of Performance, *Human Relations* 56(8): 953–81.

De Vries, M. K. 2009. The Leadership Circle. INSEAD newsletter, [http://knowledge.insead.edu/TheLeadershipcircle081215.cfm?vid=157, accessed 6th Feb 2009].

Gibbons, M., Limoges, C., Nowotny, H., Schwartzman, S., Scott, P. and Trow, M. 1994. *The New Production of Knowledge: The Dynamics of Science and Research in Contemporary Societies*. London: Sage.

Gosling, J. and Mintzberg, H. 2003. The Five Minds of a Manager, *Harvard Business Review* 81(11): 54–63.

Hadot, P. 2006. *The Veil of Isis*. London: Harvard University Press.

Hersey, P. and Blanchard, K. H. 1988. *Management and Organizational Behavior: Utilizing Human Resources*. Englewood Cliffs, NJ: Prentice-Hall.

Heifetz, R. A. and Laurie D. L. 1997. The Work of Leadership, *Harvard Business Review* Jan/Feb, 75(1): 124–34.

Hofstede, G. 1991. *Cultures and Organizations: Software of the Mind.* London: McGraw Hill.

House, R. 2005. *Culture, Leadership and Organizations: The GLOBE Study of 62 Societies.* London: Sage.

Jacob, N. 2005. Cross-cultural Investigations: Emerging Concepts, *Journal of Organizational Change Management* 18(5): 514–28.

Jokinen, T. 2005. Global Leadership Competencies: A Review and Discussion, *Journal of European Industrial Training* 29(2/3): 199–261.

Jones, A. 2005. The Anthropology of Leadership: Culture and Corporate Leadership in the American South, *Leadership* 1(3): 259–78.

Jones, A. 2006. Developing What? An Anthropological Look at the Leadership Development Process, *Leadership* 2(4): 481–98.

Jullien, F. 2004. *A Treatise on Efficacy.* Honolulu: University of Hawai'i Press.

Kets de Vries, M. F. R. and Florent-Treacy, E. 2002. Global Leadership from A to Z: Creating High Commitment Organizations, *Organizational Dynamics* 30(4): 295–309.

Knights, D. 2008. Myopic Rhetoric: Reflecting Epistemologically and Ethically on the Demand for Relevance in Organizational and Management Research, *Academy of Management Learning and Education* 7(4): 537–52.

Mendenhall, M. E., Osland, J. S., Bird, A., Oddou, G. R., Maznevski, M. L. (eds) 2008. *Global Leadership: Research, Practice and Development.* Abingdon, Oxon: Routledge.

Mintzberg, H. 2004. *Managers Not MBAs.* London: Pearson.

Monin, N. and Bathurst, R. 2008. Mary Follett on the Leadership of 'Everyman', *ephemera* 8(4): 447–61.

Moran, R. T. and Riesenberger, J. R. 1994. *The Global Challenge: Building the New Worldwide Enterprise.* London: McGraw Hill.

Osland, J. S. 2008. The Multidisciplinary Roots of Global Leadership. In M. Mendenhall, J. Osland, A. Bird, G. Oddou, M. Maznevski (eds) *Global Leadership: Research, Practice and Development.* Abingdon, Oxon: Routledge, pp. 18–33.

Rosen, R., Digh, P., Singer, M. and Philips, C. 2000. *Global Literacies: Lessons on Business Leadership and National Cultures.* New York: Crown.

Senge, P., Scharmer, C., Jaworski, J. and Flowers, B. S. 2007. *Presence: Exploring Profound Change in People, Organizations and Society.* London: Nicholas Brealey.

Sveningsson, S. and Alvesson, M. 2003. Managing Managerial Identities: Organizational Fragmentation, Discourse and Identity Struggle, *Human Relations* 56(10): 1163–93.

Sveningsson, S. and Larsson, M. 2006. Fantasies of Leadership: Identity Work, *Leadership* 2(2): 203–24.

Trompenaars, F. and Hampden-Turner, C. 2001. *Riding the Waves of Culture: Understanding Diversity in Global Business.* London: Economist Books.

Warner, L. S. and Grint, K. 2006. American Indian Ways of Leading and Knowing, *Leadership* 2(2): 225–44.

Zoller, H. M. and Fairhurst, G. T. 2007. Resistance Leadership: The Overlooked Potential in Critical Organization and Leadership Studies, *Human Relations* 60(9): 1331–60.

2
National Language and its Importance for Worldly Leadership

Doris Schedlitzki

Introduction

A worldly individual is most commonly defined as somebody who is devoted to the temporal world and experienced in human affairs (Gosling and Mintzberg, 2003). Expanding on this, one could say that a worldly individual is aware of not only his/her own but also others' belief sets, values and is able to interpret and understand different behaviours and attitudes. Within a world where especially large companies operate on a global basis, one may expect or rather hope to find increasing numbers of worldly individuals working at various hierarchical levels in such organizations. The existence of, and importance associated with, multifunctional and multicultural/national teams within organizations can almost be seen as a contextual factor enforcing the gathering of a wide range of experience in world and human affairs. For example, Gosling and Mintzberg (2003) report on the importance of a worldly mindset and its development within Shell, and research by the author of this aspect with regard to leadership in the German chemical industry has shown that it has become a prerequisite for senior leadership positions to have gathered experience as an expatriate manager in a number of other countries.

Within this global environment that is nurturing the existence of and need for worldly leaders in organizations, we can be certain of the importance of studying the phenomenon of worldliness in leadership as well as how research can inform practitioners to support and develop this worldliness in their leaders. This chapter will focus specifically on the multinational aspect of leadership in global companies and within teams and the importance of recognizing the different national languages spoken within organizations and multinational teams. It could be argued that to be a worldly leader one has to be not only aware of but also be open to and inclusive of the national and cultural differences and uniqueness of colleagues, subordinates, customers and superiors. A wealth of literature on culture and cross-cultural leadership exists (Dickson et al., 2003) and has arguably – especially through the comprehensive work of the GLOBE study (House et al., 2004) – had a significant and positive impact on adequate leadership development. Such research has, however, focused mainly on the existence and importance of value dimensions as a signifier and distinguishing factor between different countries and cultures. Acknowledging these existing contributions, this chapter will argue that we also need to pay attention to one's national language (mother tongue) and its impact on an individual's ability to speak about and understand leadership.

This chapter will address this issue through an exploration of different orders of discourse for individuals working in German and UK chemical industries, focusing especially on the importance of national differences in the language and content of individual leadership action theories. In this endeavour, the chapter draws on the linguistic relativity hypothesis (Niemeier and Dirven, 2000) to argue that an individual's national language acts as a cultural, historical voice and influence on the individual's thoughts and views of the world and specific phenomena such as leadership. It further draws a link between this hypothesis and the writing by Fairclough (2003) and others on discourse analysis and Czarniawska and Joerges' (1996) notion of individual action theories. It will argue that so far we have recognized different levels within an individual's orders of discourse and that this impacts on an individual's action theory of a phenomenon but have neglected to recognize the national language as a potentially important level and influence on action theories. The second part of this chapter will introduce empirical data from a larger study conducted in German and UK chemical industries and explore the validity of this argument regarding the importance of national language on action theories of leadership within this data set.

Taking a new lens on leadership and management – differences across national languages

Multiple definitions and lists of behaviours associated with leadership and management exist within the dominant Anglo-Saxon debate wherein scholars have discussed the relationship between these two phenomena for decades. Many of these definitions have formed an almost heroic, romantic (Meindl et al., 1985) view of leadership in comparison to the role and purpose of management. Zaleznik (2004), for example, describes a leader as a visionary, restless, experimental human being, while a manager is seen as rational, bureaucratic, dutiful, practical and unimaginative. The one uncontested assumption that this otherwise fragmented debate holds is that leadership and management are important and related phenomena that exist within organizations. Such certainty about the existence and relationship of these phenomena, however, disappears when transferring this debate to a language other than English.

German dictionaries, such as Collins or the Oxford Duden, offer a multitude of – at times overlapping or contradicting – translations for the English terms 'leader' and 'manager'. Other English organizational terms such as 'follower' and 'subordinate' do not even find a proper match in the German language, which inhibits to a certain extent the possibility of holding the above mentioned debate in German. This multitude of possible translations and interpretations of the terms 'leader' and 'manager' may be partly attributable to the functional character of the German language as the generalist English word 'manager' is supplanted by words in German that are more specifically directed at describing specific positions and functions in an organization and hierarchy. For example, both of the following German words can be translated into English as 'manager': Geschäftsführer (managing director) and Abteilungsleiter (department head). We further see, increasingly, the use of the non-translated English word 'manager' in the German language, possibly due to the difficulty of finding an equivalent generalist translation or as a sign of the pervasion of a global English business language into the German language.

Do these translation problems matter? Prince (2005) argues in favour of recognizing such problems with his work on leadership representations in Taoism and demonstrates that Chinese is a more ecologically oriented language than English and as a consequence less linear and more process-oriented. Prince (2005, p. 106) further argues that this leads to a different representation of leadership in Chinese that focuses on engagement, action and accommodation 'with circumstances as they are' rather than 'active and shaping control'. Linguistic relativity approaches agree with Prince's fundamental argument and further emphasize linguistic diversity across languages and linguistic influence on thought (Lucy, 2000). Speakers of different languages, that is different language families/national languages, are hence assumed to perceive and think about the world and specific phenomena such as leadership systematically within each language but very differently across languages.

Extending this thought further into the field of social psychology, we learn more about why language indeed has consequences on patterns of thinking about reality and as a result on behaviours and actions as suggested by linguistic relativity scholars such as Niemeier and Dirven (2000). Social psychologist Harley (2001) emphasizes that words have a denotation – a meaning attached to them – and a connotation – an emotional or evaluative association. Both the denotation and connotation of a word are context dependent and influenced by the experience and upbringing of individuals. Language is therefore not a neutral tool of communication but rather actively shapes individual thought (denotation) and action (connotation). Words like 'manager' and 'leader' are hence also influenced by both their contextually constructed denotation and connotation and will change across individuals. The context that influences the meaning of words is in itself multidimensional (national culture/institutions, organizational culture, occupation, position) and fluid, affecting the way language is shaped over time.

Fairclough's (2003) work on critical discourse analysis further stresses the importance of paying equal attention to what is said and what is not said, which encourages an investigation of whether, how and why the words 'leader' and 'manager' as well as the processes of leading and managing are embedded within a national language and to explore the influence of linguistic and discursive relativity on individuals' patterns of thought on leadership and management. Fairclough's (2003) work on orders of discourse further argues that each individual is linked into multiple levels of discourse – of which one's national language could be one – that span across different groups of individuals and again influence the meaning that leadership and management can take.

Focusing more closely on the individual's sense-making of leadership, Czarniawska and Joerges' (1996) work on travels of ideas addresses how individuals actively build their own action theories based on experience and action, which then again influence future action and behaviour. Stories, ideas, experiences, interactions all feed into and are in turn influenced by such action theories and keep these action theories in a constant flux of reinterpretation and sense-making. Recognizing the above mentioned work by Fairclough (2003) on orders of discourse reminds us that our ideas and behaviours are shaped by an invisible order of different discourses that we are linked into and that changes itself in interaction with the context we are in.

Assuming then that language matters in the Wittgensteinian sense that language is constitutive of reality and hence shapes our behaviour and actions, we need to recognize language as an inherently powerful tool that steers our interpretation of situations and our actions (Wittgenstein, 1953). Building on linguistic relativity approaches, this chapter will further make the assumption that the national language as a cultural voice (Slobin, 2000) is important as it provides the basic rules and boundaries guiding a conversation, while specific discourses affect our sense-making and theorizing within and possibly across these boundaries. Yet, we also need to recognize that both the national language as well as specific discourses change over time as individuals engage in them, reinterpret the connotations of words within them and translate them in accordance to their individual context. Language should hence be treated as a fluid phenomenon rather than static in its influence on individual action theories of leadership. This may then imply that although leadership and management may be universal in terms of existence, they certainly are not universal in meaning – an insight that has vast implications for leaders of multinational teams and certainly an aspect of worldly awareness that these leaders need to understand.

What is unclear and needs to be explored – with a view to developing future worldly leaders – is what meaning the processes of leading and managing take in different discourses and whether national language as a level of discourse really does matter.

Methods

The rest of this chapter will now discuss qualitative data and analyse them with specific focus on the importance of national, organizational, departmental and hierarchical discourses, to explore whether national language does influence an individual's theorizing of leadership and is therefore of importance to worldly leaders. These data have been taken from a wider qualitative study that encompassed 105 semi-structured interviews with employees in German and UK chemical industries, with and without managerial responsibility, targeted at understanding the participants' perceptions of their context and understanding of leadership. The subsample analysed for this chapter consists of all 27 interviews undertaken in the three UK companies and 26 interviews from three of the nine German companies. The choice of this German subsample was determined by the relative fit between UK and German company sizes, types and departments covered.

The interviews for the wider study included many questions that asked the participants to elaborate on their own opinions concerning their daily context/interactions, questions that asked what constitutes leadership in the organization, what impacts on the behaviour of a leader and what kind of leadership is displayed by their superiors and generally within their company. For this chapter, only the answers to the interview questions on participants' descriptions of ideal and existing leadership behaviour and their distinctions between managing and leading were used for in-depth analyses.

Due to the aforementioned problem of finding an equivalent translation for the generalist term 'manager', it was important to use an approximate term that would still allow for a distinction between manager and leader. For this purpose, the German word 'Vorgesetzter' was chosen although it quite specifically refers to line manager and is hence less generalist in its meaning than the word 'manager'. It was also necessary to find an approximate term for the word 'leader' to avoid the history-laden German equivalent 'Führer', and 'Führungskraft' was eventually chosen. The Duden translation for 'Führungskraft' is executive which unfortunately does not capture the composition of its two elements 'Führung' (leadership) and 'kraft' (force) and consequently affects its literal meaning.

This need to search for adequate German words to use as equivalents for the generic terms 'manager' and 'leader' tells a story of its own as it shows how a national language sets the parameters of a conversation, creating even more scope for interviewer bias to creep in when choosing specific words and setting specific questions in an interview on leadership and management. Such a possible interviewer/questioning bias has been acknowledged by the author and ought to be recognized by readers of this chapter, and its findings as well. It further reinforces the need for further focus within research on the nature and influence of national language as such.

Results

The analysis involved several readings of all 53 interviews and careful comparisons of individual accounts on leadership and management within and between several categories, such as country, organization, department and hierarchical level of the interviewees. These comparisons looked specifically for similarities in individual action theories on leadership and management and hence the presence of common discourses within these contexts.

In essence, interview accounts showed that every participant had their own action theory of leadership. This finding supports Czarniawska and Joerges' (1996, p. 16) key statement that 'organisational actors are perfectly capable of producing simplifications and stylizations – action theories – themselves'. As suggested in the literature, these theories were strongly infused with stories about their working life, their experiences and specific leadership examples they had seen and experienced over time or were striving to implement themselves.

Despite the author's difficulties in finding exact equivalent terms in German for 'manager' and 'leader', the participants talked quite easily and freely about behaviours or purposes of leaders and managers as well as differences between the two. Surprisingly, the German descriptions of management were very similar to those found in the wider Anglo-Saxon debate. It was the accounts on ideal leadership that then showed specific differences in language and meaning across the German and UK subsets. The majority of German participants believed that a leader needs to have 'Fachwissen' – functional competence/knowledge. They agreed that the leader need not be an expert on everything but must show understanding of subordinates' responsibilities and needs to know the essentials of the 'job'. Of almost higher importance was 'soziale Kompetenz' – social competence, such as the importance of communicating and informing subordinates. This also includes good and just treatment of subordinates, motivation of others as well as ana-lysing the strengths and weaknesses of each subordinate. Being able to cooperate with subordinates and acknowledge their expertise on a matter but also being strong enough to make a decision and to back up one's own decision or subordinates' decisions towards others was also mentioned.

On the other hand, UK participants defined leadership in more generic terms, using verbs such as 'inspiring', 'motivating', 'trusting', 'coaching', 'listening'. They also focused on transformational aspects of leadership such as having a vision, leading by example, setting goals and coordinating.

Similar differences between the two national data sets were apparent in the participants' descriptions of existing leadership in their organiza-tions. The focus of most German participants was on an existing type of leadership behaviour that they called 'kollegial'. The descriptions of this type of behaviour indicate quite a difference in meaning from its equivalent term in English, that is 'collegial'. It refers more specifically to somebody who is first among equals based upon social and/or func-tional competence. This is further based on a mutual respect of and trust in subordinates' expertise and a leader's superior competence and knowledge overall, allowing for a co-working relationship rather than a strict top-down relationship. Among the UK participants, there was a far greater variation in descriptions and words used to describe existing leadership. The two terms used somewhat more often than others by UK participants to describe existing leadership behaviour were 'supportive' and 'delegation/coaching'. Table 2.1 below summarizes some illustrative quotes to describe each of the relevant terms in German and English.

Interestingly, these national differences seemed to almost disappear when comparing leadership directly with management. In contrast to their definition of managing, participants tended to explain that leadership differs as it is concerned with leading through power sources other than that gained from a specific hierarchical position. Leading is rather about persuading followers to voluntarily perform well aided by the leader's expert and personal power.

> A manager leads by definition, a leader leads via competence and common goals. That is more the acceptance on the part of those who are being led. (Head of Business Line, Germany)

Table 2.1   Key leadership words and meanings in German and English

Kollegial	'I don't see myself as an authoritative person'; 'Praising but also being critical'; 'it does not mean being mates'; 'cooperative, relaxed'; 'on same level with subordinates'	Coaching	'Empowering to go beyond...to take some initiative and responsibility themselves'; 'somebody who shows other people what to do and how to do by example'
Fachwissen	'44 years of experience'; 'technical expert'; 'expert knowledge'	Supportive	'won't always necessarily give me the answer but he'll help me find it'; 'Empathic, listens to all the people'
Soziale Kompetenz	'fair treatment of subordinates'; 'acting as a role model'; 'has to communicate and work as a team'		
End-verantwortung	'taking responsibility for actions'; making decisions'		

Apart from illustrating the general distinction between managers and leaders in terms of position power, this statement also reflects the German belief in competence as the main characteristic of leadership. In summary, the German participants seem to interpret a leader's power as originating in competence and expertise, while UK participants focused more on transformational aspects and personal power.

Aside the national differences in words and meaning of leadership and management, there were also similarities in individual action theories of leadership within organizational, departmental and hierarchical subgroups. However, within these subgroups it was less the specific words or jargon that separated one group from the other but the requirements of the context on adequate leadership behaviours. For example, within departmental subgroups such as production settings the action theories of leadership focused on superior expertise and allocation of work whereas in an R&D department leaders were primarily responsible for motivation and trust building.

When further reading each individual action theory in depth it seems that foremost importance is given to the immediate context that influences these individual action theories of leadership. These action theories were infused with stories on the immediate local context and previous work experiences. Depending on the career path taken, the importance of the organization, department or hierarchical position manifested itself according to individual preferences.

Further discussion

This section will discuss further the three key findings that have arisen out of the above analyses: the national differences in language and leadership action theories; the similarities in definitions of management across the two languages; and the influence of the immediate context and career path on individual action theories of leadership. A model summarizing the influences on an individual's theorizing on leadership will be developed and its implications for worldly leadership outlined.

The strong similarities in definitions of management and the distinction of management from leadership were surprising as the concept of a manager as a profession is an Anglo-Saxon one and does not exist as such in the German language. The German word 'Vorgesetzter', used in this research to describe a line manager, is not associated as clearly with specific activities and responsibilities as the term 'manager'. Nevertheless, both German and English terms for 'manager' have been associated with the same activities, responsibilities and the slightly inferior status compared to leadership. Although further interpretations or conclusions cannot be drawn from this finding, it seems interesting as such to see these similarities in descriptions of the *process* of managing in light of the non-existence of a generalist German word for the *person* 'manager'.

Interview accounts differed most across the two languages and countries when asked to define or describe leadership and most participants did so by focusing on the process of leading. The specific meaning attached to the German words 'kollegial', 'Fachwissen', 'Soziale Kompetenz' need to be seen in light of the importance of 'Bildung' and 'Kultur' – knowledge, being cultured, deep authenticity and the like – in Germany and according to Armbrüster (2004) the importance of being up front, authentic, deep and intellectual above the significance of appearance and politeness. The German participants in this study suggested that legitimization of leadership is achieved through a mutual trust in and respect for competence – a concept that is according to Armbrüster (2004) the building block of German society. On the other hand, the UK words and meaning attached to leadership behaviour within this study show similarities to the writings on transformational leadership within the Anglo-Saxon literature on organizational leadership and may be a sign for the dominant Anglo-Saxon influence of literature on organizational leadership discourse. They could also be linked to the very different educational system in the United Kingdom that has historically favoured non-technical skills and employment (Lane, 1989), which may arguably have led to a stronger sense of managerial identity in the United Kingdom than in Germany. In a nutshell, these national language differences in accounts of ideal and existing leadership behaviour embody the cultural and institutional differences associated with education, competence and ultimately power bases in these two countries and reflect how these are captured within the resources and constraints of each language, and influence the individual's theorizing on leadership.

Of further interest are, alongside these national differences, individual differences between each individual action theory that stress the importance of the individual situation and local context within individual action theories on leaders/leading and managers/managing. Comparing broadly – at the macro level – the content and language used across the data set reveal that there are some nation-specific and language-specific aspects of leadership. Yet, when taking a closer look – micro level – at the individual action theories and influences on these, such linguistic influences are further shaped by the individual's more immediate context through experience, stories and ideas.

With reference to Fairclough's (2003) orders of discourse, the findings from this data set seem to suggest that it is the discourse of the interviewees' own experiences in their career that set the tone in these action theories, that is, one's organization, occupation, different positions, hierarchy and the like. There was, however, still a clear influence of the wider background, that is, the culture they are in and grown up with and the language they use, as it is the language individuals use that enables as well as inhibits communication and action in specific ways that is aligned with history and values embedded in this language. Figure 2.1 captures these influences on interviewees' theorizing in this data set.

This figure supports the combination of Czarniawska and Joerges' (1996) travels of ideas and Fairclough's (2003) orders of discourse as outlined earlier in this chapter. The analyses specifically support Czarniawska and Joerges' (1996) argument that stories, ideas, experiences and interactions feed into action theories and that such action theories are socially constructed and change over time through ongoing reinterpretation. These analyses have further shown that the action theories are linked into a lot of different discourses and that the order

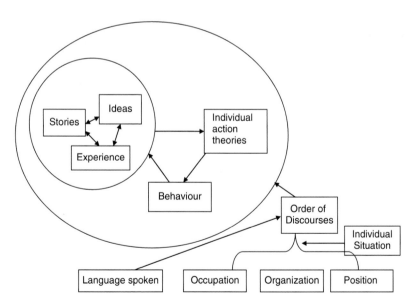

Figure 2.1 National language and individual action theories

of importance of such discourses depends on an individual's situation. Important circumstances that define a person's context at a specific point in time, such as career stage, specific experiences, organization, occupation, country and language, influence the order in which different discourses align and affect the choice of stories, ideas and experiences that are used to inform action theories of leadership. These personal circumstances and their influence on the order of discourse change over time, leading to changes in individual action theories. At the same time, it is also our own actions resulting from existing action theories of leadership that lead to new ideas, stories and experiences that then influence reinterpretation and change said action theories. What the analyses of this data set have further supported is the influence of national language on individual action theories, as it is the national language that sets the parameters, words and meanings within which conversations can take place and reality be formed.

These findings have then two implications on worldly leadership: first, national language matters and it is important to acknowledge the ways in which a mother tongue creates structures and opportunities as well as limits within which individuals grow up and come to talk and think about leadership. It is further important to see national language as a cultural voice (Slobin, 2000) and a sense-making tool that will affect interpretation and expectations of leadership. When switching between mother tongue and the language spoken in a multinational team, one switches also between two sets of structures within which to converse and meanings of leadership to interpret in light of the different cultural values embedded in the different languages. Second, every individual is linked into other discourses connected to specific contexts, such as groups, departments, occupations, organizations and so on, that change throughout life and influence and shape action theories of leadership within and across the national languages spoken. It is hence an aspect of worldliness in a leader to understand the implications of national languages and mother tongues on individuals' action theories of leadership as well as acknowledging the mediating effect that specific social contexts have on these theories.

Conclusions

This chapter has looked into the importance of national language as a cultural voice in individuals' action theories of leadership and in comparison to the influence of other discourses. This has further served to question the long held assumption that leadership and management are important and strongly related phenomena in organizations and has provided an opportunity to look at the origins of leadership and management in a country's history and language.

This questioning of the existing Anglo-Saxon discourse on leadership and management was linked to the linguistic relativity argument on the importance of language in shaping behaviour. Czarniawska and Joerges' (1996) travels of ideas and Fairclough's (2003) orders of discourse were introduced and the argument developed that as language shapes interpretation and action it is highly important for the worldly leader to know whether cultural origin, mother tongue or any other discourse affects an individual's theorizing on leadership and what order of discourses this may represent.

Empirical data from a qualitative research project in German and UK chemical industries were presented and discussed with a specific interest in uncovering existing national, organizational, departmental and hierarchical discourses across the whole data set and within individual action theories. The two main findings emerging from this are: first, individuals' tendency to draw actively from their own experience with leadership as well as the specific social context prominent within their work, that is organization, occupation, hierarchy, department and the like. While there was some overlap in the stories and examples illustrating these experiences between action theories from the same organization, department and between managers and subordinates respectively, it seemed also clear that each individual had a different order of priorities in which these discourses seemed to matter.

Second, national languages were found to matter as German interviewees were, for example, drawing on specifically German concepts such as 'kollegial' and 'Kompetenz' to define and describe leadership. The true meaning attached to these words can only be understood in the context of German national history, culture and institutions as these affect interviewees' interpretations of these words and by extension the process of leading itself. It is further clear, however, that the meaning attached to the terms 'leadership' and 'management' were not only language-specific but further dependent on the individual's translation of these within a specific context. The national languages were hence not necessarily the most influential discourse affecting individual action theories of leadership.

These findings and conclusions need to be read in awareness of the limitations and boundaries of this research. The data set is not representative of the two countries, the chemical industries in these countries, or the organizations that were sampled for the wider study. The chemical industry is further very specific with regards to its dominant features and characteristics that transcend national borders. Generalizations beyond this limited data set can therefore not be made but the findings do suggest possible lines of enquiry for future cross-cultural management and leadership research, especially in very different, and more nationally focused industry settings.

The model presented in Figure 2.1 is assumed to capture in essence the basic elements moderating and influencing an individual's theorizing on leadership based upon the literature review and data analysis presented in this chapter. It suggests that national language is one of many important discourses affecting an individual's action theory of leadership yet not always the most important one. It is rather often setting boundaries to an individual's sense-making of leadership through its fundamental influence on an individual's set of denotations and connotations. Lessons to draw for worldly leadership are hence twofold: it is important to be aware of the national languages (mother tongue) of employees within a team as these will have influenced and shaped their early action theories of leadership and may influence their current reading of leadership behaviours. Worldly leadership goes however beyond this and incorporates understanding the very specific immediate context of each individual team member in light of their careers, role and experiences beyond occupational and national boundaries.

References

Armbrüster, T. 2004. *Management and Organization in Germany.* Aldershot: Ashgate.

Czarniawska, B. and Joerges, B. 2006. Travels of Ideas. In B. Czarniawska and G. Sevon (eds) *Translating Organizational Change.* Berlin: Walter de Gruyter, pp. 13–48.

Dickson, M. W., Den Hartog, D. N. and Mitchelson, J. K. 2003. Research on Leadership in a Cross-cultural Context: Making Progress, and Raising New Questions, *Leadership Quarterly* 14(6): 729–68.

Fairclough, N. 2003. *Analysing Discourse: Textual Analysis for Social Research.* Abingdon: Routledge.

Gosling, J. and Mintzberg, H. 2003. The Five Minds of a Manager, *Harvard Business Review* 81(11): 54–63.

Harley, T. 2001. *The Psychology of Language.* 2nd edn. Hove: Psychology Press.

House, R. J., Hanges, P. J., Javidan, M., Dorfman, P. W. and Gupta, V. (eds) 2004. *Leadership, Culture and Organizations: The GLOBE Study of 62 Societies.* London: Sage.

Lane, C. 1989. *Management and Labour in Europe: The Industrial Enterprise in Germany, Britain and France.* London: Edward Elgar.

Lucy, J. 2000. Introductory Comments. In S. Niemeier and R. Dirven (eds) *Evidence for Linguistic Relativity.* London: John Benjamins, pp. ix–xxi.

Meindl, J., Erlich, S. and Dukerich, J. 1985. The Romance of Leadership, *Administrative Science Quarterly* 30(1): 78–102.

Niemeier, S. and Dirven, R. 2000. *Evidence for Linguistic Relativity*. London: John Benjamins.

Prince, L. 2005. Eating the Menu Rather Than the Dinner: Tao and Leadership, *Leadership* 1(1): 105–26.

Slobin, D. I. 2000. Verbalized Events: A Dynamic Approach to Linguistic Relativity and Determinism. In S. Niemeier and R. Dirven (eds) *Evidence for Linguistic Relativity*. London: John Benjamins, pp. 107–38.

Wittgenstein, L. 1953. *Philosophical Investigations*. Oxford: Blackwell.

Zaleznik, A. 2004. Managers and Leaders: Are They Different?, *Harvard Business Review* 82(1): 74–81.

3
Leadership Development as a Catalyst for Social Change: Lessons from a Pan-African Programme

Richard Bolden and Philip Kirk

Introduction

In recent years the call for more inclusive, 'post-heroic' perspectives on leadership has become increasingly common and relational theories that consider leadership as 'a social influence process through which emergent coordination (i.e. evolving social order) and change (i.e. new values, attitudes, approaches, behaviours, ideologies, etc.) are constructed and produced' (Uhl-Bien, 2006, p. 668) are now widely accepted within the academic literature. Despite this, much leadership training and education remains almost exclusively focused on building the 'human capital' (skills, knowledge and capability) of individuals in formal leadership roles – what Day (2000) terms 'leader development' – rather than the 'social capital' (relationships, networks and collective capacity) of the organization and/or group more widely – what Day (ibid.) refers to as 'leadership development'.

The concept of leadership development as an investment in social capital is quite different to that of developing the human capital of individual leaders. At the very least it requires consideration of the broader social and political context in which leadership occurs, and an attempt to build and sustain social relationships rather than just the personal capabilities of participants. Furthermore, it points towards the fluidity and permeability of organizational and group boundaries in that the social capital on which individuals and organizations can draw (and in most cases depend upon) stretches far beyond the direct work environment through a complex web of interrelations that extends into multiple communities.

The recognition of leadership as a process of social influence and leadership development as a mechanism for establishing interpersonal relationships and shared understandings opens new prospects for the role of both in building and strengthening communities. Leadership development, while enhancing the capacity of specific individuals, may also become a catalyst for wider scale social change. As Iles and Preece (2006, p. 337) suggest, 'leadership development platforms can thus be seen to be acting as intermediaries: facilitating bonding, bridging and brokering activities and claiming legitimacy as transformers of the space between "leaders" and other networks and institutions'.

Barker (1997) proposes that at the heart of a relational approach to leadership is an engagement with the ethical values of the community in which leadership is enacted. Drawing on Harré et al.'s (1985) three-tier construct he suggests that individual behaviour is driven largely through sub-conscious *morals*, derived from a conscious system of *ethics* which, in turn, is defined by the sub-conscious *mores* of the social system in which actors find themselves. He thus describes leadership as 'a process of change where the ethics of individuals are integrated into the mores of a community' (p. 352). From this perspective leadership development is integrally related to community development and offers a means for the surfacing and negotiation of social values and purpose.

Such concerns are the primary focus of this chapter. In it we draw on our experiences of researching a pan-African leadership development programme that had, as its objective, both personal and social change. In this chapter we consider the processes by which the programme facilitated the development of human and social capital and how, through their engagement, participants were able to fundamentally reframe their understanding of community-based leadership. It is suggested, within the context of this book, that this is an example of developing 'worldly leadership' (Gosling & Mintzberg, 2003) in that, rather than imposing a predetermined or generic model it facilitated the emergence of locally appropriate forms of leadership practice. Furthermore, through a process of collective dialogue, experimentation and 'identity work' (Sveningsson & Alvesson, 2003) it can be considered as an example of 'system leadership development' (Kirk, 2005). The chapter will conclude with further theoretical reflection on this model and the manner in which it may provide a platform for social change.

Method

The empirical research for this chapter was conducted within the context of the first cohort of a major UK-funded leadership development programme delivered to 300 participants across 19 sub-Saharan countries. As independent research partners, our intention was to gain insights into the mechanisms and processes by which this initiative built upon and challenged traditional conceptions of leadership in Africa and facilitated engagement, by Africans, with beneficial social change within their communities.

The programme was heavily informed by the principles of 'appreciative inquiry' (Cooperrider & Srivastva, 1987) and 'systems thinking' (Senge, 1990; Wheatley, 1995) and had as its focus transformational change at a personal, community, national and subcontinent level. The emphasis was very much on challenging embedded assumptions, growing collective capacity and developing a sense of shared African and community identity. It had as its central premise that leadership is a collective process in which 'everyone is a leader' and hence sought a diverse range of participants. Programme delivery was primarily through a network of African facilitators identified and trained in the first phase of the initiative, with the intention of embracing African wisdom (using local stories and examples wherever possible) and treating participants as equal partners in the learning process.

The programme comprised a series of elements including an in-country application and selection process, in-country launch, pan-African event (a 3-day conference with 100 participants selected from across all the countries) and the in-country programme (comprising three modules totalling 10 days over a period of 6–9 months). A key feature of the in-country programme was a 'community engagement' where groups of 4–5 participants spent a number of days visiting local community groups to see how they could share and disseminate the ideas raised during the programme. This engagement activity occurred during and after Module 2, with preparation in Module 1 and follow-up (including a visit and feedback from community members) in Module 3. The programme concluded with one-to-one feedback and the preparation of personal and group action plans.

The research took a narrative inquiry approach to exploring the impact of the programme both in terms of the manner in which it facilitated changing conceptions of leadership and how it impacted upon the communities in which the participants engaged. Our aim was to invite participants (and other stakeholders) to act as co-inquirers

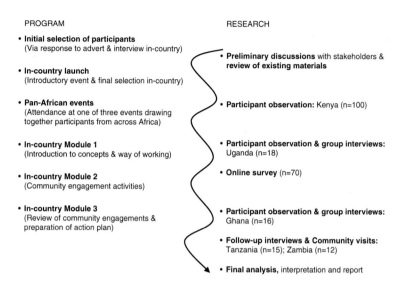

Figure 3.1   Mapping of research process against programme structure

(*Note*: figures in brackets refer to the number of participants involved in each aspect of the data collection)

into the meanings they were attaching to the notion of leadership and how they enacted these meanings, as leaders, to bring about impact within their communities.

The study was designed to triangulate a range of data and insights, including context immersion, preliminary interviews, an online qualitative survey, community visits, follow-up interviews, stakeholder interviews and analysis of secondary data (see Figure 3.1). For logistical reasons our main face-to-face data collection was restricted to Kenya, Uganda, Ghana, Tanzania and Zambia, with findings from other countries solicited through the survey.

The rich and diverse body of data called for a variety of analysis methods. The primary mechanism, however, was an inductive, qualitative approach whereby the researchers immersed themselves in the observations and narrative accounts, letting patterns, concepts and ideas emerge over time. In order to maintain a degree of rigour, the two researchers initially interpreted the data independently, drawing their own interpretations prior to a mutual process of verification and moderation, both with one another, the Programme Director and colleagues. As such, the final interpretations were the result of a cyclical process of reflection and dialogue, and the overall approach can be considered as one of 'reflexive methodology' (Alvesson & Skoldberg, 2000), whereby the researchers, in collaboration with other actors, constructed, challenged and reconstructed varying representations of the data over time.

Research findings

Our analysis of the data comprised two principal dimensions: (1) an exploration of the meanings that participants were associating with the concept of leadership and (2) evidence of the impact of their participation in this programme. Findings from the first part of this analysis are presented elsewhere (Bolden & Kirk, 2009), while the focus of the current chapter is on programme outcomes.

Almost without exception all participants who discussed their experience through conversations and questionnaires reported significant, life-changing impacts of their involvement in the programme. The range of impacts spanned the whole spectrum of life experience, from self-confidence, through relationships with partners, family members and friends, to the workplace and wider community. In order to give a sense of these outcomes they will be discussed under the following headings: impact on self, family, workplace, community and society.

Impact on self

Of the guiding principles of the programme the focus on self as a leader was seen to be the most important by a large number of participants. In effect the importance of developing and caring for oneself was seen as a fundamental precursor to taking up one's leadership role within a community. Thus the focus on self was not regarded as selfish but rather for the collective benefit, as illustrated below.

> On this programme we learnt that leadership starts with understanding yourself, realising yourself, what are your strengths, what is working and even what is not working. Then you put these things together and while it is not simple or easy, it is a good way to lead people. So you lead yourself and then you can lead others. (Male, Consultant, Tanzania)

Key elements of the impact on self included enhanced self-awareness, confidence, interpersonal skills (including listening, questioning and appreciation of the views of others), tolerance and patience. At the core of this change, however, was a shift in self-image/identity whereby participants came to realize their potential to act as leaders, capable of exerting influence and bringing about change no matter what their position in the system.

> I have confidence in myself now, I see myself as a leader, I can talk to people and listen to them and that I would enable them to listen to them rather than it is me who tells them what to do. That is why perhaps they have trust in me. I think they see that I give them the confidence to make their own decisions. (Male, Student, Tanzania)

Adopting a facilitative, inclusive approach to leadership was regarded as a way of empowering others. The leader's role was seen as one of concern, caring for and developing others rather than being directive or judgemental.

Impact on family

A distinctive feature of this programme was the holistic way in which it impacted upon participants in all aspects of their lives. Impacts within the immediate family environment were particularly commented on and, in effect, this was one of the first places where they began to apply what they had learnt during the programme.

Many spoke of improved relationships with spouses, siblings and other family members, primarily arising from the application of appreciative inquiry principles. Giving others the benefit of the doubt reopened dialogues and enabled an enhanced appreciation of the potential contribution (and personal circumstances) of different family members.

> We grew up in my family with my father not taking care of us. He never bought me a pair of shoes a T-shirt or paid my school fund but above all he was abusive to all of us including my mother, physically and emotionally. I had a great anger upon him. I never wanted anything to do with him. But because of [a communication model used on the programme] I looked into him and asked myself how was he raised was he loved by his family? Was he recognised as a person who may do something for himself? Most of the things were not there he was never loved even by his mother, she turned his sisters against him, he was very much rejected so he grew up like that. Then I asked myself this question: "How can he love if he was never loved" everything that he did was of the impact his growing up life style

had on him. My father is not stupid, he does not hate us, it is just that he does not know how to love. I took a big step I FORGAVE HIM for everything and started to look at him as somebody who needs to be loved – guess what it worked! (Female, Community Development Manager, South Africa)

There were also examples of where participants have acted as mentors for siblings and other family members – seeing it as their duty to share what they have learnt and to support those around them.

My brother who is 20 years old, for example, has no confidence. I gave him the questions I was given in [the programme] to reflect on (what are your strengths and weaknesses, what are you proud about achieving in your life, and so on). He wanted to show me his answers and talk about them. It was a powerful conversation, the first real one I had with him, because he was so honest and he was so shocking about the way he felt. [...] So I thought I would make it my mission to talk with him about what was happening to me in [the programme]. One day I gave him some money to go and deposit in the bank, into my account for me. He could not believe that I had done that. Nobody trusts him [...]. We never gave him a chance. He was so excited that I did not think he would lose it. When he came back I did not expect him to talk to me about it, but he told me about the whole process, the forms he had to fill in. It was a big boost to his confidence, his morale. (Female, Sales Executive, Tanzania)

For others the family was a powerful source of support, but one that needed continual attention in order to maintain healthy relationships.

Impact at work

Other than family, the workplace was the next context in which participants felt there had been the greatest impact of their changing approach to leadership. While these impacts were often associated with tools and skills acquired directly through the programme, they appeared most strongly influenced by a change in 'mindset' – to a more open and appreciative perspective informed by one's sense of holding a legitimate leadership role within that organization and a desire to genuinely engage with others.

With [this programme] I am able to appreciate that my colleagues could do well also, or even better than me given the chance.

I provided the opportunity and amazingly, they can do many things better than myself, and they get better with more enabling environment created. The result? My headaches have become reduced, less deadlines to meet, improved output, more satisfaction among my colleagues and more progress for the organisation. (Male, Development Worker, Nigeria)

As indicated in the previous quote, this change in style has been positively received by colleagues and bosses and, in many cases has led to improved working relationships and subsequent career progression. In some instances participants noticed a ripple effect within their organizations as more and more people adopted this inclusive approach to leadership.

As the Executive Director of the NGO, I have not only developed the ability to relate well with managers of bigger corporate organizations, but I have started a mentoring process to prepare others to succeed me with time. My colleagues in the office give me feedback in these areas all the time and with the community networking going on now, my office has become a [programme] office. (Male, NGO Director, Ghana)

Impact on community

Besides work and family, many of the participants were engaged in other social networks and groups (including church, schools, women's groups, community projects, etc.), where they found other channels to apply their learning from the programme.

It has been wonderful, at home, at work, even on the pulpit when I am preaching I now find myself ending my sermons with powerful life-giving questions. What I have noticed is that there has been a change in my approach to people and issues. (Male, CEO of IT Company and Lay-Pastor, Nigeria)

Indeed, a powerful outcome of participation in the programme was the capacity to challenge embedded cultural attitudes in an appreciative rather than confrontational manner.

The fact is that as a woman in my tradition you cannot challenge or question decisions by men. I have tried to change this. By using appreciation, goodwill and good intent and through questioning, by letting them know they are doing great things but things will be better if the women participate. Through my influence as a leader of a female association we have done this by examples of handling projects in the community where we have proved our worth. The women are now taking a leading role in community projects, which has improved a lot their status in the community. (Female, HR Director and President of Women's Association, Cameroon)

A central theme of the programme was encouraging participants to identify communities where they have influence (indeed, this formed part of the selection process) and to offer opportunities for them to spend time engaging with local communities to practise what they had learnt with the support of their peers. These engagements typically involved a small group of participants spending a day or two within the chosen community speaking with a wide range of people, asking questions, sharing insights and offering positive reflections on the work being done. Within the current chapter there is insufficient space to enter into a detailed description of the kinds of impact that were achieved in this short time, but suffice it to say a number of the changes were substantial, transformational and sustained (as reported in the feedback sessions from community members in Module 3 and community visits by the researchers some 2–3 months following the intervention). For example, two months following engagement with an artisan collective in Zambia the community had raised money and purchased a vehicle to enable development of a small farmstead recently purchased on the outskirts of the city and the chair of the Community Management Association had applied and gained a place on the second cohort of the programme. Through hands-on engagement activities such as these participants were both able to develop their own capability as well as build relationships and networks, influencing and educating others, and act as champions for the programme and the principles on which it was based.

Impact on society

Through the changes at a local level, participants began to have a wider influence at regional, national and international levels. Much of this impact was achieved in the same way as in local communities – through listening, questioning, appreciation, tolerance and improved self-confidence – and appeared to have arisen largely from changes in one's sense of identity in relation to others. For many, they now see themselves as a part of the wider society and have a sense of duty/obligation to influence policy and practice at this level.

> I have a new identity as an African – not just a Ghanaian – I am now more passionate and concerned about things that happen in other parts of Africa. I never used to look at the African column in the daily paper, I wasn't interested, but I now take that part and read it and I sit down and think and come up with ideas and solutions that I think would be an opportunity to change positions around in these countries and the situations people find themselves in. (Female, Administrator, Ghana)

Since embarking on the programme a number of participants had stood for parliamentary election; others had developed networks within and beyond Africa; yet others had used their positions in the media, broadcasting and other domains to share their learning with a wider audience; and nearly all had re-engaged with their identity as Africans.

Discussion

The examples presented above give a flavour of the kinds of effect that a programme of this type can have on participants and their communities. The intention of this chapter, however, is not to argue whether the programme has been good 'value-for-money', for such outcomes are hard to quantify, but to explore the underlying processes by which a development activity such as this can impact on individuals and their communities. To this extent we would like to begin by focusing on three elements of the programme that, we feel, make it distinct from more individually orientated initiatives, namely: relational identity, collaborative action and social construction.

Much of what has been revealed during the process of our research is how this programme offered participants the opportunity to reflect on and challenge their sense of *relational identity*. People have been able to recognize themselves as leaders, as members of their communities, as equal to others (regardless of age, gender, ethnicity, etc.) and as part of a wider 'Africa'. The opportunity of experiencing, discussing and reflecting on the nature of leadership with a diverse group of peers has challenged restrictive perspectives and replaced them with something more positive and enriching. It would seem that this may be practical evidence of what Sveningsson and Alvesson (2003) call 'identity work' – the ongoing struggle to create a sense of self and provide answers (all be they often temporary) to questions such as 'who am I?' and 'what is my purpose?' What is important within the current programme, however, is that this process of identity construction is conducted through a socialized process of dialogue and exchange, rather than through more individually orientated or 'objective' mechanisms such as the psychometric profiling, 360° feedback or one-to-one coaching more typical of 'leader development' initiatives.

A related concept at the heart of this approach is that of *collaborative action*, or 'sharing'. Whereas more academically-orientated programmes, such as MBAs, may emphasize the benefits of expertise and professionalism, the current programme attempts to break down boundaries. Thus, participants are encouraged to share and practise their learning at home as well as at work and to disseminate and exchange models and ideas within their communities for mutual benefit. The learning process is thus truly dynamic and collective, occurring through interaction and exchange rather than personal transformation alone. Indeed, the programme seems to have engaged people more at an affective than a cognitive level.

And third, is the significance of the *social construction* of leadership (Ospina & Sorenson, 2006; Fairhurst & Grant, 2010). To this extent, it can be argued that how people conceive of leadership affects how social systems operate and as a consequence affects the well-being of the social system and the people in it (Smircich & Morgan, 1982). Thus, this programme is not so much concerned with the traits or behaviours of leaders but how, through dialogue and engagement, they can collectively (re)create the environment within which they operate.

Returning to the notion of leadership development as an investment in social capital described in the introduction to this chapter it becomes clear that, in the context of a programme such as this, building social capital is about more than simply establishing relationships. It is about offering opportunities for the construction of shared identities, meanings and purpose. This distinction is identified by Willem and Scarborough (2006) who distinguish between two differing perspectives on social capital: 'the instrumental view [that] sees the establishment of social capital as based on reciprocal relationships [and] the consummatory view [that] sees social capital as the result of the development of social norms and identification with a group' (ibid., p. 1345). 'The instrumental view', they argue, 'includes the "social network" and "structural" aspects of social capital [whilst] the consummatory view emphasises that social capital is a collective attribute characterised by goal congruence, shared norms and trust' (p. 1345).

In distinguishing these two forms of social capital Willem and Scarborough (2006) posit that they will have differential impacts on knowledge sharing and learning, with the former (instrumental) having a primarily beneficial effect on knowledge sharing *within* networks and a negative effect *between* networks (largely based on role and power structures within the organization). By contrast, it is argued that 'in the consummatory view, the collective nature of social capital largely overrides individual politicking actions' (ibid., p. 1349) and that 'consummatory social capital may be a precondition for the effects which instrumental aspects of social capital have on knowledge sharing' (p. 1365).

In providing a framework through which participants can engage in the development of consummatory social capital, leadership development programmes such as the one researched in this study offer the potential of facilitating wider social change and the emergence of a more 'worldly' approach to leadership – not bounded to individual participants or organizations. The nature of such impacts, however, is necessarily emergent, somewhat unpredictable and difficult to capture empirically. Furthermore, while talk of 'transformational change' may conjure up images of heroic acts and charismatic leaders the processes set in motion through the approach described are far more subtle – a shift in values and beliefs rather than a dramatic change in behaviour (Carroll & Levy, 2010).

Towards a model of engagement

The findings from this study offer support for a relational and constructionist understanding of leadership. The narratives speak of a deeply personal appreciation and expression of leadership but one that is only meaningful *in relation* to a wider community (family, work, etc.), thereby highlighting a need to remain alert to *both* the individual *and* the collective dimensions of social influence.

The findings also support the notion that leadership development is about more than simply building the capability of individual leaders. Indeed, it implies that change occurs primarily through reconfiguration of one's personal and social identities – a form of 'identity work' – and that, through this process, it becomes possible for individuals to begin to influence wider social norms and values. The socialized learning process was supported through a series of principles and models that helped participants (and those with whom they interacted) to articulate an alternative and more inclusive perspective on leadership.

In this section of the chapter, we would like to build on Kirk's (2005) model of 'System Leadership Development' (see Figure 3.2) to explore

Figure 3.2   System leadership development

a possible mechanism through which this programme may facilitate wider social change. This model, derived from research and education in a number of community contexts, particularly with a South African NGO and wine growers' cooperative (Kirk & Shutte, 2002, 2003), presents a social constructivist model of leadership development that aims to enhance the overall leadership capacity within the system.

The model comprises three principal elements. The first, termed 'connective leadership', is mainly informed by Jean Lipman-Blumen's (1996) work on a relational, networked understanding of leadership and David Bakan's analysis of agentic and communal ways of knowing (Bakan, 1966). This notion presents leadership as a communal activity grounded in a shared sense of identity and purpose. In effect, connective leadership is about a group, organization, or community *'learning to see together'* (Kirk, 2005).

The second element of the model is termed 'collective empowerment' and is informed, primarily, by the concept of role taking (Armstrong, 1988; Reed, 2001; Triest, 1999). In Reed's words, 'to take a role implies being able to formulate or discover, however intuitively, a regulating principle inside oneself which enables one, as a person, to manage what one does in relation to the requirements of the situation one is in' (Reed, 2001, p. 2). It involves three related activities – namely role finding, role making and role taking. From Kirk and Shutte's (2003) work with a South African NGO it was found that their collective empowerment developed from (1) working to create a sense of identity, (2) the successes they achieved and (3) the crises they had come through. Collective empowerment is, therefore, about a group, organization, or community *'learning to walk together'* (Kirk, 2005).

The third element of the model is termed 'dialogue' and is informed largely through Isaacs' (1999) work on the power of dialogue and Senge's (1990) work on organizational learning. It is principally about encouraging voices to be heard, appreciating the differences in what is said, and surfacing underlying assumptions and dynamics. Dialogue, in this sense, is pluralistic yet seeks to work with differences productively, as in the case of the transitional government in South Africa who found practising dialogue led to agreement on the best course of action even though they had different reasons for this (Kirk & Shutte, 2003). To this extent it could be argued that dialogue is about a group, organization, or community *'learning to talk together'* (Kirk, 2005).

When considered in relation to the leadership development programme described in this chapter it is possible to determine how the different elements of the System Leadership Development model are supported through different developmental tools. Connective leadership, for example, is facilitated through the programmes' guiding philosophy which offers a shared language and perspective that helps participants to 'see together'. Collective empowerment is largely facilitated through the community engagements and pan-African conferences, each of which offers a powerful shared learning experience that brings participants together and gives them the chance to 'walk together' – practising their learning in a safe and supportive environment. Dialogue is enhanced through the participative approach to learning, the emphasis on equality and diversity and a number of practical tools used (including techniques for questioning, listening and communication) – thereby helping those involved to 'talk together'. Therefore, despite not being explicitly designed to these specifications it appears that the programme studied in this research contains all of the elements of a System Leadership Development initiative.

To explore how such an approach may act as a catalyst for wider social change, however, we need to extend the model beyond programme participants to other members of their communities and to consider how the tools and techniques used in the programme offer a practical means for engaging others in leadership and influencing social norms and values. It would seem that through their engagement in this programme participants are encouraged (and possibly empowered) to act as ambassadors for social change within their communities. Their impact, however, is not through directive action or personal characteristics (as might be implied by more individualistic accounts of leadership), nor necessarily through transformational or charismatic influence (although this remains a possibility), but primarily through the facilitation of a perceptual shift from the idea of the leader as an exceptional (and usually senior) individual to the notion of 'everyone as a leader' – a shift from the heroic to the collective.

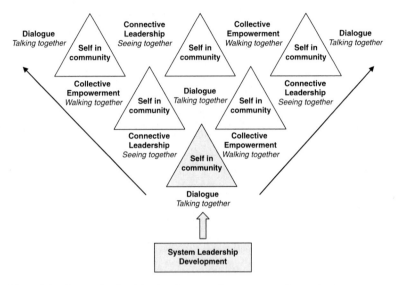

Figure 3.3   System leadership development in a community context

An inclusive and communal view of leadership, associated with a set of straightforward concepts and tools, may form the basis for a model of leadership development that can be replicated and transmitted across social groups. This process is presented in Figure 3.3 whereby, through involvement in a System Leadership Development programme, individuals become equipped with the necessary tools, language and sense of purpose to transmit their learning and shift in values to others. At the heart of this model is the concept of 'self in community'.

This model offers a framework in which leadership development can facilitate the kinds of process Barker (1997) outlined when describing leadership as community development. A fundamental element of this is the opportunity to discuss and explore personal and community values and identities and to construct new (or alternative) realities. What is also significant is how this is done in a highly contextualized environment and the way the person is treated as a whole rather than just at work.

A development initiative such as this, therefore, seems to be able to engage both with the development of self *and* community without giving precedence to one over the other. As Lawrence (1979, p. 242) argues 'social change, which implies an inspection of social realities, starts from the individual considering his or her authority for being in a role in institutions of a society'.

Limitations and areas for future research

As with all social research the findings and ideas presented in this chapter are inevitably limited in a number of ways. In this part of the chapter, therefore, we will briefly consider some of the methodological, theoretical and contextual limitations as well as likely promising areas for further research and enquiry.

From a methodological perspective, as a piece of commissioned research on a large and complex initiative, our account can only ever be a partial representation of what happened. There are key development and strategy debates to which we were not party; we only attended small parts of the programme, spoke to a limited number of people, concerned ourselves with a limited number of questions, only studied the first cohort of the programme and gave limited attention to the wider social, political and economic contexts of the intervention. Furthermore, it should be noted that both researchers were white, male and British (although a female member of the team, of different ethnicity, did attend the pan-African event in Kenya and participated in early research discussions). To this extent, what is included in this account can only represent a limited number of voices and perspectives. Despite this, however, the reflexive methodology offered many opportunities for engaging and speaking with people carrying different perspectives and agendas to verify and corroborate our interpretation of findings. Furthermore, while our cultural distance from the programme may have masked certain aspects, it is likely that it also brought others into clearer focus. It is recommended, therefore, that the account given here is treated as a preliminary exploration of the field rather than an objective statement of reality.

Theoretically our assumptions are shaped by relational theories of leadership and give precedence to socially constructed accounts of leadership practice. To this extent we are interested in how people construct a sense of purpose and identity in a social context rather than the explicit skills and behaviours they possess or exhibit. We have drawn on a range of theories in interpreting the nature of this programme and developed our own model of how it may be operating. The scope of the current project does not allow for rigorous testing of our assumptions and proposals; however, they are presented here as tentative working hypotheses – as theories under construction rather than a predictive model.

With regards to context it is important to remain aware that the research was undertaken within the context of an international development initiative for Africa. While authors such as Reynolds (2000, p. 67) warn that community development activities may 'mask darker tendencies towards coercion and the assimilation of differences' our working assumption was that the current programme was essentially benign, undertaken in the genuine pursuit of beneficial social change. Furthermore, it is important to remember that as a transcontinental initiative many of the significant contextual factors within different subcultures may have been overlooked or overgeneralized. The African concept of 'ubuntu', for example, was considered a useful mechanism for describing the interdependence of self and community in African conceptions of leadership. Despite this, however, its origins lie with the Bantu people from South Africa and are not universally accepted (Ntibagirirwa, 2003). It is also important to ask how generalizable findings from a study like this are to other initiatives and places. While our sense is that there is no reason why these principles would not be applicable elsewhere, it is possible that they may be more likely to be successful in cultures with a strong collectivist orientation and a history of verbal communication and extended social networks.

Each of these points indicates the need for further empirical research and theorizing. It would be useful to do more in-depth investigations of participants and their networks as they progress through a development programme such as this. There would be value in exploring activities such as this in a range of different contexts and cultures and for different kinds of participants and communities. And it would be illuminating to use the ideas raised to inform the design and delivery of subsequent leadership development initiatives and to compare their performance to more traditional models of engagement.

Conclusion

In this chapter we have explored a pan-African leadership development programme to consider how leadership development can act as catalyst for community-level social change. We have argued that through a process of social enquiry participants have engaged in 'identity work' – reconstructing their concept of 'self within community'. Through a combination of appreciative inquiry, systems thinking and a philosophy of collective leadership the programme has helped participants begin building 'consummative social capital' within their communities that enables a re-evaluation of social norms and group identity. Such a shift, it is proposed, may be a necessary precursor to wider social change and engagement with leadership for collective benefit.

The System Leadership Development model proposed by Kirk (2005) has been used as the basis for constructing a model of social influence within and across communities. It is argued that the programme studied in the current research may be successful by virtue of its ability to facilitate connective leadership ('seeing together'), collective empowerment ('walking together') and dialogue ('talking together') and the dissemination of these principles between different people and groups. Such a perspective extends the focus of leadership development well beyond the development of individual leaders to the establishment of networks, relationships, and a renewed sense of shared identity and purpose.

Ultimately, however, it might be argued that leadership development such as this could be conceived of as a form of catharsis that 'leaves one with a sense of being part of a moral order that is essentially "just"' (Gosling, 2000, p. 143) – a potential antidote to overly heroic or instrumental accounts of leadership but one that may also require sacrifice: the possible subordination of self-interest to that of the community.

Acknowledgements

This chapter is based on an analysis of the first cohort of the InterAction Leadership Programme. The authors would like to thank the British Council and Questions of Difference for their support in this enquiry and the contribution of all the programme participants, facilitators and trainers who spared time to speak with us.

References

Alvesson, M. and Skoldberg, K. 2000. *Reflexive Methodology: New Vistas for Qualitative Research*. London: Sage Publications.
Armstrong, D. 1988 *Professional Management*. London: Grubb Institute.
Bakan, D. 1966. *The Duality of Human Existence*. Chicago, IL: Rand McNally.
Barker, R. A. 1997. How Can We Train Leaders if We Do Not Know What Leadership Is?, *Human Relations* 50(4): 343–62.
Bolden, R. and Kirk, P. 2009. African Leadership: Surfacing New Understandings Through Leadership Development, *International Journal of Cross Cultural Management* 9(1): 69–86.
Carroll, B. and Levy, L. 2010. Leadership Development as Identity Construction, *Management Communication Quarterly* 24(2): 211–31.
Cooperrider, D. L. and Srivastva, S. 1987. Appreciative Inquiry in Everyday Organizational Life. In R. W. Woodman and W. A. Passmore (eds) *Research in Organizational Change and Development, Vol.1*. Greenwich, CT: JAI Press Inc., pp. 129–69.

Day, D. 2000. Leadership Development: a Review in Context, *Leadership Quarterly* 11(4): 581–613.

Fairhurst, G. T. and Grant, D. 2010. The Social Construction of Leadership: A Sailing Guide, *Management Communication Quarterly* 24(2): 171–210.

Gosling, J. 2000. Three Apologetics of Management Education: Utility, Emancipation and Catharsis, *Human Resource Development International* 3(2), 143–5.

Gosling, J. and Mintzberg, H. 2003.The Five Minds of a Manager, *Harvard Business Review* 81(11): 54–63.

Harré, R., Clarke, D. and DeCarlo, N. 1985. *Motives and Mechanisms*. London: Methuen.

Iles, P. and Preece, D. 2006. Developing Leaders or Developing Leadership? The Academy of Chief Executives' Programmes in the North East of England, *Leadership* 2(3): 317–40.

Isaacs, W. 1999. *Dialogue and the Art of Thinking Together*. New York: Doubleday.

Kirk, P. 2005. System Leadership Development, *21st European Group for Organizational Studies (EGOS) Colloquium,* Freie Universität Berlin, Germany, 30th June–2nd July.

Kirk, P. and Shutte, A. M. 2002. Leadership for Change Through Dialogue, *International Academy of African Business and Development*, University of Port Elizabeth, SA: IAABD Proceedings, pp.187–93.

Kirk, P. and Shutte, A. M. 2003. Community Leadership Development: Farm Worker Capacity Building in South Africa, *Proceedings of 2003 International Academy of African Business and Development (IAABD)*, University of Westminster, London.

Lawrence, W. G. 1979. A Concept for Today: The Management of Oneself in Role. In W. G. Lawrence (ed.) *Exploring Individual and Organizational Boundaries: A Tavistock Open Systems Approach*. Chichester: John Wiley and Sons, pp. 235–49.

Lipman-Blumen, J. 1996. *Connective Leadership: Managing in a Changing World*. Oxford: Oxford University Press.

Ntibagirirwa, S. 2003. A Wrong Way: From Being to Having in the African Value System. In Patrick Giddy (ed.) *Cultural Heritage and Contemporary Change – Series II, Africa, Volume 7*. [www.crvp.org/book/Series02/II-7/chapter_v.htm].

Ospina, S. and Sorenson, G. L. J. 2006. A Constructionist Lens on Leadership: Charting New Territory. In G. R. Goethals and G. L. J. Sorenson (eds) *The Quest for a General Theory of Leadership*. Cheltenham: Edward Elgar, pp. 188–204.

Reed, B. 2001. *An Exploration of Role*. London: Grubb Institute.

Reynolds, M. 2000. Bright Lights and the Pastoral Idyll: Ideas of Community Underlying Management Education Methodologies, *Management Learning* 31(1): 67–81.

Senge, P. 1990. *The Fifth Discipline: The Art and Practice of Learning Company*. London: Random House.

Smircich, L. and Morgan, G. 1982. Leadership: The Management of Meaning, *Journal of Applied Behavioural Studies* 18: 257–73.

Sveningsson, S. and Alvesson, M. 2003. Managing Managerial Identities: Organizational Fragmentation, Discourse and Identity Struggle, *Human Relations* 56(10): 1163–93.

Triest, J. 1999. The Inner Drama of Role Taking in an Organization. In R. French and R. Vince (eds) *Group Relations, Management, and Organization.* Oxford: Oxford University Press.

Uhl-Bien, M. 2006. Relational Leadership Theory: Exploring the Social Processes of Leadership and Organizing, *Leadership Quarterly* 17: 654–76.

Wheatley, M. 1995. *Leadership and the New Science: Discovering Order in a Chaotic World.* San-Francisco: Berrett-Koehler.

Willem, A. and Scarbrough, H. 2006. Social Capital and Political Bias in Knowledge Sharing: An Exploratory Study, *Human Relations* 59(10): 1343–70.

4

The Internationalization of Leadership Development

Vanessa Iwowo

Introduction

From the painstakingly edited pages of textbook manuscripts and peer-reviewed journals of social theorists to the 'best-sellers' of management development consultants, leadership studies is in a constant state of evolution. Nevertheless, the subject of leadership development is one that has remained essentially ambiguous. That this situation may have arisen from an earlier ambiguity surrounding the question of leadership and its meaning is a possibility. Indeed, Stogdill (1974) observed that there were almost as many definitions as there were persons that had attempted to define the seemingly elusive concept of leadership.

Despite the remarkable advancement in leadership studies, the actual practice of *leadership development* appears predominantly characterized by traditionalist perspectives that have included a primary recourse to pre-designed, pre-packaged modules which advocate the understanding and development of the *self* through the impartation of specific predetermined skill sets or abilities. This traditional approach is largely driven by the assumption of a pre-diagnosed problem, and offers 'readily applicable' answers in the form of packaged solutions. Indeed, Kelly et al. (2006) have observed that despite attempts made to advance the scope of leadership as a researchable phenomenon, the packaging of leadership skill sets as typically represented by pre-designed programmes and course modules, remains the dominant approach in both public and private sector organizations This continued emphasis on the development of *self* seems contradictory to the conceptualization of leadership as *process*, as *relationship*, and as essentially characterized by the social force of *influence* (Northouse, 2004).

Jones (2006) has argued that a seeming obsession with the improvement of *self* within increasingly dominant views of leadership development appears to be more or less an all-American one. He contends that the normative assumptions that underlie the business simulation processes often practised within a number of contemporary and internationally deployed leadership development programmes (LDPs), are indeed 'not culturally neutral; rather, [that] they are distinctively western in their assumptions about human behaviour and the psychological backdrop of decision making in the business context' (p. 485). As such, these essentially reflect a deeply entrenched US organizational culture of individualism and self-actualization. This preoccupation with the improvement of *self* appears more oriented towards *leader-development*, a notion that is not necessarily synonymous with *leadership development* (Iles & Preece, 2006). It is believed that the latter would largely emphasize relationship building and the development of social capital and dynamic networks within and across the organization. The understanding of leadership as *relationship* and *influence* appears consistent with this latter view.

Leadership development as a situated practice

It has further been argued that rather than associate leadership development with the development of personality traits, skills and characteristics, it could be more usefully viewed as a 'situated practice' and as one that is best understood from the perspective of the user (Ladkin et al., 2009). This infers that it should be contextually relevant and understood in terms of what it really 'means' to the user or participant. Kelly et al. (2006) also stress that this could best be regarded as a 'design' challenge wherein the prospective design of the intervention would lie in uncovering patterns of interaction, which can be achieved by developing a set of scenarios of 'teachable moments'; moments that are somewhat familiar and that resonate with participants' experiences. Ladkin et al. (2009) suggest that although LDPs may be designed to equip participants with a range of theories, insights and descriptions of leadership, 'program participants learn that the valuable knowledge about leading is that which they construct for themselves, within the context in which they operate and with those who they lead' (p. 27). It follows that for leadership development interventions to be truly effective, they must not only be understood by the intended user, but more importantly, should be contextually relevant and practicable.

Leadership development and context

As the body of knowledge on Leadership Development continues to grow, there are increasingly resounding calls for more contextualized theory and praxis. The notion of leadership as a *situated practice* requires more culturally centred models of leadership development. A major argument that is germane to this approach centres on the importance of mental programmes and the construction of 'meaning' within sociocultural reality. This argument hinges on the assumption that our understanding of social phenomena is influenced by our mental programmes, values and beliefs. As such, our understanding and practice of leadership would be continually shaped and moulded by our thought processes, interactions and experience within sociocultural reality, all of which subsequently serve to reinforce one another. This is because our thought processes often inform our interactions with one another, and these dynamic interactions with one another are what subsequently provide the basis for our experiences. These experiences are what, in turn, shape our expectations and subsequently form the frames for our terms of reference (Goffman, 1986). Frames not only provide a gestalt for viewing ongoing circumstances and for managing the understanding of events as they unfold, but they are also value-laden, rhetorical resources which minimize some aspects of a situation, while highlighting other elements of the same (Goffman, 1986; Hamilton & Bean, 2005).

Against this backdrop, *context* is defined as being made up of different sets of *competing frames* from which individuals draw resources in order to facilitate the process of sense-making (Hamilton & Bean, 2005). Subsequently, I observe that the notion of *context* does indeed seem to rest on the assumption of spatial variation, within which may be found certain forms of distinctiveness. This is best explained by an understanding of the fact that people are grounded in different realities (Hearn & Ninan, 2003), and that these realities are made up of distinct and varying *sets of frames* within which people constantly enact their unique behaviours and dynamic interactions. It is these consistently re-enacted frames and interactions within an increasingly complex social reality that may continually account for situational variation and, ultimately, contextual uniqueness.

My main argument here is that our social constructions of 'meaning' are derived from and reinforced by the rhetorical resources within our social environment. If this is the case, it follows that our understanding and practices of leadership development should equally derive from that environment. That is, what we *conceptualize*, what we *know* and what we *understand* about leadership development should flow to us from the rhetorical elements within that social environment. These include our thought processes, interactions, experiences, expectations, values and beliefs, and indeed all of the dynamic mental and relational resources which are ever present within the various contexts in which we act, and through which we make meaning.

Again, Hollander and Julian (1969) have observed that the construct of leadership is one which is not only highly contextualized, but also involves the constant interplay between leaders, followers and situations – all of which are steadily influenced by values, beliefs and deep-seated mental programmes invariably present in the given context within which they operate. Grint (2000) also proffers a social constructionist view of leadership in which he argues that every account of leadership is the product of various social representations and interpretations of episodes and events. As such, there can never be exact replications of an 'objective truth' because these accounts are impacted by people's experiences, sense-making and interpretations, which vary contextually. Northouse (2004) also suggests that *leadership* is a co-influential relationship which practically exposes the *values* and *beliefs* of both leaders and followers.

Indigenizing leadership development?

In light of the calls for more contextualized approaches to its study and practice, there have been calls, particularly by African Scholars, for a more indigenized model of leadership education (Obiakor, 2004; Mbigi & Maree, 2005; Mbigi, 2005). Ranging from the subtle to what some might consider extreme, these views contend that western theories of leadership have not done the African Continent much good, and as such should be abandoned in favour of more culturally centred models of leadership. For instance, Obiakor (2004) observes that African leadership appears still tied to European-centred frameworks, a situation he insists is 'counter-productive to the sacred existence of the African peoples' (p. 402). He contends that African leadership is struggling today mainly because such leadership lacks the required theoretical foundations required to build strong and stable societies; a situation he attributes to the absence of African-centred education in leadership development. It is argued that such African-centred leadership education is required to build the much needed values of *patriotism* and *nationalism*, which he insists are a prerequisite to improving the current leadership situation, and essential to moving the continent forward.

Consequently, the argument is made for the 'institutionalization of a pragmatic system of African-centred education that opens concrete rooms [*sic*] for African experiments and African experiences and fosters the use of the African body, mind and soul' (Obiakor, 2004, p. 404). While the idea of creating an active learning space for such experimentation is necessary, I observe that within this argument lies the allusion to an 'African' experience, mind and soul; an assumption which runs the risk of appearing simplistic and somewhat idealistic. In my consideration of this, I argue that African social and cultural reality is not necessarily homogeneous, and for want of more anthropologically detailed evidence, I draw on Hofstede's 1980 seminal study to support this claim. This is because while he studied the rest of the world on a country level, Africa was initially studied on a regional-continental level in which it was subcategorized into West, East, South and Arab Africa, a situation which in itself pre-supposes the homogeneity of culture across the countries that make up these African regions. However, despite the sweeping generalization and the geographical broadness of this study, as well as its overtly broad compartmentalization of culture, the research showed that culture across Africa was not homogeneous at the time. If this is the case and if, truly, people are grounded in multiple realities, I am curious as to what an 'African experience' or an 'African mind' would look like, especially considering that the sociocultural reality in Zimbabwe, for example, might indeed be different from that in Nigeria. Be that as it may, this does not preclude the fact that there are indeed certain aspects of sociocultural reality and experience that transcend many African societies; nevertheless, I contend that the allusion to a culturally homogenized Africa in its entirety is not only overtly simplistic, but also that it poses the risk of hasty generalization.

As such, if Africa is not socioculturally homogeneous, then there are shadows subsequently cast on the feasibility of an 'African-centred' model of leadership development. While I do not entirely reject the usefulness and importance of indigenous knowledge, values and beliefs in leadership education, I maintain that the suggestion of an 'African-centred' model of leadership development begs further clarification, and as such should not be adopted uncritically. For instance, what uniquely qualifies an experience as being entirely 'African', and how might this in turn inform an 'African mind'; and what implications would this have for an 'African Leadership model'? Indeed, in discussing the limits of western leadership theories in Africa, Blunt and Jones (1997) clearly acknowledge that it is unrealistic to suppose that *much* of what can be said about leadership will apply equally across the vast continent of Africa. Rather, they suggest that despite the existing cultural heterogeneity, similarities do exist from which a 'tentative' profile may be drawn.

Another concern with the call for entirely culturally centred models is that there might be a perceived danger of ethnocentrism. If indeed Africa appears increasingly isolated from a rapidly globalizing and technologically advanced world, does not the perception of ethnocentrism fuelled by ideological isolationism present the danger of aggravating the status quo ante? I hold that if the intellectual imperialism allegedly propagated by European-centred frameworks of learning is a major contributor to Africa's leadership crisis, then, generating *entirely* ethnocentric knowledge frameworks, particularly in the wider context of an increasingly globalized world, cannot now be advanced as a cure-all for its hydra-headed leadership problems.

Furthermore, with regards to the question of leadership research and theorizing, it has become increasingly obvious to scholars that there is a dearth in literature on leadership research touching the sphere of the African Continent. Some have recounted their search experiences in this regard as they made to access the relevant literature in the course of their work (Jackson, 2004; Malunga, 2006; Nkomo, 2008). While Jackson (2004) notes that there is 'a real absence' of articulated work and theory on leadership research in Africa, it is also observed that wherever such articulated accounts exist, these appear to be rooted in discussions around the developed–developing world dichotomy. Such a situation no doubt prevents any constructive criticism and conceptual frameworks for sustainable development (Bolden & Kirk, 2005).

Blunt and Jones (1997) note an 'absence of local alternatives' (p. 13) with regards to non-western leadership theory, observing that most modern published notions of leadership originate primarily from the West. They add that 'in the micro domains of management, there still may be more interest in the replication in developing countries of Western theory and practice than there is resistance to it' (p. 1). Malunga (2006) also acknowledges the challenge of a lack of documentation and particularly recounts that it was not easy to find the relevant literature for his study on the subject of leadership in Africa.

All the above underscore the point that research on leadership/leadership development in Africa is not always readily available. Among other reasons, this situation is most likely attributable to the ancient African practice of orally bequeathing tradition – that is, indigenous customs and cultural ways of being – from one generation to the next via the verbal medium of *storytelling*; this could begin to provide a plausible reason why there appears a lack of documentation on the subject matter.

Be that as it may, and considering the near absence of theory on leadership in Africa, a probable approach to tackling this dilemma would be to concentrate more on conducting research and theoretically articulating the subject in order to address the current dearth in literature. However, given the vast number of Graduate Business and Management Schools on the continent – from the prestigious Lagos Business School of the Pan-African University in Nigeria to the Graduate Business School at UNISA in South Africa – the crucial question of *what should be taught in the interim* remains unanswered. Pessimistic as this question may appear, I hold that it is pertinent. Observably, what is currently taught in African Business Schools appears to be drawn mainly from mainstream business/management knowledge, and as such, is arguably based on western functionalist paradigms. Furthermore, it has also been stated that due to the propagation of western management education, any 'self-respecting MBA holder' from Zimbabwe to Ecuador and beyond will generally know the same things about leadership and other aspects of HR management (Blunt & Jones, 1997, p. 10). Therefore, if indeed Africa must evolve more indigenous theoretical frameworks on leadership development, then it follows that sufficient attention must be paid to bridging the gap in knowledge; a process which can only be expected to occur gradually. In view of this, it appears that there might be only a few other options left in the short term, which include the seemingly unpopular one of continuing to teach western management theory in African Business Schools.

Be that as it may, I observe that even though maintaining the status quo appears to be one that may be realistically considered, it is necessary to explore other relevant options that can be worked with in the short term. This means that if the overall aim is to fit management and leadership development in Africa within more contextual frameworks, then immediate practical strategies are urgently needed; even as medium- and long-term research is being conducted to bridge the existing knowledge gap on the subject matter.

This is especially needful, given the current reality of business globalization and what seems like Africa's increased isolation from the global scheme of things.

In considering possible approaches to addressing this short-term dilemma, it might be helpful to examine what theoretically articulated instances of leadership may already exist within the body of knowledge. In thinking about this, the first and perhaps the most documented notion of indigenous leadership that comes to mind is the African leadership philosophy of *Ubuntu,* which is subsequently discussed in more detail.

Ubuntu – an alternative?

> Africans have this thing called UBUNTU. It is about the essence of being human, it is part of the gift that Africa will give the world. It embraces hospitality, caring about others, being able to go the extra mile for the sake of others. We believe that a person is a person through another person, that my humanity is caught up, bound up, inextricably, with yours.
>
> – Desmond Tutu, Archbishop Emeritus of Cape Town
> (cited in Battle, 1997)

Originally adapted from the *Shona* expression *umuntu ngumuntu ngabanye* meaning 'a person is a person, through others', *Ubuntu*, which is the Ndebele word for *hunhu* (Shona), is a concept that attempts to convey the humaneness of the human being. Also expressed as *izandla ziyagezana*, that is 'the left hand washes the right hand and the opposite is true' (Chinouya, 2007), *ubuntu* is a metaphor which embodies the significance of group solidarity on survival issues, particularly in the context of deprived and dispossessed communities in Africa, where resources for livelihood are low and communities must depend on each other collectively in order to stay alive. It is thus a concept of sisterhood/brotherhood and collective unity for survival (Mbigi & Maree, 2005).

The cardinal ideology of *Ubuntu* is mirrored in the philosophy that *a person is only a person, through others*, and this perspective finds practical expression in the lived values of *relationships, reconciliation, conformity, compassion, respect, human dignity* and *collective unity* (Battle, 1997; Malunga, 2005; Mbigi & Maree, 2005).

It has been argued that 'unless development structures, strategies and processes can harness these *ubuntu* values into a dynamic transformative force for reconstruction and development, failure will be almost certain' (Mbigi & Maree, 2005, p. 6). As such, there have been calls to hark back to what might seem to be a primordial heritage, where many aspects of life and community were ritualized and held sacred, and in which they were generally perceived to be essential and crucial to the sustenance and survival of entire communities; ones which created a sense of belonging and in-group inclusiveness. Indeed, not a few proponents of *ubuntu* have suggested aligning contemporary organizational life with African cultural experience. For instance, while Malunga (2005) suggests the possible ritualization of many of today's organizational practices as a practical representation of the *ubuntu* ideology in today's organizations, to enable individuals to develop a sense of belonging and inclusiveness arising out of shared practices, Mbigi and Maree (2005) advocate harnessing the traditional religious experience and sacred constitution of the African peoples. Such applications of *ubuntu* may assist in facilitating dynamic social transformative change in the reconstruction of African Society.

In short, the concept of engaging *ubuntu* within the context of work and organizations emphasizes the need to draw on traditional African collective solidarity, community networks/relationships and social sensitivity in evolving new approaches to management learning and leadership development.

As a broad suggestion, while the calls to harness the social benefits of group solidarity and increased social responsibility are commendable, the notion of *ubuntu* as it is presently advanced, rests on a number of assumptions that appear simplistic. For the purpose of this chapter, I have chosen to discuss two of which I consider to be the most prominent; namely, the twin notions of the *non-dynamism of culture* and *social stability*.

As it is presently advanced, the philosophy of *ubuntu* ideologically assumes a seeming non-dynamism of culture and society. However, research has undoubtedly proved that this is not the case. Indeed, a number of studies have shown that although some distinct cultural values of a society may endure, culture is continually constructed, negotiated and changes or evolves over time, with cultural diffusion and overlaps often occurring across the board (Schein, 1968, 1985; Smircich, 1983; Inglehart & Baker, 2000).

Such cultural diffusion is clearly mirrored in many African societies today; increasingly, there is vast cultural proliferation occurring virtually across what could previously have been referred to as fixed cultural boundaries. Examples of these abound in elements of the European and American pop culture that are constantly propagated in and through the very powerful instruments of technology and mass media (Gillespie, 1995). It is no secret that the vivid images presented have been known to appeal mainly to the younger and upcoming generations. These visions are constantly being re-enacted and, over time, have continued to find practical expression in the course of daily societal and cultural life through the vibrant agents of fashion, Hollywood, cable satellite, the Internet, and so on.

Second, the cardinal ideology of *ubuntu* appears premised on the existence of relatively *socially stable* societies and while these may have existed at some point in African history, it is certainly not the case today. The argument here is that while the idea of absolute collectivism may have worked in many traditional African societies, the diffusion of a western capitalist and consumerist culture appears to have informed new ways of sociocultural, socio-economic and sociopolitical interactions in present-day Africa. It should also be noted, however, that consumerist culture is also infused in the African context with a number of ancient but latent indigenous traditions, such as, the socio-economic indicators of achievement and materialism among the Igbo of Nigeria (see Wambu, 2007).

To further illustrate this point, I draw on the experience of a fellow African scholar during one of his visits to his native village in the Igbo speaking part of Eastern Nigeria. In this, the author recounts aspects of his interaction with some young men from the village who are having to respond to the urban encroachment of *Aba*, a fast-growing trade city, located just on the outskirts of their native village. Below is an excerpt from this account.

> Interestingly, as I wandered round the village, the young men, *Nwa Afo* (sons of the soil) I spoke to, seemed to welcome the advent of Aba. I thought I could detect a yearning. Perhaps Aba meant a space where they could make a living, earn fast money, buy their own property and escape the age-based hierarchical structure that was in our village? Power was generational in the village and many of these young men would not see power or make law for perhaps 30 years. They were frustrated that these older men who had it were not responsive to their needs. Land was commonly held, but once the old men had given you your portion to farm, you were expected to add value to it. Many of the young were no longer interested in farming, they had lots of other business ideas that they wanted capital and support for.
>
> One entrepreneurial cousin was already producing handbags and sandals in Aba and needed capital to scale up his operations. Help for him was being co-ordinated at the family levels, but resources were limited. There was no broader vision on how the village could itself support any of these activities, or plug into the other industrial activities happening in the dynamic centre of Aba. So, once given the common land, for which they were supposed to be merely custodians, many of the young people were illegally selling it to generate liquid funds.
>
> (Wambu, 2007, p. 118)

From this account, the pressure which a rapidly diffused capitalist and industrialist culture considerably exerts on a traditionally collectivist society becomes apparent. The indigenous concept of village leadership, social responsibility and communally owned resources upon which the notion of *ubuntu* inherently rests, has failed to respond to the changing needs and aspirations of the younger working population. In this case, one of the immediate fallouts is the commoditization and sale of what is otherwise communally owned land.

Against the aforementioned, it appears that this culture-mix of western capitalism and consumerism on the one hand, and indigenous materialism on the other, have collectively propelled a seemingly alien wave of economic competition and individualism; a dynamic that is proving lethal to the notions of community solidarity, material collectivism and the social sensitivity that *ubuntu* protagonists advocate. Furthermore, the current economic instability in many African nations also appears to have added a more dangerous dimension of 'survival of the fittest' to the scenario painted above.

Herein lies the dilemma of *ubuntu*: a tension between the need for collective survival in the face of *poverty* and *deprivation* – even as the people draw on collective resources – and an equally human desire to be seen to excel, to be recognized, respected and celebrated as that individual achiever who has risen above the challenge of the same socio-economic odds of *poverty* and *deprivation*.

My argument is that while the need for socio-economic stability may have fostered collectivism and group solidarity in many traditional African settings, the advent of modern capitalism and consumerism, possibly aided by an indigenous materialist ideology, seems to have occasioned a new wave of individualism and competitiveness. Although such individualism and competition may have been previously alien to many African cultures, they presently seem to be propelled by the presupposed drivers of *ubuntu* – poverty and deprivation. That is, the ideological drivers of *ubuntu* are identical to those which now appear to drive the quest for self-actualization. This is clearly seen in the Wambu extract above; the desire of the young men to 'escape' the economic, hierarchical and communal structures that fundamentally underpin the *ubuntu* ideology has merely stemmed from their exasperation with it.

Indeed, it has been acknowledged that although ubuntu values were traditionally practised in ancient stable and predictable societies, part of the limitations of this 'African model' is that it has failed to transcend the stable predictable societies of old (Malunga, 2005). Ironically, it is possible that given the advent of western capitalism and a growing materialist and consumer culture, these two factors themselves – poverty and deprivation – may have provided a perfect stage upon which the scenario of individualism, competition and a 'survival of the fittest' ideology are constantly enacted. This is so because, arguably, the propensity for the recognition and celebration of the economically privileged few, as well as the emergence of an elite class in the midst of a deprived community, remains ostensibly higher than would be the case in more economically stable societies. Unfortunately, this scenario is closer to the reality of most African societies today.

Although the idea of group solidarity and collectivism seems intuitively appealing, I contend that the possibility of making recourse to the practice of absolute collectivism as advanced by *ubuntu* appears, at worst, impracticable and at best, naively utopian. Furthermore, the romanticization of *ubuntu*, particularly with its emphasis on *conformity* and *reconciliation* may embrace the practice of group consensus or group-think at the expense of constructive criticism. Such a situation would not only be counterproductive but may be detrimental to the development of the ideologically robust conceptual frameworks that are required for any meaningful advancement of organization and society at large. Indeed, consistently taking collective responsibility for the organization may actually suffocate personal motivation and inhibit healthy competition among peers (Sinclair, 1992; Malunga, 2006).

Internationalization – towards a more practical solution

Against this background, it is clear that the advancement of an 'Afro-centric model' of leadership development, and worse still, an uncritical adaptation of *ubuntu* as a cure-all for Africa's leadership crisis, appears to be a not readily practicable option. I propose what may be considered a more practical and readily applicable solution; one which I term the *internationalization of leadership development*. This suggestion is unapologetically premised on the concept of hybridization. I propose a management learning approach in which current mainstream theories are examined and understood in the light of the prevailing environment and subsequently contextualized via creative adaptation. Although Mbigi and Maree (2005) have suggested aligning the social experiences and innovation of the African peoples with successful management techniques from the East and West, they argue that this should merely serve to 'attain comparative parity' with the rest of the world, while *ubuntu* and the concept of indigenous collective solidarity should remain the central focus of practice. However, with respect to leadership development, I advance the option of internationalization wherein existing leadership theories – as they are presently taught in contemporary Business

Schools – are merged with everyday scenario-based learning, in order to evolve more contextually relevant and effectual leadership development programmes. Pursuing this approach, existing leadership theory would be examined, understood and critically adapted in the context of the intended user's everyday work experience. I argue that this is a missing component from the design of contemporary management learning interventions, that is, not only contextualizing 'knowledges' but more specifically, addressing the practical question of 'how I can apply it *here* and *now*'. As Ladkin et al. (2009) have noted, leadership, as it is taught and learnt, must indeed be relevant to the intended user.

Therefore, I propose that well beyond the option of merely employing indigenous knowledge as the entire basis for Leadership Development interventions, particular attention could, for instance, be paid to developing and articulating *operational stories* from the daily work, social and interactional life of modern organizations within the African continent. I believe that this would not only provide the basis for proper contextualization and, as such, internationalization of leadership development, but would also allow for creative adaptation and practicable application of current theory and practice. This is because a core preoccupation of the proposed approach would be to critically examine, understand and creatively appropriate existing leadership knowledge within the social, ideological and practical frameworks of the current contextual reality. I contend that such an approach is far more practical because it would help to respectfully accommodate and experientially navigate the contextual complexities of the African organizational terrain in relation to the rest of the world, and not merely reflect traditional indigenous knowledge.

To this end, I propose the development of clearly articulated contextual case studies which would not only serve operationally to ground knowledge and make experiential learning possible, but would also quickly begin to address the current dearth in leadership and management literature on the African continent. Interestingly, this approach is quite easily premised on a most effective, time-tested and proven instrument of cultural preservation in Africa – the ancient traditional art of *storytelling*, which is not necessarily an element of *ubuntu*. This practice is indigenous to many parts of Africa, and indeed, one can still easily recall childhood memories of 'tales by moonlight' and the powerful images that these imprinted on one's young mind. It is firmly believed that the pedagogical treasures within this one tool can be effectively harnessed with a view to enhancing leadership development learning on the Continent.

Practically speaking, this means that deliberate action must now be taken to actively observe and record flexible adaptations of existing leadership theory, even as particular attention is paid to experiential *knowing*, emphasizing creative experimentation and centralizing scenario-based learning.

For instance, a practical approach to this may seek to ground existing leadership theory within learning frameworks of localized experience. Perhaps, a possible way to achieve this would be to design learning programmes that specifically allow for the critical examination of current leadership literature through the lens of 'lived' contextual experiences. That is, understanding, appropriating and even deconstructing existing leadership *theory*, in the light of *stories,* which themselves have been sufficiently articulated and suitably presented in the form of contextual experiential case studies. I believe that this would not only help merge mainstream theory with contextual practice, but it would also allow for constructive learning in the short term, as well as evolve strong conceptual frameworks for theoretical advancement.

It may be encouraging to note that a strand of such hybridization has already begun to find expression in practice. For instance, the Graduate Business School at the University of Cape Town, South Africa has had to redesign its Graduate Business programme in the post-apartheid era. In this instance, traditional MBA teaching approaches have been re-evaluated in order to become more relevant to programme participants who must operate the management principles they learn in the context of the present era. As April and April (2007) write, 'the GSB decided to pioneer a new model of a business school in Africa, one that was both international in orientation and suited to countries where there are simultaneous imperatives of socio-political transformation, international competitiveness, and economic development' (p. 216).

My hope is that such interventions will not only find practical expression in the design of future leadership development initiatives, but will also begin to promote a whole new understanding, not to mention a very *conscious practice*, of Worldly Leadership Development.

References

April, K. A. and April, R. A. 2007. Growing Leaders in Emergent Markets: Leadership Enhancement in the New South Africa, *Journal of Management Education* 31: 214.

Battle, M. 1997. *Reconciliation: The Ubuntu Theology of Desmond Tutu.* Pilgrim Press.

Blunt, P. and Jones, M. 1997. Exploring the Limits of Western Leadership Theory in East Asia and Africa, *Personnel Review* 26(1): 10–22.

Bolden, R. and Kirk, P. 2005. Leadership in Africa; Meanings, Impacts and Identities, *Conference Paper Presented at the 4th International Conference on Leadership Research, Lancaster University Management School, UK, 12–13 December 2005*.

Chinouya, M. 2007. Ubuntu and the Helping Hands for AIDS. In O. Wambu and J. Githongo (eds) *Under the Tree of Talking: Leadership for Change in Africa*. London: Counterpoint.

Gillespie, M. 1995. *Television, Ethnicity and Cultural Change*. London: Routledge.

Goffman, E. 1986. *Frame Analysis: An Essay on the Organization of Experience*. Boston, MA: North-eastern University Press.

Grint, K. 2000. *The Arts of Leadership*. Oxford: Oxford University Press

Hamilton, F. and Bean, C. 2005. The Importance of Context, Beliefs and Values in Leadership Development, *Business Ethics, A European Review* 14(4): 336–47.

Hearn, G. and Ninan, A. 2003. Managing Change is Managing Meaning, *Management Communications Quarterly* 16(3): 440–5.

Hofstede, G. 1980 [2001]. *Culture's Consequences*. London: Sage.

Hollander, E. and Julian, J. 1969. Contemporary Trends in the Analysis of Leadership Processes, *Psychological Bulletin* 71(5): 387–97.

Inglehart, R. and Baker, W. E. 2000. Modernization, Cultural Change and the Persistence of Traditional Values, *American Sociological Review* 65: 19–51.

Iles, P. and Preece, D. 2006. Developing Leaders or Developing Leadership? The Academy of Chief Executives' Programmes in the North East of England, *Leadership* 2(3): 317–40.

Jackson, T. 2004. *Management and Change in Africa: A Cross-Cultural Perspective*. London: Routledge.

Jones, A. 2006. Leading Questions: Developing What? An Anthropological Look at the Leadership Development Process across Cultures, *Leadership* 2(4): 481–98.

Kelly, S., White, M., Martin, D. and Rouncefield, M. 2006. Leadership Refrains: Patterns of Leadership, *Leadership* 2(2): 181–201.

Ladkin, D., Case, P., Gaya Wicks, P. and Kinsella, K. 2009. Developing Leaders in Cyber-Space: The Paradoxical Possibilities of On-line Learning, *Leadership* 5(2): 193–212.

Malunga, C. 2006. Learning Leadership Development from African Cultures: A Personal Perspective, *Praxis* note No. 25, INTRAC, Oxford.

Mbigi, L. and Maree, J. 2005. *Ubuntu: The Spirit of African Transformation Management*. Randburg, South Africa: Knowres Publishing.

Mbigi, L. 2005. *The Spirit of African Leadership*. Randburg, South Africa: Knowres Publishing,.

Nkomo, S.B. 2008. African Women in Leadership: Current Knowledge and a Future Agenda. Unpublished conference paper, *Leadership and Management Studies in Sub-Saharan Africa Conference, GIMPA, Accra, Ghana, July 7–9 2008*.

Northouse, P. 2004. *Leadership: Theory and Practice*, 3rd edn. Thousand Oaks, CA: Sage.

Obiakor, F. 2004. Building Patriotic African Leadership through African-Centred Education, *Journal of Black Studies* 34(3): 402–20.

Schein, E. 1968. Organizational Socialization and the Profession of Management, *Industrial Management Review* 9(2): 1–15.

Schein, E. 1985. *Organizational Culture and Leadership.* San Francisco: Jossey-Bass.

Sinclair, A. 1992. The Tyranny of a Team Ideology, *Organization Studies* 13(4): 611–26.

Smircich, L. 1983. Concepts of Culture and Organizational Analysis, *Administrative Science Quarterly* 28(3): 339–58.

Stogdill, R. 1974. *Handbook of Leadership: A Survey of Theory and Practice.* New York: Free Press.

Wambu, O. 2007. Leadership and Followership in an African Village. In O. Wambu and J. Githongo (eds) *Under the Tree of Talking: Leadership for Change in Africa.* London: Counterpoint.

5
Using the Worldly Leadership Lens to Approach the Task of Developing Women Leaders

Susan R. Madsen

Introduction

The rapid expansion of globalization in all types of businesses and organizations has forced researchers and practitioners to consider new paradigms of leadership (Robinson & Harvey, 2008). In fact, Muczyk and Holt (2008) reported that 85 per cent of Fortune 500 executives say that their firms do not currently have enough competent individuals to lead effectively in the present global environment. Many authors (e.g. Livers, 2007) agree that leading globally requires a fundamental shift in terms of thinking and behaving, but to date most researchers and practitioners have focused only on understanding and developing clearly defined skill sets or competency-based frameworks on which to base their leadership development strategies, programmes and initiatives (Byrne & Rees, 2006; Kowske & Anthony, 2007; Noel & Dotlich, 2008; Tubbs & Schulz, 2006). A compelling question arises: Will present strategies be enough to develop new leaders with the knowledge, skills and abilities needed for this dynamic, complex and challenging environment?

As leadership researchers and practitioners, we can consider development from a variety of perspectives. For example, we can focus our work on individuals in our own cultures to help them become effective in leading global organizations. The question just posed is critical to consider from this perspective because the discussion shifts to the backgrounds and experiences of the individuals being trained and the changes that need to occur in *their* thinking and behaviour so that they can become effective leaders in the global economy.

Another important task is developing and implementing leadership programmes for citizens of other countries, those who will continue to live, work and lead in their nations and cultures. In this situation, I purport that the fundamental shift in thinking and behaving needs to begin with *our* perspective or 'lens'. If leadership programmes and initiatives are not designed using the most appropriate and effective lens, long-term success of programme participants will be limited. One of the most intriguing areas of current leadership inquiry revolves around the development of female leaders in countries where women have been oppressed for centuries. Hence, it is of critical import to discover the most effective lens to use in developing women leaders who are nationals of countries that have emerging and changing perspectives of the role of women in business and government.

Developing women leaders is a highly complex phenomenon in most countries. Consideration must be given to culture, tradition, religion, values, backgrounds, education, work – family issues, self-concept, gender barriers, expectations, previous opportunities and perceived future opportunities; otherwise, the effectiveness of structured development programmes will not meet their potential. I would argue that there are many more layers or worlds to understand in developing women leaders in global settings, and that unless we understand the layers of complexity within cultures, traditions, and perspectives – and a woman's 'world' is much different from a man's 'world' in any culture – we cannot be effective in designing and implementing relevant leadership development programmes. For example, I am currently doing research on women in the United Arab Emirates (UAE). Although there are at present few Emirati women leaders, women are now receiving education and are being encouraged by many to join the workforce (Al Abed et al., 2007; *Khaleej Times*, 2007). There also seems to be an emerging openness towards the involvement of UAE women in management and leadership roles; consequently, there is an increasing need for leadership programmes that will assist in the development of Emirati women who want to become influential in their communities, governments and businesses. The complexities listed previously must be explored before leadership programmes are developed and implemented.

I am also researching on women in China and have worked with women leaders from Russia. I know there is a need for a guiding approach in preparing for and designing leadership programmes for women in these countries. I argue that, for these and other such opportunities, the 'global leadership' perspective is limiting, and instead Mintzberg's (2004) concept of 'worldly leadership' is more effective. Therefore, the purpose of this chapter is to investigate the utility of using the worldly leadership lens to approach the task of developing women leaders, particularly in non-Western cultures. This chapter explores (1) the concepts of wholeness to worldly perspectives, (2) the need for a change of lens, (3) examples of studies that provide insight for a more 'worldly' lens within specific cultures, (4) a supporting theory that provides a framework for acquiring a worldly leadership lens and (5) theory to practice.

Wholeness to worldly perspectives

Amidst the plethora of writings on leadership, there is a 'call' for looking at leadership development in a more holistic manner (Bennis, 1989; Madsen, 2008a, 2008b; Mintzberg, 2004). Palmer (2004) argued for the importance of discovering one's own 'hidden wholeness' as a 'journey toward an undivided life' or, as Bennis termed, towards becoming an 'integrated human being' (p. 4). Bennis said that the process of becoming an integrated human being (i.e. finding wholeness) is much the same process as becoming a leader. Systems theory can also be used to explore wholeness because it helps us understand the interconnectedness of each component within an organization. Systems theory can also illuminate the complexity of developing people both internally (our emotional, intellectual, physical and social facets) and externally (our relationships, contexts and behaviours). Although the whole is more powerful than the sum of its parts, an understanding of the function and connectedness of the parts can lend to a more holistic look at what Dewey (1944) called the 'whole person'. John Dewey argued that individuals need to be understood from various perspectives, which include knowledge, intellect, emotion, endeavour, capacity and interests. Further, Dewey (1962, p. 152) explained that learning and development need to be approached with awareness of the complexities of 'the interaction of man, with his memories and hopes, understanding and desire'. Approaching the development of women leaders in the framework discussed in the introduction lends itself to this holistic approach. The question then becomes, which lens is most useful – global or worldly – in developing women leaders through a holistic approach?

The global lens, as Mintzberg (2004) outlined, views individuals, situations, opportunities and challenges from a distance, and encourages homogenization of behaviour. Hence, if one looks at the development of people in various cultures, from this perspective, checklists of generic competencies needed for global leadership can be used as an outline for one's development plan. But how effective can this be for individuals and cultures that have layers of complexity? Many with this perspective tend to approach development with individuals in various countries in the same way and with the same set of predetermined competencies. Leaders who use this lens are 'conditioned by Western- and US-centric leadership theories and methodologies' (The Leadership Trust, 2009, p. 1), and this thinking is 'driven through our global business schools and business cultures, often to the exclusion of non-Western traditions and cultures' that offer valuable insights and wisdom. This lens neither provides the flexibility and leadership wisdom that 'lies hidden in ancient, indigenous societies and cultures' nor the encouragement to explore in-depth backgrounds and experiences of specific populations from which the potential programme participants emerge.

In his writings, Mintzberg (2004) argued that we should consider the worldly mindset to develop leaders and managers. The word 'worldly' in the context of leadership development can be defined in a variety of ways (Dictionary.com, 2009; The Free Dictionary, 2009). It can be used to describe one who is experienced, practical and sophisticated, or as one who 'knows' and is connected with or directed towards the affairs and interests of the world. 'Worldly' can describe someone who possesses a practical understanding of human affairs and is knowledgeable about and experienced in human society and life. Mintzberg explained that our globe is actually made up of all kinds of worlds – even worlds within worlds – and we need a worldly leadership lens to be truly successful in working with people of other cultures. In fact, he argues that to truly understand our own world, we needed to understand other cultures and worlds. I argue that Mintzberg's worldly perspective is particularly useful in developing leadership in women from the non-Western cultures to which I referred.

What constitutes a worldly lens for those who develop women leaders in various countries? Such a developer would reflectively design and implement leadership programmes based on her wealth of experience in understanding and applying knowledge in practical ways. She would have an in-depth understanding of human learning and behaviour in the cultures and circumstances for which she is developing programmes. Recent studies suggest a growing need for her to understand human development and adult development perspectives (Hoppe, 2007). She can use this lens only if she understands human society within the specific contexts of country, work and community. In addition, viewing worldly leadership through a comprehensive developmental lens also considers the various elements within an external environment: governmental relations, societal trends, economic challenges, legal climate, industry dynamics, international development and technological advancements (Mintzberg, 2004; Porter & McKibbin, 1988). Finally, because there are layers of complexity within each society and culture, the experiences of women are typically quite different from those of their male counterparts. Designing effective programmes for women in these countries requires a unique set of insights into specific gender dynamics and their interplay within each culture.

Need for a change of lens

Many leadership researchers and practitioners continue to use cluster models to guide their design of global leadership development. Bass (1990) summarized various models nearly two decades ago as a way, in part, for leadership developers to determine how to teach and train individuals within the United States and beyond. He argued that 'some behaviour, attributes, causes, and effects are found everywhere in similar fashion' but that 'other elements tend to be concentrated in some cultures and countries rather than others' (p. 761). The generalizations summarized in his seminal *Handbook of Leadership* continue to be helpful in many ways; however, most provide 'global' rather than 'worldly' insights. For example, Bass summarized the styles for leaders in various regions and countries (autocratic versus democratic leadership, participative and directive leadership, relations-oriented and task-oriented leadership, initiation versus consideration, laissez-faire leadership versus the motivation to manage and transformational and transactional leadership).

Interestingly, Kowske and Anthony (2007) present evidence that practitioners and researchers can make serious mistakes when they classify expectations for leadership style and behaviour by geographical regions: 'Generalizing the interaction between leadership roles and culture by region may be, at best, insufficient, but at worst, may be harmful to at-work relationships and work practices' (p. 39). They further note that differences exist between countries within the same region and that the 'definitional nature of leadership can change both between and within countries' (p. 22).

Research (Ardichvili & Kuchinke, 2002; Kowske & Anthony, 2007) shows that many cultures do not share basic assumptions regarding what leaders may or may not do, what their status and influence levels are, what is expected of them and even what attributes are seen as leadership characteristics. Hoppe (2004) warned that when leadership programmes and products based on one country's set of leadership values are used for people in other cultures, the results often yield confused participants, unreliable data and unsatisfactory outcomes. I would argue that even if slight to moderate changes are made to leader development programmes for women based on global models (e.g. Hofstede's Cultural Dimensions), results may still be disappointing, for not only do assumptions and expectations vary by region and country, they can also vary substantially from individual to individual within a particular country depending on their background experiences, individual upbringing, religion, community environment, social status, personal challenges and expected opportunities.

I do admit that generalizations based on existing cultural models can be helpful in providing some initial insights, but they cannot provide the depth of perspective needed for the worldly lens. Research provides some general criteria. For example, Malaysian culture disdains assertive, confrontational behaviour, and therefore maintaining harmony is of utmost importance (Kennedy, 2002). Though somewhat useful, global models and competency-based studies do not provide the best tools to probe deeply enough to view development through a worldly lens.

Examples

To develop leadership programmes for women in non-Western countries, the worldly lens requires a much more individualized and in-depth analysis of the participants and the numerous complexities that embody and surround them: culture, traditions, religion, values, backgrounds, education, work – family issues, self-concept, gender barriers, expectations, previous opportunities, perceived future opportunities. The literature related to gender issues provides examples of frameworks that can be useful in the analysis or needs assessment stage, which takes place before the programme is designed. For example, Ruderman (2004) argues that it is important to understand the context in which women leaders operate to discover what leadership development strategies might best serve them. She stated that to understand how to develop high-achieving women leaders, it is critical to consider the forces that shape their careers. Although these forces may differ for women in different countries, cultures and social classes, Ruderman's five themes reveal the factors that may influence the development of women leaders and 'capture the issues faced by high-achieving women as they approach their careers and their lives' (p. 275). She suggested that understanding these themes can help determine the 'suitability of the typical techniques organizations used to develop women leaders' (p. 275). These themes include (1) *authenticity:* the 'degree to which daily actions and behaviours are in concert with deeply held values and beliefs' (p. 275); (2) *connection:* 'need to be close to other human beings – family, friends, community, and co-workers' (p. 276); (3) *agency:* desire to control one's own destiny; (4) *wholeness:* desire to 'feel complete and integrated as a full human being' (p. 276); and (5) *self-clarity:* 'need to understand themselves within the context of the world in which they operate' (p. 277). Understanding these themes within specific cultures would provide insightful information that would help one develop a more worldly lens from which to facilitate the development of leadership.

The distinction between worldly and global lenses appears in studies that detail the unique situations of women within specific nations. For example, Gvozdeva and Gerchikov (2002) studied women in Russia and found that women regard power and influence negatively, and, in fact, more than half of those surveyed saw no opportunity for advancement. Their motives for management and leadership included self-realization instead of profit; interesting, meaningful work instead of independent decision making; money instead of the desire to lead; and concern for associates rather than career. They are also motivated by professional growth and self-assertion. The researchers note that Russian women managers typically employ moral and psychological persuasion rather than administrative measures when dealing with a subordinate who needs to be disciplined. Women managers, researchers discovered, are better at resolving conflict than are Russian men, and women tend to pinpoint the basis of conflict and want to remedy the causes to help eliminate future conflicts. The surveyed Russian women clearly had the following:

> (1) high intelligence; (2) the ability to achieve set goals; (3) a willingness to assume responsibility; (4) the ability to act in the role of wise advisor and counsellor; (5) a sense of confidence in the web of organizational relations and events; and (6) a friendly, courteous, but decisive way of dealing with people. (Gvozdeva & Gerchikov, 2002, p. 66)

Another Russian study (Chirikova & Krichevskaia, 2002) found that women entrepreneurs are more 'oriented toward controlling their own time, often at the expense of greater profit, and their attempt to find a happy balance between work and home limits the expansion of the enterprise' (p. 39). This and other Russian research studies (see Zaslavskaia, 2007) reveal some of the layers needed for a worldly lens.

Worldly leadership supporting theory

Throughout the past few years, I have conducted three studies in the UAE with female Emirati college students and successful female leaders in business and government. Through this journey I have acquired a worldly lens for UAE culture that has already proven invaluable, giving me critical information and insights to begin developing leadership programmes for UAE women nationals. I developed this lens primarily through using the transformational learning theory to guide my work, and I discovered that this theory can provide a particularly useful framework for exploring how to design effective leadership programmes. The theory can help practitioners and researchers develop a worldly lens. In fact, it may be an ideal theory to anchor the movement from a global to a worldly lens, especially regarding the development of women managers and leaders. To understand 'worlds within worlds', we must understand the complexity of development so we can design leadership programmes for women in specific cultures. Effective leadership development requires change, and I propose that worldly vision occurs through transformative learning. In 1978, Jack Mezirow introduced transformational learning theory (transformative theory) and the associated perspective, transformation construct. Mezirow (1990) defined learning as 'the process of making a new or revised interpretation of the meaning of an experience, which guides subsequent understanding, appreciation, and action' (p. 1). Merriam and Caffarella (1995) stated that 'transformational learning theory is about change – dramatic, fundamental change in the way we see ourselves and the world in which we live' (p. 318). Clark (1993) stated that 'Transformational learning shapes people; they are different afterward, in ways both they and others can recognize' (p. 47). Transformational learning is anchored in life experience. Mezirow's theory is about how adults make meaning from and interpret their experiences. According to Taylor (1993),

Transformative learning attempts to explain how an individual's expectations, framed within cultural assumptions and presuppositions – meaning perspectives, directly influence the meaning an individual derives from his or her experiences ... When an individual has an experience that cannot be assimilated into his or her meaning perspective, the experience is rejected or the perspective changes to accommodate the new experience. It is the revision and change of these meaning perspectives that is explained by the theory of perspective transformation. (pp. 7–8)

Transformational learning focuses on three core components (Merriam & Caffarella, 1995; Mezirow, 1991):

1. *Mental Construction of Experience*: Engaging with each life experience to make meaning provides opportunities for changes in perspective and behaviour.
2. *Critical Reflection*: 'Effective learning does not follow from a positive experience but from effective reflection' (Criticos, 1993, p. 162). To reflect critically, individuals must not only think about their experiences, but they must also examine the underlying beliefs and assumptions that influence how they make sense of their experiences.
3. *Development/Action*: Individuals must explore options for forming new roles, relationships, or actions. To truly transform, they need to try out their new knowledge, skills, or roles and then build new competence and self-confidence.

For an individual to 'transform' through a learning experience, she needs to have opportunities to fully engage in all three core components throughout the process. Development is about improving and changing oneself in some way, and leadership development is anchored in this change. Reflection is the central component in transformative learning. Mintzberg (2004, p. 307) stated that 'worldliness puts analysis and reflection into context'. Reflection is at the heart of transformational learning, and it lies at the heart of the worldly leadership lens (Mintzberg, 2004). Thus, I propose a model that aligns the worldly leadership concept with analysis and reflection to bring context to the worldly lens.

Mezirow (1991) first applied the 'perspective transformation' construct to adult learning, arguing that perspective transformation shows how learning can lead to change. He defined perspective transformation as

> The process of becoming critically aware of how and why our assumptions have come to constrain the way we perceive, understand, and feel about our world; changing these structures of habitual expectation to make possible a more inclusive, discriminating, and integrative perspective; and finally, making choices or otherwise acting upon these new understandings. (p. 167)

Mezirow articulates ten phases of the perspective transformation process, which he acknowledges need not occur in the sequence he outlined (see Merriam & Caffarella, 1995; Mezirow, 1991). First, the transformation is initiated by a disorienting dilemma (a life event or experience – often a crisis) that cannot be resolved through problem-solving skills or strategies one has used in the past. Second, the individual engages in some type of self-examination process, which (third) leads to a critical assessment of his or her assumptions. Fourth, exploring one's assumptions leads to a recognition that others have experienced similar discontentment, transformation and change. Fifth, the individual explores options for change (forming new roles, relationships and actions) and (sixth) formulates a plan of action. Seventh, the plan or strategy includes the acquisition of applicable knowledge and skills needed for implementation. Eighth, individuals need to manifest these new roles and/or behaviours and (ninth) build competence and self-confidence in the resulting new roles or relationships. Finally (tenth), the individual needs to integrate these changes into his or her life (Merriam & Caffarella, 1995).

Transformational learning theory has been used as a theoretical framework for a variety of studies in a multitude of unique learning environments from dying patients to healthy graduate students or working professionals (see King, 2003; Taylor, 2007; Young et al., 2006). To date, no research has been published on Mezirow's theory providing a basis for research in learning environments within most non-Western countries and particularly to research related to women and leadership development; however, it does provide an intriguing outline for researching and learning details that can help us develop a more worldly lens for distinct populations, particularly emerging women leaders.

Theory to practice

The three core components can help us carefully craft our own experiences towards strategically transforming our thinking and behaviours from the global to worldly lens. First, we must engage with each potential learning experience related to the culture and country in which we would like to work. No detail is too small to learn. We need to make meaning from what we see, hear and read so we can change our own perspectives and behaviours. Second, we must learn to reflect more deeply and critically about our own beliefs and assumptions and ponder their influences on how we are making sense of others' experiences. Finally, we need to explore our own options for forming new roles, relationships and actions. Developing our worldly lens is a transformation we must undertake. We too must try out our new roles, skills and knowledge to build confidence in studying and practising leadership in new settings.

The perspective transformation process also provides an interesting framework for leadership researchers and practitioners towards the development of a worldly leadership lens. Although Mezirow's ten-phase process was not designed to provide a framework for the acquisition of a comprehensive worldly leadership lens, it provides a loose structure for facilitating leadership. Through research studies, interviews and observations, one can develop a worldly lens specific to a culture and understand in more depth the women leaders one will be assisting. In the following section, I will highlight each phase and provide insights into how each can guide us to collect information that will strengthen our worldly lens so we can facilitate effective leadership growth.

1. *Disorienting dilemma:* Figure out what the critical life events or crises women in a culture may experience. Discover trigger events that tend to facilitate and initiate the desire for change within potential women leaders. The situations are new to these women, who initially are not sure how to resolve them. Disorienting dilemmas are the catalysts that force these women to develop new skills and/or strategies that will help them in overcoming a crisis and move forward in strengthening themselves and developing new skills.
2. *Self-examination:* Discover how women within a particular culture analyse and examine themselves. In some cultures women are very hard on themselves, and negative feedback from others is devastating. It is important to find out whether the women are taught to examine their own thoughts, behaviours and actions. If they are not, then self-examination skills should be added to the curriculum of leadership development programmes. Some cultures have reflection at their core, while others do not teach this naturally – particularly to the upcoming generation of leaders. It is critical to learn about women's habits, behaviours and understanding of the need to reflect on their own experiences. The phase aligns well with the first of Ruderman's (2004) themes, *authenticity,* and it considers the degree to which actions and behaviours parallel deeply held beliefs and values. Self-examination is the first step in this personal assessment.
3. *Critical assessment of assumptions:* Reflection is crucial in this phase. We need to understand when and how women typically assess personal assumptions within their culture. In some cultures women are taught not to challenge their assumptions – values, habits and long-held opinions. Leadership development requires change; discover

appropriate, culture-specific ways to challenge women to analyse their assumptions. This phase also parallels Ruderman's (2004) *authenticity* theme in analysing the assumptions that lie at the heart of beliefs and values and their influence on personal behaviour.

4. *Recognition of others:* Discovering how and what women see in others can help one design effective leadership programmes. In most cultures women find solace in hearing others' experiences; they want to know they are not alone in their struggles and challenges, and researching stories of other women's successes within a particular culture may provide helpful material in designing programme sessions. Also, providing ample time for women to share experiences and transformational moments is generally helpful. Women in all cultures like connecting with others; most have a need to be close to family, friends, community and co-workers (see Ruderman, 2004, theme two).

5. *Change options:* Explore the options for change that women believe they have had or will have. Understand the options women have had for leadership roles and recognize the traditional and emerging cultural assumptions for women in management and leadership in each culture. Explore how new roles are formed and recognize general resistance to change. To develop leadership, women will need to form new roles and relationships. Understanding the history and perceptions of change within a culture can help provide a general outline for change strategies within a leadership programme.

6. *Plan of action:* To implement change, there must be a plan of action. Women in different countries and cultures view structured plans of action in varying ways. If structured plans are uncommon in a particular culture, then foundational materials should be developed with strategies for change. However, in other cultures women desire strict accountability for plans of action. We must customize culture-specific development programmes to incorporate strategies that will be effective. Ruderman's (2004) third theme, *agency*, relates to this phase: we must understand women's perspectives towards their ability and desire to control their own destinies. For example, curriculum for women who do not believe they can control their destinies will vary greatly from programmes designed for women who believe they have control of their destiny.

7. *Acquiring the knowledge and skills to implement the plan:* Explore how women have acquired knowledge and skills within their cultures to design experiences for the acquisition of new skills. Identify potential role models. The more information one has into women's past experiences within a particular culture, the more one can provide

valuable insights into the design of developmental curriculum. Understanding how women transform leads to understanding how they learn and develop.

8. *Trying out these new roles and/or behaviours:* A comprehensive long-term leadership programme must shift women from learning about something to actually implementing new roles and behaviours. If a programme does not require implementation, it is unlikely to result in long-term change for its participants. Developing a comprehensive worldly leadership lens from which to design effective leadership programmes requires an in-depth understanding of how women can safely try out roles and behaviours within training, workplace and community settings. This information will not only provide helpful examples, scenarios and cases for discussion within the programme, but it will also provide a foundation for conversations with women participants regarding how they can manifest change in their lives.

9. *Building competence and self-confidence in new roles or relationships:* Women need to have time to try out new roles long enough to build competence and self-confidence. Conducting culture-specific research on women's past experiences can provide beneficial insights in understanding programme design for future leadership development efforts. Ruderman's (2004) *wholeness* theme aligns with phases eight and nine of the perspective transformative process. Women have a desire to feel complete and integrated as people, and this requires taking new knowledge and applying it. To be 'whole', one must align one's thoughts, words, actions and behaviours.

10. *Integrating changes into his or her life:* The final theme in Ruderman's (2004) work is *self-clarity*. Women in all cultures have a need to understand themselves in their myriad functional contexts and 'worlds'. Understanding how women navigate their cultures can be helpful. By integrating changes fully within their workplaces, homes, families and communities, women may create permanent changes – particularly if the changes are supported by others in their environment. In any culture, women can find self-clarity, but new experiences provide opportunities for new self-discovery, which fosters an ongoing process of change as long as women have a continued desire for growth, learning and improvement. Leadership practitioners should understand how women need support to generate long-term change. Implementing these findings within a leadership programme is important.

Highlighting each of the ten phases provides a guide to use in exploring cultures to glean critical information that can help one design effective and comprehensive leadership programmes. I argue that transformational learning theory can provide an important foundation for the worldly leadership lens, and that through this lens we can approach the task of developing women leaders more effectively. In fact, I have found through my experiences that researching and discovering the 'lived experiences' of women's upbringings and adulthood environments (e.g. culture, expectations, traditions, challenges, opportunities) before designing leadership development initiatives can lead to life-changing experiences for programme participants. This is clearly an example of using a worldly instead of a global lens. These phases and themes can help us understand how to shift our own lens so that we can understand the layers and 'worlds within worlds' needed for the leadership programmes we should be developing for women living in any country, but particularly in regions where the oppression of women has been commonplace or is culturally sanctioned. The ten phases can also be helpful in and of themselves as a flexible guide to the actual design of a leadership programme, just as each phase is important in developing and transforming any person. A thorough, long-term, comprehensive programme should ensure that all phases are integrated into the curriculum.

Conclusion

At the beginning of this chapter I asked the following question: Will the global lens be enough to develop new leaders with the knowledge, skills and abilities needed for this dynamic, complex and challenging environment? The answer is 'No'. The rate at which globalization has occurred in all types of organizations has forced researchers and practitioners into considering new paradigms of leadership – and it should force us into manifesting new paradigms of leadership development. The Center for Creative Leadership (Hernez-Broome & Hughes, 2004) agreed, highlighting trends that will have a major role in future understanding and practice of leadership development. New ways of thinking about the nature of leadership and leadership development typify one such trend. Leading in various cultures across the globe requires a fundamental shift in terms of our thinking and behaving, which will influence the design and development of future leadership programmes and initiatives. With these shifts, the new paradigm will be more difficult to design and implement, and the next steps in development will require a deeper understanding of complex elements, including the culture of leadership development.

To address this challenge, there are emerging new perspectives – such as the worldly leadership lens – that may profoundly affect our thinking on developing future leaders. The worldly lens, through the frameworks I have introduced, can meet the leadership challenges of the future in varying cultures around the world.

Leadership development opportunities are needed for individuals and organizations around the world. These should not be limited to businesses; leaders are needed in all sectors and settings – business, government, non-profit, education, homes, communities and churches. Worldly leadership development should not just be focused on those who are already in middle to upper management. Providing opportunities for many girls, young women and mature women in various settings within non-Western cultures can eventually change countries for the common good. The shift in perspectives must begin with us. When we use the worldly lens to approach the task of developing women leaders, we can provide experiences that will give women around the world a better chance of making the critical differences that are needed by all.

References

Al Abed, I., Vine, P. and Potts, D. (eds) 2007. *United Arab Emirates*. London: Trident Press.

Ardichvili, A. and Kuchinke, K. P. 2002. Leadership Styles and Cultural Values Among Managers and Subordinates: A Comparative Study of Four Countries of the Former Soviet Union, Germany, and the U.S. *Human Resource Development International* 5(1): 99–117.

Bass, B.M. 1990. *Bass & Stogdill's Handbook of Leadership: Theory, Research & Managerial Applications*, 3rd edn. New York: The Free Press.

Bennis, W. 1989. *On Becoming a Leader*. Reading, MA: Addison-Wesley Publishing.

Byrne, J. C. and Reese, R. T. 2006. *The Successful Leadership Development Program*. San Francisco: Pfeiffer.

Chirikova, A. E. and Krichevskaia, O. N. 2002. The Woman Manager: Business Strategies and Self-image, *Sociological Research* 41(1): 38–54.

Clark, M. C. 1993. Transformational Learning. In S. B. Merriam (ed.) *An Update on Adult Learning Theory: New Directions for Adult and Continuing Education, No. 57*. San Francisco: Jossey-Bass.

Criticos, C. 1993. Experiential Learning and Social Transformation for a Post-apartheid Learning Future. In D. Boud, R. Cohen and D. Walker (eds) *Using Experience for Learning*. Buckingham, England, and Bristol, PA: Society for Research into Higher Education and Open University Press.

Dewey, J. 1944 [1916]. *Democracy and Education: An Introduction to the Philosophy of Education*. New York: The Free Press.

Dewey, J. 1962 [1934]. *A Common Faith*. New Haven, CT: Yale University Press.

Dictionary.com, *Definition of worldly*. [http://dictionary.reference.com/browse/worldly, accessed 8th April 2009].

Gvozdeva, E. S. and Gerchikov, V. L. 2002. Sketches for a Portrait of Women Managers, *Sociological Research* 41(1): 55–68.

H.E. Sheikha Lubna Bint Khalid Al Qasimi 2007. Women in the Mainstream. In T. A. Kamali (ed.) *An Anthology Celebrating the Twentieth Anniversary of the Higher Colleges of Technology*. Abu Dhabi: The HCT Press.

Hernez-Broome, G. and Hughes, R. L. 2004. Leadership Development: Past, Present, and Future, *Human Resource Planning* 27: 24–32.

Hoppe, M. H. 2004. Leader Development Across Gender. In C. D. McCauley and E. V. Velsor (eds) *The Handbook of Leadership Development*, 2nd edn., pp. 331–60.

Hoppe, M. H. 2007. Adult Development Theory May Boost Global Leadership, *Leadership in Action* 27(3): 21.

Kennedy, J. C. 2002. Leadership in Malaysia: Traditional Values, International Outlook, *Academy of Management Executive* 16(3): 15–24.

Khaleej Times 2007. Women Active Partners in Nation's Development. 19th November.

King, K. P. 2003. Understanding Adult Learners Amidst Societal Crisis: Learning and Grief in Tandem, *Journal of Continuing and Higher Education* 51(2): 13–23.

Kowske, B. J. and Anthony, K. 2007. Toward Defining Leadership Competence Around the World: What Mid-level Managers Need to Know in Twelve Countries, *Human Resource Development International* 10(1): 21–41.

Livers, A. 2007. Leading Globally Requires a Fundamental Shift, *Leadership in Action* 27(3): 23.

Madsen, S. R. 2008a. *On Becoming a Woman Leader: Learning from the Experiences of University Presidents*. San Francisco, CA: Jossey-Bass.

Madsen, S. R. 2008b. *Developing Leadership: Learning from the Experience of Women Governors*. Lanham, MD: University Press of America.

Merriam, S. B. and Caffarella, R. S. 1995. *Learning in Adulthood: A Comprehensive Guide*, 2nd edn. San Francisco: Jossey-Bass.

Mezirow, J. 1990. How Critical Reflection Triggers Transformative Learning. In. J. Mezirow and Associates (eds) *Fostering Critical Reflection in Adulthood: A Guide to Transformative and Emancipatory Learning*. San Francisco: Jossey-Bass, pp. 1–20.

Mezirow, J. 1991. *Transformative Dimensions of Adult Learning*. San Francisco: Jossey-Bass.

Mintzberg, H. 2004. *Managers Not MBAs: A Hard Look at the Soft Practice of Management and Management Development*. San Francisco: Berrett-Koehler Publishers.

Muczyk, J. P. and Holt, D. T. 2008. Toward a Cultural Contingency Model of Leadership, *Journal of Leadership & Organizational Studies* 14(4): 277.

Noel, J. L. and Dotlich, D. L. (eds), 2008. *The 2008 Pfeiffer Annual Leadership Development*. San Francisco: Pfeiffer.

Palmer, P. J. 2004. *A Hidden Wholeness: The Journey Toward an Undivided Life*. San Francisco: Jossey-Bass.

Porter, M. E. and McKibbon, L. E. 1988. *Management Education and Development: Drift or Thrust into the 21st Century*. New York: McGraw-Hill.

Robinson, D. A. and Harvey, M. 2008. Global Leadership in a Culturally Diverse World, *Management Decision* 46(3): 466.

Ruderman, M. N. 2004. Leader Development Across Gender. In C. D. McCauley and E. V. Velsor (eds) *Handbook of Leadership Development*, 2nd edn., pp. 271–303.

Taylor, E. W. 1993. *A Learning Model of Becoming Interculturally Competent: A Transformative Process.* Unpublished doctoral dissertation. Athens: University of Georgia.

Taylor, E. W. 2007. An Update of Transformative Learning Theory: A Critical Review of the Empirical Research (1999–2005), *International Journal of Lifelong Education* 26(2): 173–91.

The Free Dictionary. *Definition of worldly.* [http://www.thefreedictionary.com/worldly, accessed 8th April 2009].

The Leadership Trust 2009. *The 'Worldly Leadership' Project: Uncovering Ancient Leadership Wisdom for a More Sustainable World.* Ross-on-Wye: The Leadership Trust.

Tubbs, S. L. and Schulz, E. 2006. Exploring a Taxonomy of Global Leadership Competencies and Meta-competencies, *The Journal of American Academy of Business,* 8(2): 29–34.

Young, M., Mountford, M. and Skrla, L. 2006. Infusing Gender and Diversity Issues Into Educational Leadership Programs: Transformational Learning and Resistance, *Journal of Educational Administration* 44(3): 264–77.

Zaslavskaia, T. I. 2007. The Vanguard of the Russian Business Community: The Gender Aspect (I), *Sociological Research* 46(5): 6–25.

6
Worldly Leadership and Concepts of Community

Gareth Edwards

Introduction

This chapter is an exploration of the concepts of community as related to the worldly leadership perspective. It is based on a reading of Delanty's major review of the literature on community (Delanty, 2003) and therefore represents an initial exploration with some tentative suggestions for further research (all references to Delanty in this chapter are to that of his work *Community* in 2003). The chapter explores community as a basis for theorizing and researching the worldly leadership perspective. The suggestion being that if the worldly leadership perspective is about gaining insight regarding leadership practices in indigenous cultures, then the concept of community could help to uncover important elements of what leadership means to these indigenous cultures through how they present themselves as a community. The indigenous cultures to be investigated represent the development and maintenance of community; indeed, the very essence of community or the loss of community appears to provide an underlying rationale for the shift towards worldliness as a lens by which to investigate leadership. It appears that the loss of a sense of community in postmodern times (Delanty, 2003; Pawley, 1973) could be a contributory factor in the rise of the Westernization of popular thinking and theory with regards to leadership (Turnbull, 2009) and hence, the turn of focus towards a worldliness perspective. This chapter extends the debate towards developing tentative research criteria in relation to the study of leadership from this worldliness perspective.

Leadership from a worldliness perspective

As highlighted in previous chapters, the concept of worldly leadership challenges current thinking on global leadership and enables further conceptualizations of leadership to emerge based on understanding deep-rooted, indigenous perspectives from around the world (Turnbull, 2009). The concept has been developed from the literature concerning the 'Worldly Mindset' and 'Worldliness' (Mintzberg, 2004; Mintzberg & Gosling, 2003). 'Worldliness' according to Mintzberg (2004) is quite different from the idea of globalization, in that it involves taking a closer, as opposed to a distant, look at the world. Turnbull (2009) suggests an alternative view to 'global leadership' is needed owing to four limitations: (1) global leadership is often shorthand for the application of Western management practices in non-Western contexts, (2) defining a set of universal traits for leadership is impossible, (3) leadership is contextually driven and (4) leadership can be seen as a dynamic social process (Turnbull, 2009, p. 91). The worldly leadership concept addresses these shortcomings and has been defined as 'seeing all kinds of different worlds (often worlds within worlds) from close up and taking action...aiming for unity and collaboration...through a shared humanity'. Above all it can be seen as being about 'shared power, dispersed and flexible networks, stewardship, integrity, responsibility for good, and an emphasis on a sustainable world' (2009, p. 91). The push for investigating leadership through the worldliness lens appears warranted on these grounds. However, from Turnbull's comment above it appears to be shifting towards the very concept it is challenging since, rather like 'global leadership', it seems in abstract to be concerned with developing lists of desirable outcomes or characteristics. By taking community as a core concept, additional contextual nuances may be developed to the findings already uncovered in this area.

The central tenet of this chapter is that the definition 'seeing all kinds of different worlds (often worlds within worlds)' is a crucial element for the worldly leadership concept and the contribution the concept makes to the general leadership literature. For this contribution to be developed fully a good understanding of 'community' is needed, as exploring the notion of 'community' may be one way of accessing the 'world within a world'. Indeed Mintzberg talks of the futility of discussing leadership without 'community-ship', especially on an international scale (Turnbull & Ghosh, 2009). This chapter, therefore, unravels the ideas behind 'community' to inform the growing development of a research stream concerning the idea of 'worldly leadership'. If the worldly leadership concept concerns understanding deep-rooted philosophies of leadership from indigenous cultures for the development of leadership theory, then an idea of how these philosophies are developed and how they are bounded by a sense of community is needed.

In addition this chapter suggests that by taking community as a core concept the view of 'worldly leadership' can develop a broader theme of investigating leadership within indigenous cultures. It appears the worldly leadership research agenda is trying to develop concepts of leadership that are pro-eastern, moving away from the Western-dominated literature, theory and research concerning leadership. This chapter contends that while this is a useful push towards developing fresh and new ideas and conceptualizations regarding the phenomena of leadership, we must not lose sight of this approach and logic applying equally to Westernized indigenous communities and subcultures, for example, Celtic, Gaelic and Flemish cultures. The use of community as a basis for investigation and theorizing regarding worldly leadership concepts can therefore contribute to developing themes across broader geographical areas by providing a consistent framework of investigation.

Tensions in community and worldly leadership

Delanty (p. 14) describes a tension in understanding the concepts of community as – '...in the critical juncture of Greek and Christian thought two senses of community emerge which are fundamentally contradictory: community as local and therefore particular and, on the other side, community as ultimately universal. This conflict has never been resolved and has endured to the present day when we find two kinds of community in conflict: the cosmopolitan quest for belonging on a global level and the indigenous search for roots.' This description relates to the idea of developing a worldly view of leadership, in fact this quote epitomizes the tension described in the leadership literature between universalistic or global ideas and the worldliness perspective. It appears that we are researching leadership from a worldliness perspective in response to an over-elaboration and concern for what Delanty describes as 'community as ultimately universal'. The debate regarding community appears to parallel that of 'worldly' leadership. For example, the following quote, also from Delanty, invokes a familiar picture to that of the worldly leadership literature and yet he is concerned with an historical account of the degradation of community. 'The break of medieval guilds and corporations, the commercialisation of agriculture that came with the emergence of capitalism and the decline in the autonomy of the cities following the rise of the modern centralized state led to a disenchantment with community' (p. 15). Here we see the concept of community or the loss of ideas around community being part of the drive towards capitalism and, in turn, a drive towards universalistic, global

views on leadership, largely driven by Western thinking overshadow-
ing local wisdom and leading to the call for a worldliness perspective
to be adopted. Investigating leadership through the lens of 'worldliness'
therefore may be interpreted as the search for community, or indeed,
rediscovering 'community'.

Concepts of community

There appear to be four broad positions regarding community: (1)
informed by communitarian philosophy, there is the community of
urban localities and civic voluntarism, (2) informed by cultural sociology and anthropology, there is a position of community as a search
for belonging and identity, (3) informed by postmodern politics and
radical democracy, community is seen as political consciousness and
collective action and (4) based on technological advancement, community is seen as being cosmopolitanized and represents new relations of
proximity and distance (Delanty). This chapter will not review each of
these positions in detail, but will identify core themes from these concepts of community and relate them to the study of leadership and, in
particular, the study of leadership through the worldliness lens.

A sense of belonging

What appears to be common among views on community is a sense of
belonging (Delanty). This represents an important element in researching worldly leadership. For example, one may need to ask the question:
What makes you feel a sense of belonging in this community and why?
This represents a solid foundation from which to identify key leadership constructs in differing indigenous cultures and communities. As
an example I have cited a description by Delanty from a classic study
of modern urban communities, *Tradition and Change: A Study of Banbury*
(Stacey, 1960) – 'It is even doubtful whether there is a sense of community among all of those who were born and brought up in the town.
For those who are still part of the traditional small-town society, who
own, manage, or work in its traditionist shops and smaller factories,
who provide the traditional services, who belong to the close-knit and
long-standing groups in clubs and pubs and who accept the traditional
standards, there is certainly some sense of loyalty to the town and its
established institutions. Groups of immigrants who shared together the
experiences of coming to the town and settling down there and especially those who live as neighbours have a sense of belonging to a group
within the town and not the town itself' (Stacey, 1960, p. 177, cited

in Delanty, pp. 40–1). Delanty also points to evidence from studies in other towns by Moore (1974, 1982) as illustrating this sense of belonging that is not necessarily linked to a geographical location. There is an element here of not just seeking a township or geographical area for study with regards to leadership through the worldliness lens, instead the study of 'belongingness' appears to be key. Hence, the worldly leadership project could be guided towards identifying indigenous cultures through a sense of belonging, that is by asking questions such as, What does belongingness mean in differing cultures? How do members of indigenous cultures identify with a sense of belonging? These questions appear to be important in identifying leadership from a worldliness perspective and in essence indicate the need to move away from identifying culture through geography and move towards identifying culture through a sense of belonging.

Indeed a recent paper has described the role of leadership as confirming and maintaining a group member's sense of belonging and a group's identity – described as *genius loci* – an expression from Greek mythology (Neri, 2006). *Genius loci* can be described as a protective spirit of a place and Neri goes on to describe the *genius loci* of a group as having the function of domesticating objects and healing wounds in a community's social fabric and syncretic sociality. An interesting thread therefore for the worldly leadership project could be to try and understand how *genius loci* is represented in differing indigenous cultures and as part of further research could be linked to the cultural geographical literature on space and place and community (e.g. Low & Lawrence-Zúñiga, 2003).

A sense of community (SOC)

Linked to a sense of belonging and largely found in the psychology literature is a further concept regarding community, that of having a 'sense of community'. A sense of community has been defined as an individual's experience of community life (Hyde & Charvis, 2007) or the sense that one is part of a readily available mutually supportive network of relationship (Sarason, 1974). A model has also been posited that includes four dimensions (membership, influence, integration and fulfilment of needs and shared emotional connection) (McMillan & Charvis, 1986). Although empirical research regarding this model is mixed (see Mannarini & Fedi, 2009 for a review) it may be a useful framework to use when researching leadership through the worldliness perspective as it indicates possible categories for researchers to investigate. Further to this Mannarini and Fedi (2009) conclude that what seems reasonable is to consider 'sense of community' as a *shared narrative* (Mankowski & Rappaport, 1995). This appears connected to more post-modern interpretations of community discussed below. Furthermore, Mannarini and Fedi (2009, p. 218) suggest from their empirical research that 'the concept of participation seems intertwined with the concept of community and ... being a community implies that members undertake action to better their lives and solve common problems'. An additional area that the worldly leadership project could take, therefore, is to study how differing cultures develop and talk about 'a sense of community' and what leadership means within this sense of community.

Individualism and community

The literature on new social movements (e.g. Lichterman, 1996) offers a different perspective on community. Notions of community based on communitarianism suggest that individualism is detrimental to a sense of community. Delanty, however, points out that research on new social movements reveals individualism to be a core element of building communities. Here self-fulfilment and individualized expression can be highly compatible with collective participation. Indeed, French et al. (2009) have recently deconstructed the meaning of 'individual' back to its original Latin and Greek meaning. From their paper we can see that the very meaning of the word engenders community in that it means '... we cannot be 'divided' from those around us ... we are indeed individual: literally we cannot be separated or cut apart' (p. 149). In relation to the worldliness perspective on leadership, it would be important to understand what individualism means in differing cultures. Also linked to this literature on community is the idea that participation in community life can reinforce the quest for personal achievement (Lichterman, 1996). This links directly to the leadership literature that relates effective leadership to concepts such as self-development (Bennis, 1984, 1990; Day et al., 2009; Edwards et al., 2002; Goffe & Jones, 2000), self-awareness (Fletcher & Baldry, 2000), self-confidence and self-coping (Edwards et al., 2002). Indeed, one theorist (Melucci, 1996), suggests that self-realization can be enhanced by collective action. Community can reinforce personalism, giving to an individual a stronger sense of identity (Delanty). This also links us back to the concept of leadership as identity (Ford et al., 2008). Here, therefore, we see the need for researchers to identify what indigenous cultures view as self-development, self-improvement, self-realization, self-coping, self-confidence and self-awareness.

Community as communicative

In his text Delanty suggests that community can be viewed as communicative in the sense of being formed in collective action based on place; he goes on to assert that it is not merely an expression of an underlying cultural identity. Another critical issue arises therefore for the worldly leadership project, which appears to be guided by cultural identity as opposed to collective action based on place. How the project might develop this theme is again expressed by Delanty (p. 71), when he states that 'Local communities [as opposed to political or cultural community] are important vehicles for the recovery and expression of moral recognition and the building of personal identities...This idea of community is a constructivist one, whereby community is socially constructed by society as opposed to being identified simply with a locality'. This idea of community, therefore, has parallels with leadership not least in the idea that community drives moral recognition and personal identity, which could well have links to concepts such as ethical leadership (Mendonca & Kanungo, 2006) and leadership as identity (Ford et al., 2008), respectively. Indeed, community has been defined as a moral order or moral force (Delanty, 2003; Durkheim, 1957). Therefore, an investigation of the morals and ethics that bind an indigenous culture and how identity is constructed is as important for the worldly leadership project as for the wider leadership literature.

Indeed, some social theorists (Bauman, 2001; Habermas, 1984, 1987; Touraine, 1995, 1997) go further and have a marked distrust of the very idea of community (Delanty). Touraine's (1995, 1997) critique is based on community being closely aligned with nationalism suggesting that community and nationalism are close and that community may have been debased by nationalism (Delanty). Bauman's (2001) critique is based on community being a nostalgic or utopian discourse. Habermas' (1984, 1987) view is more ambiguous (Delanty), but actually holds a critical discussion in relation to the study of worldly leadership. For example, Habermas suggests that social action is based on language and that society is linguistically created. From Habermas' (1984, 1987) work developed the idea of 'communication communities', which means that social relations in modern society are organized around communication rather than by other media such as authority, status or ritual (Delanty). First, therefore, this emphasizes the importance of language research in leadership and how this language can be colonized or anglo-ized through professional/business discourse (Jepson, 2009) and second, relates the current shift in the leadership literature away from positional aspects of leadership towards more emergent frames of reference. This is epitomized by the current theme of 'dispersed' or 'distributed' leadership (Gronn, 2002).

Community through symbolism

Influenced by the seminal books by Anderson (1983) and Cohen (1985) community as a concept has made a shift in recent years from being conceptualized as a social interaction concerned with meaning and identity towards community as a symbolic structure (Delanty). Although the worldly leadership concept could be indicating a shift back towards the understanding of community based on identity and meaning which reflects some of the already existing literature on leadership (e.g. Ford, 2010; Smircich & Morgan, 1982), it is an important point for the project to take forward – the understanding of indigenous cultures through symbolism. The literature on community appears to be epitomized with a tension regarding community representing differences (through symbolic meaning or being imagined) and community representing what people have in common which derives from the more traditional social interaction viewpoint (Delanty).

Cohen (1985) sees community as a symbolic construction of boundaries and that this can entail different interpretations as to the meaning of communitas. He defines community in terms of particular kinds of awareness groups have of themselves in relation to other groups. Here we see an important aspect for understanding leadership through the worldliness lens. First, it offers another piece of evidence to suggest the importance of using a methodology that highlights broad and aesthetic representations of leadership such as the 'Leaderful Moment' (Wood & Ladkin, 2008). The idea behind the leaderful moment is to take a snapshot of leadership in practice through photographs or film and then deconstruct what represents leadership in context. The use of this form of data collection will enable a more comprehensive understanding of leadership through symbolism and second, it suggests a level of investigation that identifies indigenous cultures through what appears similar or different to other cultures or groups, identified by those within that cultural group. 'How do you see yourself compared to other groups?' appears to be a critical question to ask when conducting this form of research. What symbols are evident in communities will, therefore, be important in developing an understanding of leadership. It is recommended, therefore, that researchers use the methodology of the 'leaderful moment' to capture symbolism in the 'worlds with worlds' that are being investigated.

Community, friendship and betrayal

A further interpretation of the postmodern community is that of friendship. Delanty draws on the work of Pahl (2001) to describe how communities are moving away from family and kin relationships, and as Delanty points out the concept of 'personal communities' has been developed in response to friendship being viewed as a purely personal relationship between two people. It would appear, therefore, that it is important to investigate concepts of friendship as part of a worldliness investigation of leadership. Work is already being developed in looking at friendship and leadership; French (2008), for example, initiates a discussion regarding linking the two concepts by drawing on the western tradition of friendship. This is also expanded to discuss the role of friendship and betrayal in organizations in a more general sense (French et al., 2009). In this paper French et al. describe how friendship in particular and subsequently betrayal have been divorced from organizational research into a more private sphere and they are therefore '... not reflected in the official discourse of organisations – nor of university departments of organisation studies or in management and leadership training' (French et al., 2009, p. 149). The worldly leadership project, therefore, would be an ideal opportunity to develop an understanding of what friendship and betrayal mean in indigenous cultures and how this relates to leadership and subsequently how this relates back to organizations and management in an international sense.

Liminality

Liminality is described by Delanty (p. 44) as '... moments in and out of time ...' and refers to the 'between' moments, such as carnivals, pilgrimages, rites of passage or rituals in which normality is suspended. These events symbolize moments of symbolic renewal when a society or group asserts its collective identity. These shifts are described as structure and anti-structure. Turner (1969), for example, who developed the concept of liminality further from the earlier work of Van Gennep (1960), argues that community needs to be understood in opposition to structure. There appears to be an important discussion here, therefore, that relates to research in the worldliness and 'worldly' leadership vein. For example, if one researches events such as rites of passage and carnivals and holds them as symbols of culture, it must be recognized that they are outside normality for communities and may represent a different picture as to leadership in a more routine process in communities. The learning point with regards to understanding leadership through the lens of worldliness may be not to understand various indigenous cultures through their structures *per se*. Indeed, Delanty goes on to highlight other 'in-between' places that are beginning to have growing importance in people's lives – the airport lounge, the commuting train or shopping centres. Delanty also highlights other kinds of communities based on more explicit liminality, such as New Age Travellers, where communities are built on 'places on the margin'. To the fullest extent, therefore, this concept would work up towards 'virtual' communities (Bateman Driskell & Lyon, 2002; Castells, 2001; Jones, 1995; Rhiengold, 1993; Shields, 1996; Smith & Kollock, 1999), where communities are technologically mediated. To what extent can we view leadership within these spaces? Would these be classed as taking a worldliness perspective? It certainly broadens the worldliness perspective outside the investigation of eastern cultures in response to westernization.

A more critical view of liminal spaces and liminality is provided by Sturdy et al. (2006). They researched business meals between senior mangers in an organization and some visiting consultants as liminal space. They conclude that liminal spaces could be highly structured and conservative spaces as well as being creative and unsettling. They argue that the business dinner opens up an important liminal space which is used in tactical ways to assess trustworthiness, explore and shape political dynamics, test out and sell issues and as a safety valve for pent up cynicism and frustration. They suggest, contrary to the above representation, that liminal space while transitory and betwixt and between, it is not isolated from either organizational or other social routines, norms and structures. This therefore suggests that identifying, investigating and deconstructing liminal space in community and hence worldly leadership dynamics is an important area for further research. Important questions, therefore, include – how can we identify these areas of liminal space in indigenous cultures and how is it related to leadership?

The postmodern community

A critical point for the study of leadership from a worldliness perspective is the understanding of community in the postmodern society (Agamben, 1993; Blanchot, 1988; Corlett, 1989; Maffesoli, 1996; Nancy, 1991) where group membership is more fluid and porous – an age of multiple belongings (Delanty). Drawing on the works of Urban (1996) and Nancy (1991), Delanty (p. 136) posits that '...community is "inoperative"; it can never be instrumentalized or institutionalized'. This creates some difficulty in identifying leadership through the worldliness lens. For example, if we identify leadership in an indigenous culture, first, there must be recognition of other cultures to which they have been exposed, and second, the term 'indigenous culture' could be seen as instrumental. This therefore questions the use of indigenous cultures as a basis for investigating the worldliness perspective.

Researchers studying leadership in these indigenous cultures, therefore, should be sympathetic to the idea of multiple belongings, and an investigation into the level to which this impacts on an indigenous culture is paramount. This is an area described and discussed further in Chapter 11 of this book, on Seth organizations in Pakistan by Khakwani and Case. An important point for research in the 'worldly' leadership area, therefore, is that the very presence of a westernized researcher in an eastern culture may represent a new belonging within the culture which highlights the importance of using ethnographic or even auto-ethnographic forms of data collection. There is already some work in this area of ethnographic research on leadership and leadership development (e.g. Kempster, 2009; Kempster & Stewart, 2010), which would be a useful reference point for the worldly leadership project.

In addition, Delanty goes on to use the work of Lash (1994) to highlight an important element of postmodern community which is that of 'reflexive composition'. Reflexive communities have three aspects: (1) one is not born or 'thrown' but, rather, throws oneself into them, (2) they may be widely stretched over abstract space and sometimes over time and (3) they consciously pose themselves the problem of their own creation, and are subject to constant re-invention. In addition, the tools and products tend not to be material but abstract and cultural (Lash, 1994). This highlights the importance of heeding the need to be open-minded and to cast a wide net when gathering information regarding leadership from a worldliness perspective, as suggested above. It also points to the importance of aesthetics in understanding leadership (e.g. Schroeder, 2008). Researching leadership from a worldliness perspective, therefore, should gather evidence of the aesthetics of leadership in differing settings. Relating to the aesthetic element elaborated above is the idea of 'emotional communities' (Maffesoli, 1996). It appears that these emotional communities are marked by an aesthetic sensibility rather than by symbolic codes (Delanty). Here we see the importance of understanding not just how the aesthetic is developed in the cultures in which leadership is being investigated but also how the aesthetic is understood and agreed upon within cultures, that is, what is commonly understood by cultural aesthetics by the inhabitants of the culture? This is an important question in understanding leadership within 'indigenous' cultures and from a worldliness perspective in general.

Multiculturalism

An indirect notion that has arisen from reading around the subject of community is that of multiculturalism. First, it appears important for the worldliness literature to position itself alongside or even against other notions of multiculturalism. A number of differing views are represented in the literature; Delanty distinguishes between Traditional Multiculturalism (Monoculturalism, Republican Multiculturalism, Pillarization and Liberal Multiculturalism) and Modern Multiculturalism (Communitarian Multiculturalism, Liberal Communitarian Multiculturalism, Interculturalism, Radical Multiculturalism, Critical Multiculturalism and Transnational Multiculturalism). These differing views are considered in more detail by Delanty. A further development of the worldly leadership theme therefore would be to compare these views to the worldliness perspective. Second, it will be important to identify worldly groups and their interpretation of multiculturalism. For example, does an indigenous group have a particular take on multiculturalism and, if so, what does this mean for leadership. Finally, an important point is raised within the discussion regarding multiculturalism which provides a challenge to the worldliness perspective and hence the search for worldly leadership; the boundaries between social groups are more diffuse than previously found in cultural terms – 'It is more difficult to demarcate ethnic groups – the boundary between ethnic groups and the majority culture is not always so clearly defined' (Delanty, p. 108).

This presents a challenge. For example, how will understanding leadership from a worldliness perspective demarcate groups to ensure that groups are not replaying the 'global' or 'westernized' viewpoint. It appears that most ethic groups have been tainted by the overriding Western view. Ong (1999), for example, has suggested that many immigrants are middle-class professionals, and that was in the late 1990s; this may well have increased exponentially by now, increasing the problems associated with the investigation of indigenous cultures. I believe that the worldliness perspective is much broader than indigenous culture investigation and, therefore, once a culture has been tainted by Westernization, it has developed into a slightly different culture, which in turns needs investigation with regards to the worldliness perspective and in particular leadership.

Limitations and further development

A limitation of this chapter is that it is based on a limited literature review, being largely based on one core text – Delanty (2003). Further development of this theme therefore would take into account a wider literature and a critical review of empirical research in this area. Also the concept of community could be expanded to critically review the more general leadership literature beyond the worldliness perspective. The chapter draws on the wider leadership literature to understand how the worldliness perspective could be developed and therefore a wider scope for these ideas appears to be warranted.

Finally, a deeper review of the postmodern view of community would be beneficial. The leadership literature appears to be moving towards this body of literature (e.g. Grint, 2001) and a deep review of the works of Agamben (1993): *The Coming Community*: Blanchot (1988): *The Unavowable Community*; Corlett (1989): *Community Without Unity*; Maffesoli (1996): *The Time of the Tribes*; Urban (1996): *Metaphysical Community*; and Nancy (1991): *The Inoperative Community* in particular may provide further development of leadership theory and practice. Further reading and deliberation would also be beneficial on relating leadership in the worldliness vein to virtual world (Bateman Driskell & Lyon, 2002; Castells, 2001; Jones, 1995; Rheingold, 1993; Shields, 1996; Smith & Kollock, 1999) and transnational communities (Delanty). Within this chapter I have not explicitly reviewed this literature as the concepts of world community and transnational community appear in direct opposition to the idea of worldliness. However, a review of the literature may prove useful in expanding the concept and providing a critical perspective on the worldliness concept itself. For example, although globalization has been the precursor for the development of the idea of worldly leadership, the very development of globalization has brought about new and distinct communities (world, transnational and virtual), which deserve the time to be researched as much as indigenous cultures.

Conclusions

As Delanty has featured so heavily throughout the chapter I believe it is fitting to conclude on his main points. First, he emphasizes that '... an understanding of community is neither a form of social integration nor one of meaning but is an open-ended system of communication about belonging' (p. 187) and '... community is communicative – communicative of new cultural codes of belonging' (p. 191). I conclude therefore that understanding leadership could be viewed through the lens of this communication about belongingness and this is particularly important for the worldly leadership project. Second, Delanty concludes that

'... the vision of community to come has remained and has become more powerful today. This is not of nostalgia for something that has been lost but because the question of belonging has become more acute' (p. 193). The response to the *question of belonging* may be held in the phenomenon of leadership and relating the worldliness concept to leadership appears to be responding to the increased acuteness of the situation.

This chapter has reviewed literature regarding community and related it to the leadership literature investigating the worldliness perspective. It concludes that to gain a truly worldly perspective research will need to investigate crucial elements of community-ship – a sense of belonging and multiple belongings, language, ethics, identity, multiculturalism, individualism, self-development, aesthetics, participation, friendship, betrayal and a sense of community. The study of these cultures may also need to be sympathetic towards the postmodern community represented by multiple belongings and recognize the need for ethnographic, and probably more importantly, auto-ethnographic approaches to data collection similar to some recent research on leadership and leadership development (e.g. Kempster, 2009; Kempster & Stewart, 2010). By exploring concepts of community, this chapter, has developed some tentative suggestions for researching leadership from a worldliness perspective in indigenous cultures. The chapter has also suggested that community can be the basis for developing a wider remit for the worldly leadership perspective further to eastern indigenous cultures.

References

Agamben, G. 1993. *The Coming Community*. Minneapolis: University of Minnesota Press.

Anderson, B. 1983. *Imaginary Communities: Reflections on the Origin and Spread of Nationalisation*. London: Verso.

Bateman Driskell, R. and Lyon, L. 2002. Are Virtual Communities True Communities? Examining the Environments and Elements of Community, *City and Community* 1: 373–90.

Bauman, Z. 2001. *Community: Seeking Safety in an Insecure World*. Cambridge: Polity Press.

Bennis, W. 1984. The Four Competencies of Leadership, *Training and Development Journal* 38(8): 14–19.

Bennis, W. 1990. *Why Leaders Can't Lead*. San Francisco: Jossey-Bass.

Blanchot, M. 1988. *The Unavowable Community*. Barrytown, NY: Station Hill Press.

Castells, M. 2001. *The Internet Galaxy: Reflections on the Internet, Business and Society*. Oxford: Oxford University Press.

Cohen, A. *The Symbolic Construction of Community*. London: Tavistock.

Corlett, W. 1989. *Community Without Unity: A Politics of Derridan Extravagance.* Durham, NC: Duke University Press.

Day, D. V., Harrison, M. M. and Halpin, S. M. 2009. *An Integrative Approach to Leader Development: Connecting Adult Development, Identity and Expertise.* New York: Routledge.

Delanty, G. 2003. *Community.* Abingdon: Routledge.

Durkheim, E. 1957. *Professional Ethics and Civic Morals.* London: Routledge and Kegan Paul.

Edwards, G. P., Winter, P. K. and Bailey, J. 2002. *Leadership in Management.* Ross-on-Wye: The Leadership Trust Foundation.

Fletcher, C. and Baldry, C. 2000. Self-awareness in the Context of Multi-source Feedback, *Journal of Occupational and Organisational Psychology* 73: 303–19.

Ford, J. 2010. Studying Leadership Critically: A Psychosocial Lens of Leadership Identities, *Leadership* 6: 47–65.

Ford, J., Harding, N. and Learmonth, M. 2008. *Leadership as Identity: Constructions and Deconstructions.* Basingstoke: Palgrave.

French, R. 2008. Sharing Thoughts on Leadership and Friendship. In K. Turnbull James and J. Collins (eds) *Leadership Perspectives: Knowledge into Action.* Basingstoke: Palgrave, pp. 43–57.

French, R., Case, P. and Gosling, J. 2009. Betrayal and Friendship. *Society and Business Review* 4: 146–58.

Goffee, R. and Jones, G. 2000. Why Should Anyone Be Led By You?, *Harvard Business Review* 78: 62–70.

Grint, K. 2001. *The Arts of Leadership.* Oxford: Oxford University Press.

Gronn, P. Distributed Leadership as a Unit of Analysis, *Leadership Quarterly* 13: 423–51.

Habermas, J. 1984. *The Theory of Communicative Action, Vol. 1: Reason and Rationalisation in Society.* London: Heinemann.

Habermas, J. 1987. *The Theory of Communicative Action, Vol. 2: Lifeworld and System: A Critique of Functionalist Reason.* Cambridge: Polity Press.

Hyde, M. and Charvis, D. M. 2007. Sense of Community and Community Building. In R. A. Cnaan and C. Milofsky (eds) *Handbook of Community Movements and Local Organisations.* New York: Springer, pp. 179–92.

Jepson, D. 2009. Studying Leadership at Cross-country Level: A Critical Analysis, *Leadership* 5: 61–80.

Jones, S. (ed.) 1995. *Cybersociety: Computer Mediated Communication and Community.* London: Sage.

Kempster, S. 2009. *How Managers Learn to Lead.* London: Palgrave.

Kempster, S. and Stewart, J. 2010. Becoming a Leader: A Co-produced Autoethnographic Exploration of Situated Learning of Leadership Practice, *Management Learning* 41: 205–19.

Lash, S. 1994. Reflexivity and its Doubles: Structures, Aesthetics, Community. In U. Beck, A. Giddens and S. Lash *Reflexive Modernisation: Politics, Tradition and Aesthetics in the Modern Social Order.* Cambridge: Polity Press.

Lichterman, P. 1996. *The Search for Political Community: American Activists Reinventing Commitment.* Cambridge: Cambridge University Press.

Low, S. M. and Lawrence-Zúñiga, D. (eds) 2003. *The Anthropology of Space and Place: Locating Culture.* Malden, MA: Blackwell.

Maffesoli, M. 1996. *The Time of the Tribes: The Decline of Individualism in Mass Society*. London: Sage.

Mankowski, E. and Rappaport, J. 1995. Stories, Identity and the Psychological Sense of Community. In R. S. Wyer, Jr (ed.) *Knowledge and Memory, the Real Story: Advances on Social Cognition*. Hillsdale, NJ: Erlbaum, pp. 211–26.

Mannarini, T., and Fedi, A. 2009. Multiple Senses of Community: The Experience and Meaning of Community, *Journal of Community Psychology* 37: 211–27.

McMillan, D. and Charvis, D. M. 1986. Sense of Community: A Definition and a Theory, *Journal of Community Psychology* 14: 6–23.

Melucci, A. 1996. *Challenging Codes: Collective Action in the Information Age*. Cambridge: Cambridge University Press.

Mendonca, M. and Kanungo, R. 2006. *Ethical Leadership*. Milton Keynes: Open University Press.

Mintzberg, H. 2004. *Managers Not MBAs: A Hard Look at the Soft Practice of Managing and Management Development*. San Francisco: Berrett-Koehler.

Mintzberg, H. and Gosling, J. 2003. The Five Minds of a Manager, *Harvard Business Review* Nov: 54–63.

Moore, R. 1974. *Pit-men, Preachers, and Politics: The Effects of Methodism in a Durham Mining Community*. Cambridge: Cambridge University Press.

Moore, R. 1982. *The Social Impact of Oil: The Case of Peterhead*. London: Routledge and Kegan Paul.

Nancy, J. L. 1991. *The Inoperative Community*. Minneapolis: University of Minnesota Press.

Neri, C. 2006. Leadership in Small Groups: Syncretic Sociality and the *Genius Loci*, *European Journal of Psychotherapy and Counselling* 8: 33–46.

Ong, A. 1999. *Flexible Citizenship: The Cultural Logics of Transnationality*. Durham, NC: Duke University Press.

Pahl, R. 2001. *On Friendship*. Cambridge: Polity Press.

Pawley, M. 1973. *The Private Future: Causes and Consequences of Community Collapse in the West*. London: Thames and Hudson.

Rheingold, H. 1993. *The Virtual Community: Homesteading on the Electronic Frontier*. Reading, MA: Addison-Wesley.

Sarason, S. B. 1974. *The Psychological Sense of Community: Prospects for a Community Psychology*. San Francisco: Jossey-Bass.

Schroeder, J. E. 2008. Aesthetic Leadership. In A. Marturano and J. Gosling (eds) *Leadership: The Key Concepts*. London: Routledge, pp. 5–7.

Shields, R. (ed.) 1996. *Cultures of the Internet*. London: Sage.

Smircich, L. and Morgan, G. 1982. Leadership: The Management of Meaning, *Journal of Applied Behavioral Science* 18: 257–73.

Smith, M. and Kollock, P. (eds) 1999. *Communities in Cyberspace*. London: Routledge.

Stacey, M. 1960. *Tradition and Change: A Study of Banbury*. Oxford: Oxford University Press.

Sturdy, A., Schwarz, M. and Spicer, A. 2006. Guess Who's Coming to Dinner? Structures and Uses of Liminality in Strategic Management Consultancy, *Human Relations* 59: 929–60.

Touraine, A. 1995. *Critique of Modernity*. Oxford: Blackwell.

Touraine, A. 1997. *What is Democracy?* Oxford: Westview Press.

Turnbull, S. 2009. 'Worldly' Leadership for a Global World. In M. Harvey and J. D. Barbour (eds) *Global Leadership: Portraits of the Past, Visions of the Future.* Maryland, MD: ILA, pp. 82–94.

Turnbull, S. and Ghosh, S. 2009. Influences, Tensions, and Competing Identities in Indian Business Leaders' Stories. Paper presented at the *British Academy of Management Conference,* Brighton, 15th–17th September.

Turner, V. 1969. *The Ritual Process: Structure and Anti-Structure.* London: Routledge.

Urban, G. 1996. *Metaphysical Community: The Intellect and the Senses.* Austin: University of Texas Press.

Van Gennep, A. 1960. *The Rites of Passage.* London: Routledge.

Wood, M. and Ladkin, D. 2008. The Event's the Thing: Brief Encounters with the Leaderful Moment. In K. Turnbull James and J. Collins (eds) *Leadership Perspectives: Knowledge into Action.* Basingstoke: Palgrave, pp. 15–28.

Part II
Worldly Leadership Research

7
Children's Image of Leadership in China

Liwen Liu, Roya Ayman and Saba Ayman-Nolley

Introduction: children's implicit leadership theories in China

Leadership has been a focus in the Chinese culture and philosophy since antiquity. Philosophers such as Confucius (Ware, 1995) and Mencius (Lau, 1970) advised the emperors and leaders of the time. Now, China is transformed from the world's greatest opponent of globalization into a committed advocate of globalization (Overholt, 2005). The opening of the People's Republic of China, together with the steady economic growth in the past few years, has aroused an increasing interest in Chinese leadership and culture (Fu et al., 2007).

In the study of leadership, the impact of culture can be evaluated through either the etic or emic cross-cultural research approaches (Ayman & Korabik, 2010; Gelfand et al., 2002). The etic approach in its purest form, 'imposed etic', takes the knowledge and measures of one culture and applies them to another, with the aims of validation and of potentially developing a universal concept of leadership. The 'derived etic' approach explores similarities among cultures, with the same goal of identifying a universal concept, an example being the Global Leadership and Organizational Behavioural Effectiveness (GLOBE) project (for more detail, see House et al., 2004).

Though this is an important approach, the perspective of worldly leadership is focused on the uniqueness of leadership within each culture. It encourages scholars to learn about each culture and its approach to leadership (Jepson, 2009). The emic cross-cultural research approach develops the measures and knowledge from within a culture to understand the phenomenon, thus allowing for the phenomenon to be explored with the endogenous perspective. With this method, the uniqueness of a culture can emerge or be noticed. Recently, both endogenous and exogenous researchers providing insight into Chinese leadership from an emic perspective have concentrated on the description of overt leadership behaviour. Their primary focus has been on the role of *guanxi* (e.g. Chen et al., 2004; Wong et al., 2003; Wood et al., 2002; Yi-Feng et al., 2008) or paternalistic leadership (e.g. Cheng et al., 2004).

Very little information, however, is available about the mental image Chinese people have regarding leadership (except Ling et al., 2000). Without knowing the true Chinese meaning of *leader* or *leadership*, we cannot have an authentic picture of leadership in China. Implicit leadership theory is a paradigm that studies leadership through the vantage point of the layperson (Schyns & Meindl, 2005). Though studies of implicit leadership theory in various cultures are meagre, what has been done shows that expectations of leadership are different in different cultures (Ayman & Korabik, 2010; Gerstner & Day, 1994).

Children are an important part of a society. In addition, they have a unique culture. So it is important to understand how these future adults perceive this social role and its characteristics. Also, children mirror the reality of the society in which they are raised and are often able to 'tell the truth' about social arrangements that adults have come to accept as second nature (Nemerowicz & Rosi, 1997). Therefore, much can be learned about leadership from young children, including the stereotypes that might impede advancement. Yet, hardly any information exists about Chinese children's mental image of a leader. In exploring the children's expectations, we used the most emic method of investigation: drawings. Children use drawing very naturally as a means for expression (Ayman-Nolley & Ayman, 2005). This, using the implicit leadership theory paradigm, gave us a window into the minds of Chinese children.

This study examines the implicit leadership theory (ILT) of children in China. We focus on gender stereotype and leader's assigned roles, as they are the primary categories that have emerged in the study of ILT (Lord et al., 2001. Also, in her review, Korabik (1994, 2006) stated that in China, due to communist-regime policies, women are represented in management roles to a greater extent than in the United States. However, both her work and Schein et al.'s (1996) provided evidence that gender stereotyping of leadership as a masculine social role is prevalent in China. This may be indicative of the deep-rooted confusion in ideology regarding women's lower status and weakness that makes them ineligible for primary leadership roles (Korabik, 2006). In addition, these scholars among others have argued that stereotyping is based in socialization and thus needs to be addressed by early child-hood educators.

Implicit leadership theories

There are different types of schemas: person schemas, self-schema and role schemas. Of particular interest in this study are role schemas, which contain our understanding of the behaviours and attributes expected of people in particular social positions. Schemas for roles are also equivalent to stereotypes, which are expectations about people who fall into particular social categories (Fiske & Taylor, 1991; Martin & Halverson, 1981; Rudman et al., 2001). Therefore, both *gender* and *leader* could be considered as social groupings. In the case of gender, evidence shows that people do have distinct expectations for women and men.

Based on the categorization theory, Lord and colleagues (e.g. Lord et al., 1984) suggested that cognitive representations of leaders can also be differentiated into three hierarchical levels. At the highest level, perceivers made the simple dichotomous distinction of leader or non-leader. At the middle level, which is the basic level, perceivers classified target persons into different types of leaders based on the context, such as business leader, sport leader and so on. At the lowest and most specific level, leaders were differentiated within each of the contexts, providing a contextually defined leadership prototype (e.g. female military leader versus male military leader) (Brown et al., 2004). It is interesting to note that though gender effect was included in the most specific level, very few studies actually looked at gender across different contexts. Most studies of gender and leadership have focused on the manager as the leader where, as Schein (2001) has stated, there is a common 'think manager, think man' paradigm that prevails.

Effect of perceiver's characteristic and implicit leadership theories

Various characteristics of perceivers may influence their expectations of a leader. In this section, we will review the impact of gender, culture and age on implicit leadership theories.

Gender

Studies on gender in implicit leadership theories are concerned with the gender of the perceivers (followers) and the gender of the target (leader). Few studies have examined the effect of the gender of the perceivers on implicit leadership theory. On the one hand, among adults, implicit leadership theories were found to be similar both in the United States (Offermann et al., 1994) and in China (Ling et al., 2000). On the other hand, when men and women across several cultures, including China (Schein et al., 1996), were asked to describe a typical man, woman, or manager, they mostly described the manager in the image of a man. However, in the more recent studies in the United States, women seem to hold less of a male image of a manager (Duehr & Bono, 2006; Schein et al., 1996). Therefore, the role of the gender of the perceiver in forming the image of a leader needs further examination, particularly across cultures.

Culture or country of origin of the perceiver

In addition to gender stereotyping, researchers are also interested in different cultures' implicit leadership theories. Within the implicit leadership theory research paradigm, Gerstner and Day (1994) used a measure that was developed in the United States, and applied it in other cultures. The results showed that different cultures had different images of a leader.

In contrast, in China, Ling et al. (2000) developed the Chinese Implicit Leadership Scale (CILS) and administered the CILS to Chinese participants from five occupation groups. This study is of great importance, as not only was it an emic approach but it was also conducted by endogenous researchers. The impact of culture in the interpretation of the results has not gotten much attention thus far (Ayman, 2004), but it will be a secondary interest of this study.

Cross-cultural studies on implicit leadership theories showed that some of the leaders' characteristics were shared across cultures while other characteristics were more culture-specific (Ayman & Korabik, 2010). For instance, the result of the GLOBE project indicated that attributes summarized as charismatic leadership were considered important for successful managers in all cultures (Dorfman et al., 2004). Conversely, some characteristics seemed to be specific to some clusters of countries. For example, when the implicit leadership theories were studied with an emic method, Ling et al. (2000) reported that Chinese implicit leadership theory included personal morality, goal efficiency, interpersonal competence and versatility. Ling's results were different from the eight factors which emerged from Offermann et al.'s (1994) for US participants. Similarly, Ayman and Chemers (1983) demonstrated that Iranians' concept of leadership combined considerate and initiating-structure behaviours, which loaded on the same factor as 'leader is a father figure to me'. This one factor was labelled as 'benevolently paternalistic' and did not fit the same pattern as that of the US population. These results suggest that people in each culture have a unique expectation of their own leaders.

Most of the implicit leadership studies discussed above were conducted among adults and college students. Studies on children's implicit leadership theories are quite limited, probably because it is believed that the concept is not well-formed in children or that it does not have much significance for them. However, as we mentioned in the introduction, this is not true and it is really important to understand children's mental image of a leader in their culture. In the next section, we will review the studies on children's implicit leadership theories conducted in and outside the United States.

Children's Implicit Leadership Theories

In the United States, existing studies have shown that children as young as those in kindergarten have implicit leadership theories (Ayman-Nolley & Ayman, 2005). Two interview studies conducted around 1990 demonstrated a strong male image of the ideal leader in the minds of children in both grades 3 and 6, though girls rather than boys held a strong image of a male ideal leader. This male image of a leader was stronger in grade 6 than in grade 3. Also, the leader's categories varied across a child's gender and grade. However, some researchers have shown concern that the use of interviews may interfere with the child's verbal ability (e.g. Matthews et al., 1990).

To overcome this limitation, later studies by Ayman-Nolley and Ayman used a less intrusive method: children's drawings. Starting in the 1990s, many studies have used children's drawings to tap into their social concepts (Andersson, 2005; Bombi & Pinto, 1994; Dickson et al., 1990; Dunn et al., 2002; Falchikov, 1990; Gramradt & Staples, 1994; Holmes, 1992; Mietkiewicz & Jolliot, 2004; Pinto et al., 1997). There are many advantages to using drawing methodology over structured interviews. First of all, it alleviates some of the developmental challenges faced by researchers when using written or verbal expression to assess children. It also increases the amount and accuracy of contextual information about the leader prototypes held by young children. Finally, it allows researchers to ask children about social phenomena with very little influence from the adult researchers' own perspective and therefore provides a more emic set of information on children's implicit leadership theories.

Drawings help children to overcome the difficulties in fully disclosing their opinions, thoughts and feelings to an adult researcher (Ayman-Nolley & Ayman, 2005; Leffler et al., 2006). Children's enjoyment of drawing activity reduces their inhibitions and increases their verbal production (Gross & Hayne, 1998; Klepsch & Logle, 1982). It has been clearly shown that, in their drawings, children reveal their own understanding of the world around them (Benveniste, 2005; Dennis, 1966). This method provides a worldly leadership perspective on the Chinese children's image of leadership.

In the previous drawing studies of implicit leadership theory, children were asked to produce pictures of 'leadership' or 'a leader leading' (e.g. Ayman-Nolley & Ayman, 2005; Nemerowicz & Rosi, 1997). The results showed that children of different gender, ethnicity, or age held different images of leaders (Ayman-Nolley & Ayman, 2005). Specifically in regard to gender, differences were found in that boys' images of leaders were depicted by predominately male figures, while girls' images of leaders showed both male and female figures (Ayman-Nolley & Ayman, 2005). In another study examining drawings of leaders, although both boys and girls tended to depict their own gender as the leader, boys did so at twice the rate (Nemerowicz & Rosi, 1997). However, no significant relationship was found between the drawn leader's gender and the child's grade in the drawing studies (Ayman-Nolley & Ayman, 2005).

As to social roles, Nemerowicz and Rosi (1997) found that children obtained their mental image of leaders primarily from government and politics (e.g. US Presidents as leaders). Family and school were a second source of examples (e.g. parents and teachers as leaders). Though both boys and girls drew generic persons as leaders, they differed in the categories of leaders they chose to draw. Girls drew more authority figures such as religious leaders, teachers and parents, whereas boys drew more masculine roles such as from sports and the military (Ayman-Nolley & Ayman, 2005). Similar results were found in Leffler et al. (2006), in which boys' images of a leader were primarily represented by traditional leadership roles such as military or head of state, whereas girls' images of a leader were primarily represented by self and teacher roles. Older children drew more sophisticated leader categories than younger ones. The choice of stereotypic known leaders also increased by grade (Ayman-Nolley & Ayman, 2005).

Differences of gender and social role in the children's implicit leadership theories were also found in a cross-cultural study conducted in Costa Rica (Ayman-Nolley et al., 2006). The result revealed that the majority of the children in both the United States and Costa Rica drew mostly male leaders, representing a traditional leader image. But US girls drew more female leaders than girls in Costa Rica, representing a less traditional leader image. Moreover, American children's implicit leadership theories represented more exemplars of specific historical figures, whereas those of Costa Rican children were represented by generic leadership roles. The result might be explained by cultural differences such as individualism versus collectivism and power distance. It is also interesting to note that Costa Rican children drew more military figures even though the country does not have a military.

At this time, the differences in drawn leader's gender between boys and girls seem to be well established, but there is very little knowledge about how this characteristic differs across age groups. Very few drawing studies looked at the variable of the children's grade, or they did not find a significant relationship between child's grade and leader's gender (Ayman-Nolley & Ayman, 2005). There is general evidence that children's stereotypes, such as those of ethnic and racial differences, are well established by age 5; but variations are found between age groups (Augoustinos & Rosewarne, 2001; McKown & Strambler, 2009; McKown & Weinstein, 2003). In general, young children seemed to demonstrate increasing knowledge of gender stereotypes at least through kindergarten (e.g. Edelbrock & Sugawara, 1978; Levy et al., 1995; Signorella et al., 1993). After this age, however, there were mixed developmental trends. Many studies showed a sharp increase in knowledge, while others suggested decreases or curvilinear relationships of stereotyping with age (Miller et al., 2009; Ruble, 1988; Ruble et al., 2006). For example, some researchers have found that children between the ages of 4 and 8 embraced gender stereotypes more strongly, while children between the ages of 8 and 10 seemed to accept a wider range of behaviours, occupations, objects and characteristics for their gender (Trautner, 1992). In another study on gender-based restrictions on occupations, a majority of 4-year-olds and a majority of 9-year-olds believed that there should be no gender-based restrictions on one's choice of occupation. Between these ages (e.g. 6- and 7-year-olds), however, children held more rigid opinions (Damon, 1977; Ruble et al., 2006).

In their meta-analysis, Signorella et al. (1993) suggested that inconsistencies in past research on developmental changes in gender schemas might be a consequence of different ways of conceptualization and measurement. On forced choice measures, in which children must select one gender or the other for each item (e.g. 'Who is the strong one?'), 'correct' matches to societal stereotypes increased with age. Increases were not, however, related to the type of question used (e.g. 'Who is...?'

versus 'Who can...?'). In contrast, on non-forced choice measures, the type of question did affect results. Children showed increases in non-stereotyped responses with age, but especially when asked 'Who should...?' or 'Who can...?' In summary, the results of the developmental changes in gender schemas are mixed, and most research used either verbal interview or questionnaire. The current study will examine the effect of the child's grade on the perceived leader's gender using the drawing methodology, which can shed some light on the developmental pattern of gender stereotype or gender schema.

Studies such as those by Lobel et al. (2001) have shown that there are clear cultural differences in gender-related inferences and judgments. Comparing Israeli and Taiwanese children, they found that children in more traditional and collective societies have stronger and more restricted gender schema than those in more individualistic and less traditional societies. For this current study, China was chosen because of its unique culture. Although the United States and Costa Rico, used in our previous studies, share some geographical similarities, these two countries are different in terms of culture and presence of military. While the United States has an individualistic culture and its own military, Costa Rico is collectivist and has no military. In contrast to these two countries, China is a collectivist country with its own military. By comparing the results of these studies, we may be able to see how cultural and social factors might influence children's implicit leadership theories.

The focus of the current study, therefore, was to examine Chinese children's image of a leader based on gender and social roles. In addition, we were interested to examine the children's characteristics (i.e. gender and grade) that can contribute to this image. Finally, we also explored the drawn leader's gender across different social categories. The following hypotheses are based on the previous research conducted in China and on ILT in other cultures. By supporting these hypotheses, we can demonstrate that on some dimensions Chinese children are more similar to their counterparts in other countries while on others they have a unique point of view. The specific hypotheses were:

Hypothesis 1: The gender of the drawn leaders is different across children's gender.
Hypothesis 2: The gender of the drawn leaders is different across children's grade.
Hypothesis 3: The role category of the drawn leaders is different across children's gender.

Hypothesis 4: The role category of the drawn leaders is different across children's grade.

Hypothesis 5: The gender of the drawn leaders will differ across various leader-role categories.

Method

Sample

At the beginning of 2008, drawings were collected from two schools in a large city of northeastern China. One of the schools was an elementary school (grades 1 through 6) with 600 students, of which 491 from all six grades participated in the study. The other was a high school (grades 7 through 12) of about 2000 students, of which 100 from grades 7 and 8 participated.

As this study was focused on a leader leading, we only analysed data from children who (a) drew a human figure(s) and (b) identified the gender of the leader. Of the 591 drawings collected, 514 met these criteria. Of the children who participated in the selected drawings, 50.8 per cent were boys and 49.2 per cent were girls. The distribution of children across grades was 15.6 per cent in first, 11.5 per cent in second, 12.6 per cent in third, 14.8 per cent in fourth, 16.9 per cent in fifth, 12.1 per cent in sixth, 8.8 per cent in seventh and 7.8 per cent in eighth grade (see Figure 7.1).

Materials

The students were given a sheet of A4 white paper (about 8 × 11 inches), one #2 pencil and a box of 12 coloured pencils.

Data collection procedure

For all grades, data were collected in the home classroom during a 45-minute art class. Two experimenters were present at each class session. One of the experimenters had gone through training for data collection and had participated in one session in the United States. The other experimenter was fully informed about the process and was mainly responsible for materials distribution. Once the class began, the art teacher introduced the experimenters and explained that they were there to do a study. One of the experimenters then wrote on the blackboard in Chinese: 领导者正在领导 (which means: DRAW A LEADER LEADING). The students were given verbal instructions to use the coloured pencils, the #2 pencil and the white paper to draw a leader leading. In order to avoid sharing ideas, students were asked not to talk to each other in the classroom, and to raise their hand if they had any questions.

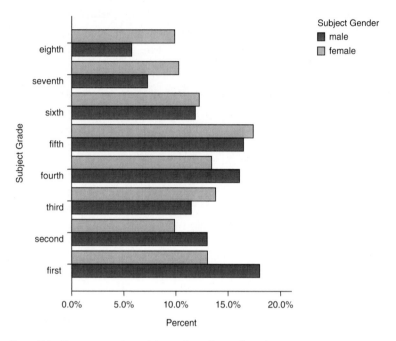

Figure 7.1   Frequency of participants' gender and grade

Instead of explaining what a leader was, experimenters only repeated the phrase 'draw a leader leading' and told the students to draw whatever came to mind. If a student expressed concerns about their drawing abilities, the experimenters assured the student that this was not a drawing contest and asked them to do their best.

Upon completion of the drawing, each student was asked to turn over his or her paper and write one or two short sentences describing the drawing and identifying which figure in the drawing was the leader. Those in grade 1 and 2 received an experimenter's or the art teacher's assistance in writing these sentences. Drawings were then collected and checked for interpretable information about the leader. With the help of the art teacher, each student's gender and grade level were recorded on the back of the drawing. Drawings were then filed in an envelope labelled for each session.

Coding procedure

Ayman-Nolley and Ayman (2005) developed a coding manual which contained detailed coding procedures for the previous studies in the United

States. Some of the categories were revised based on the drawings from the Chinese children. For example, 'Chairman Mao' and 'manager/supervisor' were added to the social role category. All identified leaders were coded for gender, skin colour and social role. As suggested by Coles (2003), to keep both the observer's and the child's view in mind, both the drawings and the children's descriptions of them were used for all coding.

For the current study, using the Ayman-Nolley and Ayman (2005) coding manual, leader's gender and leader's social role were coded. Leaders were classified as male or female based on predetermined masculine and feminine characteristics. Representation of male leaders consisted of drawn figures wearing pants, having short hair and void of any characteristics typical of a female such as long eyelashes, skirts and jewellery. Drawn leaders coded as female displayed characteristics typical of a female. If no such characteristics of either gender were present, the leader was coded as 'neutral'. However, if the child's written description identified the drawn leader as a male or female, the drawn leader was coded accordingly. This also included gender pronouns, labels such as *mother* or *father*, and/or identifying the drawing as oneself. As for role categories, in addition to examining the details of the drawings, the coder read the description of the leader on the back of the drawing and categorized the leader as one type of person, such as military personnel, generic person, child, teacher, parent, head of the state and so on.

Inter-coder agreement

The coding process included inter-coder agreement from two Chinese and two American coders. Based on written rules of analysis presented in the coding manual, inter-coder agreement was evaluated on a randomly selected 3 per cent sample of drawings (16 drawings). Inter-coder agreement was collected from four independent coders: two Chinese and two American graduate students. The two Chinese coders showed agreement of 94 per cent for leader's gender and 81 per cent for leader's role category. The two American coders were in complete agreement, 100 per cent, on leader's gender; but on leader's role category the agreement was at 69 per cent. The agreement between Chinese and American coders was first calculated between one Chinese coder and one American coder. Then it was averaged with the agreement between the other pair of Chinese and American coders. The average agreement between Chinese and American coders on leader's gender was 91 per cent, and on leader's role category was 72 per cent.

To explore the research questions, two of the seven coded variables were included as the drawing characteristics in the following analyses: leader's gender and leader's role category. The average reliability was 95 per cent for leader's gender and 74 per cent for leader's role category. Prior to analysis of the drawings, a chi-square test was conducted to examine potential confounding relationships between children's gender and grade. The result was not significant (χ^2 (7, N = 514) = 8.53, $p = .29$), so there were no confounding relationships between these two independent variables.

To examine the effects of grade on children's drawings of a leader leading, we analysed the variables against a combined range of grades (1–2, 3–5, 6–8). Combining grades gave us larger cell sizes as well as a general comparison across the Piagetian developmental levels of early concrete operational (grade 1 and 2), well-established concrete operational (grade 3 through 5, middle childhood) and early formal operational (grade 6 through 8) (Ayman-Nolley & Ayman, 2005). Given all these advantages, only the combined grade analysis is presented in the current study.

Results

The following analyses explored the relationship between the child's characteristics (i.e. gender and grade) and the drawing characteristics (i.e. leader's gender, leader's role category). For each variable, we first presented the frequency of the drawing characteristics. Then we ran a series of chi-square tests to examine how the drawing characteristics were different across child's gender and grade. To assist in further clarifying the most salient relationships, we also conducted several logistic regressions on the drawing characteristics and children's characteristics. Finally, the relationship between leader's gender and leader's role category were examined by another chi-square test.

Leader's gender and child's characteristics

The majority of children drew a male leader (75.9%), while 24.1 per cent drew a female leader. The effect of the child's gender and grade was examined against the drawn leader's gender. The results showed that both gender and grade of the child differed significantly on the drawn leader's gender. Boys drew more male leaders (90.0%) than female leaders (10.0%), whereas 61.3 per cent of the girls' drawings included male leader figures χ^2 (1, N = 514) = 58.11, $p < .001$ (see Table 7.1 and Figure 7.2).

Table 7.1   Summary statistics: leader's gender by child's gender

Statistics	Value	df	p
Pearson chi-square	58.11*	1	< 0.001
Likelihood ratio	60.95	1	< 0.001
Linear-by-linear association	57.99	1	< 0.001
Cramer's phi	0.34		< 0.001

Note: N = 514.

*No cells (0.0%) have an expected count less than 5. The minimum expected count is 61.04.

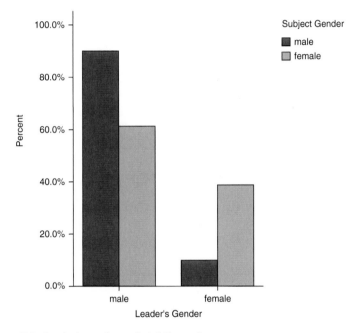

Figure 7.2   Leader's gender and child's gender

Table 7.2   Summary statistics: leader's gender by child's grade

Statistics	Value	df	p
Pearson chi-square	15.67*	2	< 0.001
Likelihood ratio	15.65	2	< 0.001
Linear-by-linear association	0.03	1	0.86
Cramer's phi	0.18		< 0.001

Note: N = 514.

*No cells (0.0%) have an expected count less than 5. The minimum expected count is 33.53.

The analysis examining the relationship between child's grade and leader's gender yielded significant result χ^2 (2, N = 514) = 15.67, $p < .001$ (see Table 7.2). While 67.5 per cent of students in the middle grades (grades 3 through 5) drew a male figure for the leader, those in other grades drew even more male leaders (83.5% for grades 1 and 2 and 81.6% for grades 6 through 8, respectively) (see Figure 7.3).

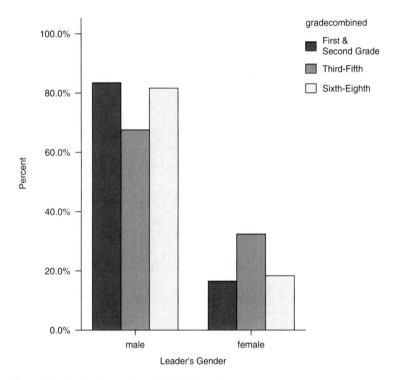

Figure 7.3 Leader's gender and child's grade

Table 7.3 Logistical regression analysis predicting drawn leader's gender

	B	SE	Wald	df	Exp. (B)
Child's gender	1.77	0.25	51.91***	1	5.87
Child's grade	−0.01	0.01	1.06	1	1.00
Constant	−2.01	0.27	53.84	1	0.13

Note: N = 514.
***$p < 0.001$, **$p < 0.01$, *$p < 0.05$.

When we regressed the leader's gender on the child's characteristics, the model with gender as the predictor was significant χ^2 (2, N = 514) = 62.01, $p < .001$. This result showed that if the child was a boy, he was more likely to draw a male leader (Wald = 51.91, B = 1.77, $p < .001$). Grade, however, was not a significant predictor of drawn leader's gender (Wald = 1.06, B = – 0.01, $p = .30$) (see Table 7.3).

Leader's category and child's characteristics

Overall, children identified 17 categories of leaders' social roles: military personnel, generic person, child, teacher, parent, parade/band, head of state, fantasy-story, religious, sports leader, famous politician, self, Chairman Mao, manager/supervisor, mayor, tourist guide and journalist. The three categories with the highest frequency were generic person (37.4%), manager/supervisor (23.9%) and teacher (12.8%) (see Figure 7.4). To meet the assumptions surrounding the use of chi-square (e.g. each cell within a contingency table having at least 80% expected count exceeding 5.0), the 11 categories with a percentage lower than 2 per cent (i.e. child, parent, parade/band, fantasy-story, religious, sports leader, self, mayor, tourist guide, principal and journalist) were combined in one category labelled as 'others'. Therefore, in the subsequent analysis there were eight social role categories: military personnel (7.4%), generic person (37.4%), teacher (12.8%), head of state (2.3%), famous politician (2.7%), Chairman Mao (5.8%), manager/supervisor (23.9%) and others (7.6%).

The leader's role categories varied significantly due to the child's gender χ^2 (7, N = 514) = 20.53, $p < .01$ (see Table 7.4). Boys (55.7%) and girls (44.3%) drew almost equal percentages of generic persons (e.g. see Figure 7.5). For the other categories, boys and girls varied in the frequency of their depictions. For example, boys drew 65.8 per cent of military personnel (e.g. see Figure 7.6), 66.7 per cent of head of state, 64.3 per cent of famous politician and 66.7 per cent of Chairman Mao. On the other hand, girls drew 60.6 per cent of teacher, 59.3 per cent of manager/supervisor (e.g. see Figure 7.7), and 59.0 per cent of the 'others' category that included a variety of social roles (e.g. tourist guide, fantasy-story etc.) (see Figure 7.8).

The result of leader's category was also different across grades, χ^2 (14, N = 514) = 111.05, $p < .001$ (see Table 7.5). The presence of a generic person became progressively less frequent as grade level increased, from 65.5 per cent for grades 1 and 2 to 23.8 per cent for grades 6 through 8. Students in grades 3 through 5 drew the most teachers (20.2%) and those in grades 6 through 8 drew the most manager/supervisors (43.5%) (see Figure 7.9).

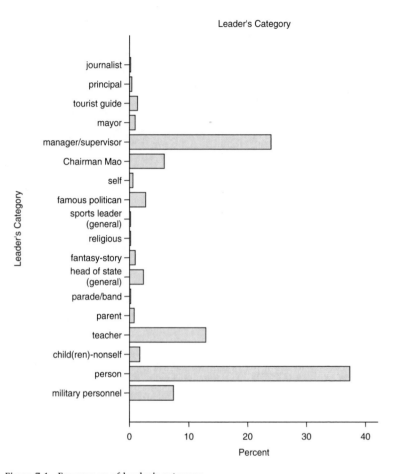

Figure 7.4   Frequency of leader's category

Table 7.4   Summary statistics: leader's category by child's gender

Statistics	Value	*df*	*p*
Pearson chi-square	20.53*	7	< 0.01
Likelihood ratio	20.76	7	< 0.01
Linear-by-linear association	4.48	1	< 0.05
Cramer's phi	0.20		< 0.01

Note: N = 514.

*No cells (0.0%) have an expected count less than 5. The minimum expected count is 5.91.

Figure 7.5 The generic leader drawn by 2nd grade girl

Figure 7.6 Military leader drawn by a 6th grade boy

Figure 7.7 Drawn by 8th grade girl

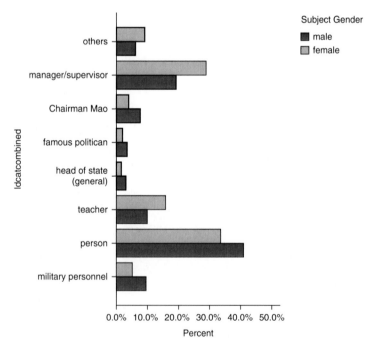

Figure 7.8 Leader's category and child's gender

Table 7.5 Summary statistics: leader's category by child's grade

Statistics	Value	df	p
Pearson chi-square	111.05*	14	< 0.001
Likelihood ratio	107.14	14	< 0.001
Linear-by-linear association	29.00	1	< 0.001
Cramer's phi	0.33		< 0 .001

Note: N = 514.
*Four cells (16.7%) have an expected count less than 5. The minimum expected count is 3.25.

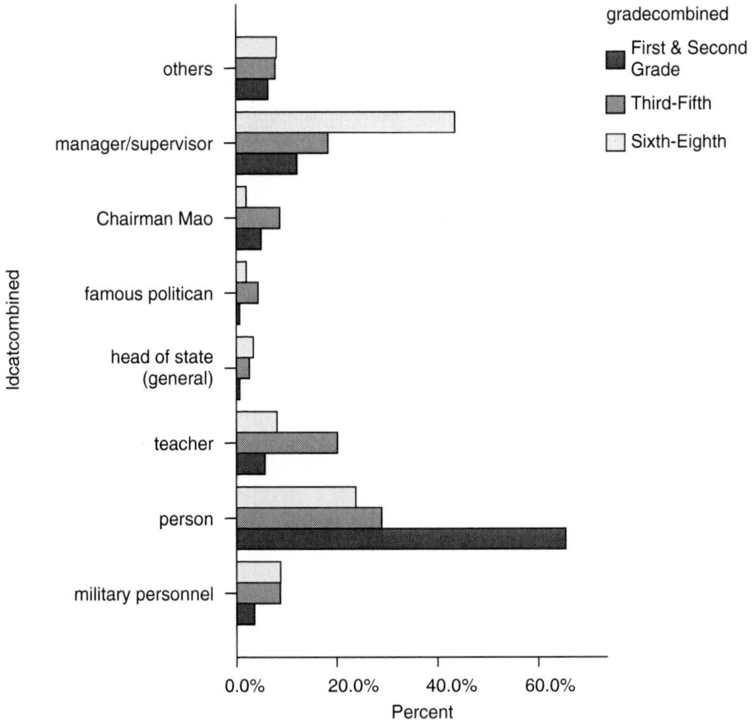

Figure 7.9 Leader's category and child's grade

Using multinomial logistic regression, we regressed leader's category on children's characteristics. The model was significant with both gender and grade as predictors χ^2 (14, N = 514) = 87.80, $p < .001$. See Table 7.6 for detailed results on each child characteristics. Role categories that differed significantly across child's gender or grade were military personnel, generic person, Chairman Mao and manager/supervisor. When the

Table 7.6   Multinomial logistic regression for leader's role categories and children's characteristics

Effect	-2 log likelihood of reduced model	Chi-square	df
Intercept	340.39	157.37***	7
Child's gender	201.12	18.09*	7
Child's grade	250.07	67.04***	7

Note: N = 514.
***$p < 0.001$, **$p < 0.01$, *$p < 0.05$.

Table 7.7   Summary statistics: leader's category by leader's gender

Statistics	Value	df	p
Pearson chi-square	120.59*	17	< 0.001
Likelihood ratio	116.52	17	< 0.001
Linear-by-linear association	2.56	1	0.11
Cramer's phi	0.48		< 0.001

Note: N = 514.
*Twenty-two cells (61.1%) have an expected count less than 5. The minimum expected count is 0.24.

child was a boy, he was more likely to draw military personnel (Wald = 4.89, B = –1.05, $p < .05$) and Chairman Mao (Wald = 3.94, B = –1.01, $p < .05$). Also, the older the child was, the less likely that he or she drew a generic person (Wald = 7.48, B = –0.02, $p < .05$) and the more likely that he or she drew a manager/supervisor (Wald = 5.67, B = 0.02, $p < .05$).

Leader's gender and leadership role

Here, we focused on drawn leader's gender across different social categories. The result of a chi-square analysis was significant χ^2 (7, N = 514) = 97.50, $p < .001$ (see Table 7.7). The drawn leader was more likely to be a male when it was drawn as military personnel (92.1%), generic person (83.3%), head of the state (83.3%), famous politician (85.7%) and manager/supervisor (81.3%). Only when the drawn leader was a teacher was it depicted more often as a female (65.2%) (see Figure 7.10 and e.g. Figure 7.11)

Discussion

The main purpose of this study was to explore the mental image of a leader held by Chinese school children. We approached this with an

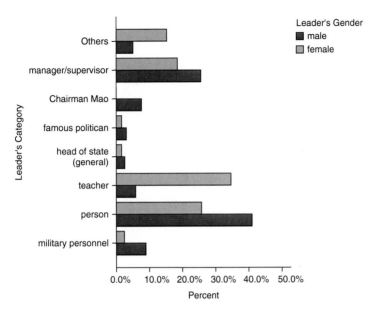

Figure 7.10 Leader's gender and leader's category

Figure 7.11 A teacher drawn by 4th grade girl

emic approach with the aim of adding to the worldly leadership literature. We found that both leader's gender and role category differed across child's gender and grade. We also found a relationship between drawn leader's gender and role category. Overall, leaders were predominantly perceived as male figures, which is consistent with the results of previous drawing studies in America (Ayman-Nolley & Ayman, 2005; Ayman-Nolley et al., 2006; Leffler et al., 2006). This finding also supports the male stereotype of leadership in adult literature (e.g. Heilman et al., 1989; Powell et al., 2002; Schein et al., 1996). Therefore, this study confirms that Chinese children as young as elementary school already (and similar to the children from the other cultures studied) had an implicit idea of a leader, and more often than not the leader was portrayed as a male image (Ayman-Nolley & Ayman, 2005). These findings parallel those of Liben et al. (2001), who found that 6- to 11-year-olds attribute higher status to masculine jobs.

It is also important to notice that boys almost always drew male leaders, whereas girls' drawings included a less skewed distribution of male and female leaders. On the one hand, this confirms previous findings that boys' images of leaders were depicted by predominantly male figures, whereas girls' images of leaders included both male and female figures (Ayman-Nolley & Ayman, 2005). However, about two-thirds of Chinese girls still drew a male leader. This is different from the most recent findings that girls in the United States actually drew more female leaders than male leaders (Ayman et al., 2004; Ayman-Nolley & Ayman, 2005; Leffler et al., 2006). On the other hand, similar results were already found in some cross-cultural studies in both children and adult literature. Ayman-Nolley et al. (2006) found that, while children in both the United States and Costa Rica drew mostly male leaders, American girls drew more female leaders than any other groups (i.e. American boys, Costa Rican boys, Costa Rican girls). In Schein et al. (1996), the managerial male stereotype was found in all groups except American women, who saw men and women as equally likely to possess management characteristics. In fact, the Weisgram et al.,(2010) finding that boys more often than girls prefer the high powered jobs is an applied indication of this male-leader image they hold.

Child's grade also influenced drawn leader's gender, but the pattern was not a consistent one. The results showed more similarity between the youngest grades and oldest grades in contrast to either one compared to middle grades. Although no drawing studies had found such a relationship between child's grade and leader's gender, Ayman-Nolley and Ayman (2005) reported the relationship between grade and other implicit leadership theories as 'U' shaped or 'J' shaped changes across grades. Our result also supported previous findings that children between ages 6 and 8 held a stronger gender stereotype than children between ages 8 and 10 (Damon, 1977; Ruble et al., 2006; Trautner, 1992). However, it is important to note that older children (between ages 12 and 14) again held a stronger gender stereotype than those in the middle grades. This unusual pattern might be explained by the fact that, with their increasing knowledge of gender stereotypes in real life, older children tend to more accurately reflect such reality on their drawings. This movement from more stereotypic images in youngest children to flexibility in middle childhood, followed by a return to more stereotyping in pre-teens and early adolescents, is evidence for the 'J' shape development: the early stereotyping is based on mimicking what is available to the youngest children, whereas the later forms of stereotyping by older children is a parallel to the gender intensification of their pubertal tendencies towards more self-gender-specific behaviours and attitudes (Larson & Richards, 1994; McHale et al., 2004). This return is therefore more internalized than that seen in the early childhood years. In fact, post-puberty there is consistency in these stereotypic attitudes within individuals into their adult years (Golombok et al., 2008; Kagan & Moss, 1962). However, some more recent studies show less gender intensification and less constrained-gender-stereotyping in adolescents (Priess, 2009).

As for leader's social category, a substantial portion of Chinese children drew a manager or a supervisor. However, the category of manager/supervisor was not even included in the American studies (e.g. Ayman-Nolley & Ayman, 2005; Ayman-Nolley et al., 2006). Meanwhile, the drawings of Chinese children showed less variety of leader's social roles. In comparison to their American peers, for example, very few Chinese children identified themselves, other children, or parents as leaders. Also, they did not draw leaders as a sportsman, religious person, or entertainer. Overall, the Chinese children's drawings showed more images of actual leaders in their community (teachers, managers, Chairman Mao) and less of either people close to them or fantastical/idealized leaders, which were more common in the American children's drawings.

Though both boys and girls drew generic leaders, boys drew more traditional authority and masculine figures such as head of the state and military personnel, again consistent with occupational preferences found by Weisgram et al. (2010). This result is also consistent with those of the studies in the United States (e.g. Ayman-Nolley & Ayman, 2005).

In contrast, girls drew more teachers and manager/supervisors, which are more commonly seen in the child's everyday life. Girls also drew more 'others' category, which included a greater variety of social roles. This can be a further indication of the more flexible and inclusive view of leadership that girls may hold, even in more traditional societies such as China. With the increase of the grade level, the presence of a generic person became progressively less frequent. It makes intuitive sense that as children's general knowledge of the world increases, so does their inclusion of more categories of leaders and more socially recognizable leaders (Ayman-Nolley & Ayman, 2005).

The results also showed that children held different implicit leadership theories regarding the role category of a drawn male or a drawn female leader. Male leaders were more likely to be military personnel, manager/supervisor, head of state and famous politicians; but female leaders were more likely to be teachers, which is a less traditional leadership role. Therefore, this result, that traditional leaders such as managers and head of the state were perceived as male by children, can also be interpreted from the well-established phenomenon of male leadership stereotype in adult literature.. This again confirmed the previous findings that school children already held a male leadership stereotype. These results also again parallel those of Liben et al. (2001) showing children's preference for masculine jobs. So the think-manager-think-male phenomenon can be traced back even to elementary school.

Although the current study was mostly conducted by an endogenous investigator, we were interested in finding out whether cultural differences influence the interpretation of drawing characteristics. Therefore, we also investigated the inter-coder agreement between Chinese and American coders. The result showed that when the drawing characteristics were not culture-related (e.g. leader's gender), the agreement between Chinese and American coders was as high as the agreement between coders from the same culture. However, when the characteristics were more related to the leading context (e.g. leader's role category), the agreement between Chinese and American coders was lower than the agreement between the Chinese coders. One example would be a drawing described as 'a female conductor leading her students who are singing happily'. While Chinese coders coded it as *teacher*, American coders coded it as *band*. Using the coding instructions the Chinese coders coded it as a teacher since in China singing in a class setting is common. American coders saw the drawn leader as a choir conductor and therefore used the code *band* for this image. This finding emphasizes the importance of indigenous collaborators when exogenous researchers are doing research on leadership topics, particularly when an emic approach is undertaken (Ayman, 2004).

Conclusion

We believe that the current research has theoretical, methodological and applied significance. As far as the authors know, this is the first research to address implicit leadership theories among children in China. This study provided both descriptive data and empirical evidence to highlight the need for future research on implicit leadership theories in China. For instance, our result shed some light on the male leadership stereotype held by school children, especially by boys. By examining the mental image of a leader held by Chinese young adults, future researchers can find out whether the stereotype ever changes as the children mature. This study also contributed to research on the generalizability of implicit leadership theory across cultures. While in both cultures children perceived leaders as male figures, Chinese girls held more of a male leadership stereotype than American girls did. This might be explained by the finding that Chinese society scores low on gender egalitarianism, indicating that the society favours men more than other cultures do (Fu et al., 2007).

In addition, this study once again has confirmed and helped refine the drawing methodology as a tool for studying children's social concepts and schemas. And increasing the variety of study topics and populations in which this methodology is used in future will clearly help to further improve the technique.

Since gender stereotype was found among Chinese children, their educators can make every effort to address this in early schooling (as for example American educators have done and still need to do). More female leaders can be depicted on books and made more prominent in the classroom. By exposing children to a multitude of diverse leaders at an early age, Chinese society will have the opportunity to eliminate the male stereotype of leadership and its influence on the children's leadership prototype. Finally, it is the society's responsibility to emphasize equal representation of both genders in all societal roles by employment regulation and media campaigns. We expect that creating equal opportunities for career advancement will lead to less male-leader stereotyping and more women leaders in future generations.

This study is only the beginning of understanding implicit leadership theories among the people of China. Due to accessibility issues, the drawings were collected from only two schools in one large city in China. As Chinese people are by no means homogeneous among themselves (Fu et al., 2007), the result should be interpreted only as a useful reference for understanding Chinese children's implicit leadership theories rather than as an overview of the topic in the country. In future studies, it would be beneficial to look at multiple schools in different communities. This would increase the generalizability of our findings beyond the school population studied.

This study sought to examine and discover unknown dimensions of an important and ancient quality of Chinese culture, that of leaders and leadership. In this chapter, we have only scratched the surface of this line of inquiry. To uncover the details of the implicit theories about leadership styles and other characteristics in both children and in adults, much remains to be addressed beyond our findings about gender and grade. As China becomes more integrated into the world economy and culture, these studies will become more important and valuable to help that transition be more fruitful and effective for them and for the global community at large.

References

Andersson, S. B. 2005. Social Scaling in Children's Family Drawings: A Comparative Study in Three Cultures, *Child Study Journal* 25(2): 97–121.

Augoustinos, M. and Rosenwarne, D. L. 2001. Stereotype Knowledge and Prejudice in Children, *British Journal of Developmental Psychology* 19: 143–56.

Ayman, R. 2004. Leadership and Culture. In C. Spielberger (ed.) *Encyclopedia of Applied Psychology*, vol. 2. San Diego, CA: Elsevier, pp. 507–19.

Ayman, R. and Chemers, M. M. 1983. The Relationship of Supervisory Behavior Ratings to Work Group Effectiveness and Subordinate Satisfaction Among Iranian Managers, *Journal of Applied Psychology* 68: 338–41.

Ayman, R. and Korabik, K. 2010. Leadership: Why Gender and Culture Matter, *American Psychologist* 65(3): 157–70.

Ayman, R., Ayman-Nolley, S. and Leffler, H. 2004. Children's Gender and Their Implicit Theory of a Leader. In B. Schyns (chair), *Leadership: Implicit Theories and Perception*, symposium conducted at the International Congress of Psychology in Beijing, China (August).

Ayman-Nolley, S. and Ayman, R. 2005. Children's Implicit Theory of Leadership. In B. Schyns and J. R. Meindl (eds) *Implicit Leadership Theories: Essays and Explorations*. Greenwich, CT: Information Age Publishing, pp. 189–233.

Ayman-Nolley, S. Ayman, R. and Leone, C. 2006. Gender Differences in the Children's Implicit Leadership Theory: Costa Rican and American Comparison. In R. Littrell (convener), *Empirical Studies: Qualitative and Quantitative Analyses of Leadership and Culture*, symposium conducted at the International Congress of Cross-cultural Psychology in Isle of Spetses, Greece (July).

Benveniste, D. 2005. Recognizing Defenses in the Drawings and Play of Children in Therapy, *American Psychological Association* 22(3): 395–410.

Brown, D. J., Scott, K. A and Lewis, H. 2004. Information Processing and Leadership. In J. Antonakis, A. T. Cianciolo, and R. J. Sternberg (eds) *The Nature of Leadership*. Thousand Oaks, CA: Sage, pp. 125–47.

Bombi, A. S. and Pinto, G. 1994. Making a Dyad: Cohesion and Distancing in Children's Pictorial Representation of Friendship, *British Journal of Developmental Psychology* 12: 563–75.

Chen, C. C., Chen, Y.-R. and Xin, K. 2004. Guanxi Practices and Trust in Management: A Procedural Justice Perspective, *Organization Science* 15(2): 200–9.

Cheng, B. S., Chou, L.-F., Wu, T.-Y., Huang, M.-P. and Farh, J.-L. 2004. Paternalistic Leadership and Subordinate Responses: Establishing a Leadership Model in Chinese Organizations, *Asian Journal of Social Psychology* 7: 89–117.

Coles, J. 2003. *Signals from the Child*. Denver, CO: EMBA House.

Damon, W. 1977. *The Social World of the Child*. San Francisco, CA: Jossey-Bass.

Dennis, W. 1966. *Group Values through Children's Drawings*. New York, NY: Wiley.

Dickson, J. M., Saylor, C. F. and Finch, Jr, A. J. 1990. Personality Factors, Family Structure, and Sex of Drawn Figure on the Draw-a-person Test, *Journal of Personality Assessment* 55: 363–6.

Dorfman, P. W., Hanges, P. J., Brodbeck, F. C. and Project GLOBE research team. 2004. Leadership and Culture Variation: The Identification of Culturally Endorsed Leadership Profiles. In R. J. House, P. J. Hanges, M. Javidan, P. W. Dorfman and V. Gupta (eds) *Culture, Leadership, and Organizations: The GLOBE Study of 62 Societies*. Thousand Oaks, CA: Sage, pp. 669–719.

Duehr, E. E. and Bono, J. E. 2006. Men, Women, and Managers: Are Stereotypes Finally Changing?, *Personnel Psychology* 59: 815–46.

Dunn, I., O'Connor, T. G. and Levy, I. 2002. Out of the Picture: A Study of Family Drawings by Children from Step, Single-parent, and Non-step Families, *Journal of Clinical Child and Adolescent Psychology* 31: 505–12.

Edelbrock, C. and Sugawara, A. I. 1978. Acquisition of Sex-typed Preferences in Preschool-aged Children, *Developmental Psychology* 14: 614–23.

Falchikov, N. 1990. Youthful Ideas About Old Age: An Analysis of Children's Drawings, *International Journal of Aging and Development* 31(2): 79–99.

Fiske, S. T. and Taylor, S. E. 1991. *Social Cognition*. New York, NY: McGraw-Hill.

Fu, P. P., Wu, R., Yang, K. and Ye, J. 2007. Chinese Culture and Leadership. In J. S. Chhokar,

F. C. Brodbeck and R. J. House (eds), *Culture and Leadership across the World*. Mahwah, NJ: LEA, pp. 877–908.

Gramradt, J. and Staples, C. 1994. My School and Me: Children's Drawings in Postmodern Educational Research and Evaluation, *Visual Arts Research* 20: 36–49.

Gelfand, M. J., Raver, J. L. and Ehrhart, K. H. 2002. Methodological Issues in Cross-cultural Organizational Research. In S. Rogelberg (ed.) *Handbook of Research Methods in Industrial and Organizational Psychology*. Malden, MA: Blackwell, pp. 216–46.

Gerstner, C. and Day, D. V. 1994. Cross-cultural Comparison of Leadership Prototypes, *Leadership Quarterly* 5(2): 121–34.

Golombok, S., Rust, J., Zervoulis, K., Croudace, T., Golding, J. and Hines, M. 2008. Developmental Trajectories of Sex-typed Behavior in Boys and Girls: A

Longitudinal General Population Study of Children Aged 2.5–8 Years, *Child Development* 79: 1583–93.

Gross, J. and Hayne, H. 1998. Drawing Facilitates Children's Verbal Reports of Emotionally Laden Events, *Journal of Experimental Psychology: Applied* 4(2): 163–79.

Heilman, M. E., Block, C. J., Martell, R. F. and Simon, M. C. 1989. Has Anything Changed? Current Characterizations of Men, Women, and Managers, *Journal of Applied Psychology* 74: 935–42.

Holmes, R. M. 1992. Children's Artwork and Nonverbal Communication, *Child Study Journal* 27(3): 157–65.

House, R. J., Hanges, P. J,. Javidan, M., Dorfman, P. W. and Gupta, V. 2004. *Cultures, Leadership, and Organizations: The GLOBE Study of 62 Societies.* Thousand Oaks, CA: Sage.

Jepson, D. 2009. Studying Leadership Across Countries: A Critical Analysis, *Leadership* 5: 61–80.

Kagan, J. and Moss, H. A. 1962. *Birth to Maturity: A Study in Psychological Development.* New York, NY: Wiley.

Klepsch, M. and Logle, L. 1982. *Children Draw and Tell.* New York, NY: Brunner/ Mazel.

Korabik, K. 1994. Managerial Women in the People's Republic of China: The Long March Continues. In N. J. Adler and D. N. Israeli (eds) *Competitive Frontiers: Women Managers in the Global Economy.* Oxford: Blackwell, pp.114–26.

Korabik, K. 2006. China at the Crossroads: A 25 Year Retrospective of Women Leaders in the People's Republic of China. A Working Paper for the Centre for Studies in Leadership, Guelph, ON, Canada: University of Guelph [http:// csl.uoguelph.ca/attachments/Working%20papers/Korabik%20China%20 Working%20Paper.pdf].

Larson, R. W. and Richards, M. H. 1994. *Divergent Realities: The Emotional Lives of Mothers, Fathers and Adolescents.* New York, NY: Basic Books.

Lau, D. C. 1970. *Mencius.* Harmondsworth: Penguin Books.

Leffler, H., Ayman, R. and Ayman–Nolley, S. 2006. *Do Children Possess the Same Stereotypes as Adults? An Exploration of Children's Implicit Leadership Theories,* poster presented at the International Congress of Applied Psychology, Athens, Greece (July).

Levy, G.. D., Taylor, M. G. and Gelman, S. A. 1995. Traditional and Evaluative Aspects of Flexibility in Gender Roles, Social Conventions, Moral Rules, and Physical Laws, *Child Development* 66: 515–31.

Liben, L. Bigler, R. S. and Krough, H. R. 2001. Pink and Blue Collar Jobs: Children's Judgments of Job Status and Job Aspirations in Relation to Sex of Workers, *Journal of Experimental Child Psychology* 79(4): 346–63.

Ling, W., Chia, R. and Fang, L. 2000. Chinese Implicit Leadership Theory, *The Journal of Social Psychology* 140(6): 729–39.

Lobel, R., Gruber, T. E., Govrin, N. and Mashraki-Pedhtzur, S. 2001. Children's Gender-related Inferences and Judgments: A Cross-cultural Study, *Developmental Psychology* 37(6): 839–46.

Lord, R. G., Brown, D. J., Harvey, J. L. and Hall, R. J. 2001. Contextual Constraints on Prototype Generation and their Multilevel Consequences for Leadership Perception, *The Leadership Quarterly,* 12: 311–38. [http://www.elsevier.com/ wps/find/journaldescription.cws_home/620221/description#description].

Lord, R. G., Foti, R. J. and de Vader, C. L. 1984. A Test of Leadership Categorization Theory: Internal Structure, Information Processing, and Leadership Perceptions, *Organizational Behavior & Human Performance* 34(3): 343–78.

Martin, C. L. and Halverson, C. F. 1981. A Schematic Processing Model of Sex-typing and Stereotyping in Children, *Child Development* 52: 1119–32. [http://www.wiley.com/bw/journal.asp?ref=0009–3920].

Matthews, A. M., Lord, R. G.. and Walker, J. B. 1990. *The Development of Leadership Perception in Children*, unpublished manuscript, University of Akron.

McHale, S. M., Shanahan, L., Updegraff, K. A., Crouter, A. C. and Booth, A. 2004. Developmental and Individual Differences in Girls' Sex-typed Activities in Middle Childhood and Adolescence, *Child Development* 75: 1575–93.

Mckown, C. and Strambler, M. J. 2009. Developmental Antecedents and Social and Academic Consequences of Stereotype Consciousness in Middle Childhood, *Child Development* 80: 1643–59.

McKown, C. and Weinstein, R. S. 2003. The Development and Consequences of Stereotype Consciousness in Middle Childhood, *Child Development* 74: 498–515.

Mietkiewicz, M.-C. and Jolliot, C. 2004. Grand Parents, Great Grand Parents and Step Grand Parents: The Young Children's Representations [French], *Neuropsychiatrie de l'Enfance et de l'Adolescence* 52(5): 330–6.

Miller, C. F., Lurye, L. E., Zosuls, K. M. and Ruble, D. N. 2009. Accessibility of Gender Stereotype Domains: Developmental and Gender Differences in Children, *Sex Roles* 60: 870–81.

Nemerowicz, G. M. and Rosi, E. 1997. *Education for Leadership and Social Responsibility*. London: Farmer.

Offermann, L., Kennedy, J. and Wirtz, P. 1994. Implicit Leadership Theories: Content, Structure, and Generalizability, *Leadership Quarterly* 5(1): 43–55.

Overholt, W. H. 2005. *China and Globalization*. Santa Monica, CA: RAND Corporation.

Pinto, G., Bombi, A. S. and Cordioli, A. 1997. Similarity of Friends in Three Countries: A Study of Children's Drawings, *International Journal of Behavioral Development* 20(3): 453–69.

Powell, G.. N., Butterfield, D. A. and Parent, J. D. 2002. Gender and Managerial Stereotypes: Have the Times Changed?, *Journal of Management* 28: 177–93.

Priess, H. A., Lindberg, S. M. and Hyde, J. S. 2009. Adolescent Gender-intensification Identity and Mental Health: Gender Intensification Revisited, *Child Development* 80: 1531–44.

Ruble, D. N. 1988. Sex-role Development. In M. H. Bornstein and M. E. Lamb (eds) *Developmental Psychology: An Advanced Textbook*. Hillsdale, NJ: LEA, pp. 411–60.

Ruble, D. N., Martin, C. and Berenbaum, S. 2006. Gender Development. In W. Damon and R. M. Lerner (series eds) and N. Eisenberg (vol. ed.) *Handbook of Child Psychology, Volume 3: Social, Emotional, and Personality Development*, 6th edn. Hoboken, NJ: Wiley, pp. 858–932.

Rudman, L. A., Ashmore, R. D. and Gary, M. L. 2001. 'Unlearning' Automatic Biases: The Malleability of Implicit Prejudices and Stereotypes, *Journal of Personality and Social Psychology* 81: 856–68.

Schein, V. E. 1973. The Relationship Between Sex Role Stereotypes and Requisite Management Characteristics, *Journal of Applied Psychology* 57: 95–100.

Schein, V. E. 2001. A Global Look at Psychological Barriers to Women's Progress in Management, *Journal of Social Issues* 57: 675–88.

Schein, V. E., Mueller, R., Lituchy, T. and Liu, J. 1996. Think Manager—Think Male: A Global Phenomenon?, *Journal of Organizational Behavior* 17: 33–41.

Schyns, B. and Meindl, J. R. 2005. An Overview of Implicit Leadership Theories and their Application in Organization Practice. In B. Schyns and J. R. Meindl (eds) *Implicit Leadership Theories: Essays and Explorations.* Greenwich, CT: Information Age, pp.15–36.

Signorella, M. L., Bigler, R. S. and Liben, L. S. 1993. Developmental Differences in Children's Gender Schemata About Others: A Meta-analytic Review, *Developmental Review* 13: 147–83.

Trautner, H. M. 1992. The Development of Sex-typing in Children: A Longitudinal Study, *German Journal of Psychology* 16(3): 183–99.

Ware, J. R. 1995. *The Sayings of Confucius: A New Translation.* New York, NY: New American Library.

Weisgram, E., Bigler, R. and Liben, L. 2010. Gender, Values, and Occupational Interests Among Children, Adolescents and Adults, *Child Development* 81(3): 778–96.

Wong, C. S., Tinsley, C., Law, K. S. and Mobley, W. H. 2003. Development and Validation of a Multidimensional Measure of Guanxi, *Journal of Psychology in Chinese Societies* 4(1): 43–69.

Wood, E., Whiteley, A. and Zhang, S. 2002. The Cross Model of Guanxi Usage in Chinese Leadership, *Journal of Management Development* 21(4): 263–71.

Yi-Feng, N. C., Tjosvold, D. and Peiguan, W. 2008. Effects of Relationship Values and Goal Interdependence on Guanxi Between Foreign Managers and Chinese Employees, *Journal of Applied Social Psychology* 38(10): 2440–68.

8

Implicit Leadership in Iran: Differences between Leader and Boss and Gender*

Roya Ayman, Alan D. Mead, Afshin Bassari and Jialin Huang

Introduction

Globalization has increased the interest in understanding leadership within and across cultures around the world. Adding to this is the political dynamics in the world, which further enhance the need to better understand major cultural expectations people have of those in decision-making roles in society. As we consider leadership around the world, we can reflect on the scholars of previous centuries around the world who advised their rulers and the leaders of their time, such as Confucius in China, Machiavelli in Europe and Saadi, Nasir Toosi, Nezamolmolk in Iran. In more modern times Thomas Carlyle, Mao Zedong, Karl Marx and Max Weber are some who have written about the leader and leadership in various parts of the world. In the last century, the empirical approach has added to these philosophical endeavours, emphasizing the importance of the layperson's expectations about leadership, which in turn guide their judgment and behaviours as they interact with or as a leader. This line of research is known as the implicit leadership theory (Lord & Maher, 1991; Lord, 2005).

With the increased interest in the geopolitics of Iran, a closer observation of Iranians' image of a leader seems to be of value. In examining leadership within a particular culture, two initial approaches can be considered: etic and emic. While an etic approach uses the constructs developed in other cultures in assessing leadership in a culture, an emic approach develops constructs from within the culture under investigation (Ayman & Korabik, 2010). Most empirical studies that have examined

---

* This chapter is based on Afshin Bassari's Master's thesis

135

aspects of Iranians' implicit leadership theory (e.g. Dastmalchian et al., 2001) have used various forms of etic approach. The study presented in this chapter used an emic approach, which provides an approach closer to the worldly leadership perspective (Jepson, 2009; Turnbull, 2009).

Implicit leadership theory and culture

Implicit leadership theory (ILT) is the schema, or mental image, that people hold regarding a leader or leadership (Lord & Maher, 1991). In essence, ILT includes traits and behaviours that people expect when they think of the leader (Schyns & Meindl, 2005). Depending on the focus of the studies, this schema could be about a typical leader (Offermann et al., 1994), an ideal leader, or a successful leader (e.g. Heilman et al., 1989; Epitropaki & Martin, 2005). The presence of implicit leadership theory was first introduced by Eden and Leviatan (2005). Its impact on people's judgment of a leader is also illustrated by a series of studies (Lord & Maher, 1991). The importance of this concept in measuring leader behaviour and leadership effectiveness has been extensively discussed (Lord & Emrich, 2001; Meindl, 1995).

The focus of this study is on the content of ILT. To understand the content of ILT, several major studies were conducted. They started with Lord, de Vader, and Alliger (1986) who, through a meta-analysis of previous studies on leadership characteristics, showed that intelligence, masculinity-femininity and dominance are what differentiated leaders from non-leaders. However, because this study was dependent on what previous scholars had included in their leadership studies, one important point remained unclear: Were these the only characteristics that *laypeople* considered when thinking of leaders? Or were these merely reflecting the ILT of the *scholars* of leadership? Subsequently, Offermann et al. (1994) studied the expectations of men and women, both with and without work experience, about a leader, a successful leader and a supervisor. Their results showed that the characteristics of sensitivity, dedication, tyranny, charisma, attractiveness, masculinity, intelligence and strength seemed to be stable regardless of the gender of the perceiver and type of leader. Leaders and effective leaders were perceived with higher ratings than the supervisors.

Though the 1994 Offermann et al. study did not find the gender of the perceiver affecting ILT, others have acknowledged that perceiver characteristics do have an impact on ILT (Foti & Luch, 1992). The potential cultural difference on ILT, tested by Gerstner and Day (1994) using a different method, demonstrated that people from various cultures – such as China, France, Germany, Honduras, India, Japan and Taiwan – held varying implicit leadership theories. This finding provided some possibility that the content of ILT will vary due to the perceiver's culture. Using a different paradigm and primarily focusing on expectations of people related to a manager instead of a leader in general, Schein's series of studies (e.g. Schein, 1973; Schein et al.,1989; Schein, 2001) demonstrated that people's image of a manager is more aligned with their image of a man than a woman. However, more recent studies reported that in the United States, women's image of a manager was less aligned with a man than had been true in the past (Duehr & Bono, 2006; Schein et al., 1996). Additionally, Runkle and Ayman (1997) found that the image held by Caucasian respondents of a manager was more aligned with their image of a prototypical Caucasian than of an African American. However, the African American respondent's image of a leader was more often Caucasian than African American, thus showing that followers' experiential background may affect their ILT content.

The leadership categorization theories (Hall & Lord, 1995; Lord et al., 2001) have demonstrated that ILT is context-bound. Similar to social psychological theory of connectionist models, evidence showed that these expectations are dynamic, flexible and sensitive to the real-time constraints of social interaction. Lord et al. (2001) acknowledged four contextual constraints for the formation of the ILT content: culture, leader's role, follower's characteristics and the nature of the task. Thus, it is not surprising that the perceiver's gender or culture may have an impact on their expectation of the leader (Hanges et al., 2000).

The Global Leadership and Organizational Behavioural Effectiveness (GLOBE) project (House et al., 2004) included about 62 societies and studied perception of leadership behaviours in three different types of industries. It also addressed culturally endorsed implicit leadership theory (CILT). From an ILT perspective, GLOBE assessed expectations of an ideal leader, not a prototypical leader (House et al., 2002). The problem with studying people's expectations of an ideal image of a leader is that people mostly agree on that image compared to their expectations of a typical leader (e.g. Heilman et al., 1989). In addition, GLOBE's main goal was to find universals; and to that end it used a uniform measure in all countries, thus losing the potential elements of uniqueness within a culture (Jepson, 2009).

Most of the studies on ILT or leadership categorization were initiated from North America. Thus, from a cross-cultural study approach, they were more etic. However, to fully understand the ILT of a people due to their culture, a more emic approach is preferable – that is, an exploration of the indigenous definition of leadership attributes (Ayman, 2004). The only study today, which has replicated the 1994 study by Offermann et al. of ILT in the United States in another country, is the work in China (Ling et al., 2000). The findings by Ling et al. described the prototypical Chinese leader as having personal morality, goal efficiency, interpersonal competence and versatility. They also reported that perceivers put the highest value on interpersonal competence. These findings did not show similarity with the Offermann et al. ILT content in the United States. Thus, this further emphasizes the importance of an emic approach to ILT in various cultures.

Leadership in Iran

The present study is an emic approach to implicit leadership theory in Iran. In order to appreciate this study and its value, we will provide a short overview of the country and some cultural aspects before reviewing some of the leadership studies that have been conducted in Iran.

The country of Iran, known as Persia until 1935, has historically been the cradle of culture, civilization and trade in the Middle East, with a written history of over 2500 years. Iran has always served as a link between the West and the East. With an area of 1,648,195 sq km and an estimated population of 76,923,300 (Central Intelligence Agency, 2010), the country enjoys a wide range of climates and landscapes with a mostly semi-arid terrain. Some 21.7 per cent of the population are very young, ranging in age from 0 to 14 years; 72.9 per cent are 15–64 years; 5.4 per cent are 65 years and over (CIA, 2010). The ethnic groups are Persians 51 per cent, Azeri 24 per cent, Gilaki and Mazandarani 8 per cent, Kurd 7 per cent, Arab 3 per cent, Lur 2 per cent, Baloch 2 per cent, Turkmen 2 per cent, and others 1 per cent (CIA, 2010). The official language in Iran is Persian (Farsi), an Indo-European language written with the Arabic alphabet, though local symbols and dialects are widespread and permitted. As to religion, 98 per cent of the population adhere to Islam (89% Shia and 9% Sunni), and the remaining 2 per cent are Bahá'í, Zoroastrian, Jewish and Christian (CIA, 2010). Iran seems to have the largest market in the Middle East. The country's GDP (purchasing power parity) in 2009 was $827.1 billion, making the per capita figure $12,500 (CIA, 2010). Petroleum and petrochemical products account for more than 80 per cent of Iran's exports (CIA, 2010). The most populous cities of Iran are Tehran (the capital), Mashad, Tabriz, Isfahan and Shiraz. Iran became an Islamic Republic in 1979 after the ruling monarchy was overthrown, and the new regime rejected the programmes of modernization and westernization of Iran. The country has experienced pronounced social and economical changes since 1979 (Dastmalchian et al., 2001). The Iranian government and leadership is a theocracy and rule by fear which has penetrated all aspect of social life in the country.

The following explanation of the changes in Iran was inspired by articles published in Persian. Socially, religion has become predominant in all aspects of life and politicized as a means in the service of political ends. It serves as a facade or justification for legitimizing the autocratic behaviour of the ruling group. Economically, mineral resources, particularly oil and gas in international market, have become the main source of national income; and sharp increases of some household items to be exported to Central Asian countries and steel products to be sold in international markets have become a second source of income but to a much smaller scale compared to minerals export. Rapid demographic changes such as the population doubling in less than three decades and rejuvenation of population have increased the capacity of the domestic market. Industrial development, however, is lagging behind resulting in the increase of the number of young educated unemployed. As a result there is a dichotomy of leadership patterns in Iran: traditional autocracy in the public sector and a more western pattern of management in the private sector (e.g. Zandian, 2010; Majidi, 2010; Amuzegar, 2010).

Empirical research about leadership in Iran published outside the country is meagre and is mostly based on etic approach (e.g. Ayman & Chemers, 1983; Dastmalchian et al., 2001). Zonis (1971), through observation and interview technique, conducted an emic approach to leadership in Iran. He concluded that Iran is a high power distance culture. He also mentioned that two factors play an important role in Iranian leadership: formality and attention to relationship.

The two etic studies published on Iranian leadership occurred in two very different socio-political environments. Ayman and Chemers (1983) conducted their study prior to the 1979 revolution. They used a modified version of a North American measure (Leader Behaviour Description Questionnaire) to assess the subordinates' perceptions of their managers in Iran. Their results showed that subordinates described their middle-level managers' leader behaviours as both structuring and considerate. This leadership was also highly related to the satisfaction and effectiveness of the manager. Comparing this finding to early work by Chemers in Iran (Chemers, 1969), where the Iranian subordinates were describing their American supervisors, led Ayman and Chemers to conclude that the Iranians perceived the effective leader as a 'benevolent paternal leader'.

After the 1979 revolution, as part of the GLOBE research project, Dastmalchian et al. (2001) examined culture and leadership in Iran. The participants were 300 mid-level managers in three different industries – food processing, banking and telecommunications – and GLOBE leadership behaviour measurement was the instrument. The authors concluded that the results showed seven scales: supportive, dictatorial, planner, familial, humble, faithful and receptive.

The present study examined the content and factors of the implicit leadership theory of Iranian laypeople in present day Iran. This expands the previous studies which primarily examined the perception of managers or executives or workers (e.g. Ayman & Chemers, 1983; Dastmalchian et al., 2001) on ideal leadership and perception of managers in companies. Additionally, it explored people's ILT due to leader's role, examining the leadership categorization by comparing ILT of a leader, a manager or a boss. Finally, it compared the effect of the respondent's gender on their implicit leadership theory.

Methodology

Inspired by the Offermann et al. (1994) and Ling et al. (2000) methodology, this study was conducted in two parts. A pilot study was conducted to identify the Persian terms for *leader* and also to develop an Iranian implicit leadership scale. The main study, with a larger sample, examined the implicit leadership theory of Iranians as they think of a typical leader or a *boss*.

Pilot study

Initially, we had trouble selecting an accurate and explanatory word for *leader* in the Persian language. The equivalent word originally would have been *rahbar*. However, in recent decades since the Islamic Revolution, the political meaning of the word *rahbar* in Iran refers to a *supreme leader*, specifically Ayatollah Ruhollah Khomeini. Therefore, to avoid this confusion, we examined the newspapers and chose the recently coined word *raahbar* instead. (Many Iranian newspapers using this word follow it with the English word *leader* written with the Arabic alphabet.) Additionally, we were interested in leadership categorization; therefore, in the pilot study, we compared the three roles: (1) *leader* or *raahbar*, (2) *manager* or *modir* and (3) *boss* or *raiis*. With the comparison of the descriptions of the three different words, we hoped to obtain our best target word.

Of the 30 adults between the ages of 25 and 65 years who participated in the pilot study, all 15 women and 15 men resided in Tehran, Iran. On three separate sheets of paper labelled, respectively, *raahbar* (leader), *modir* (manager) and *raiis* (boss), we asked each participant to write up to ten words or phrases describing characteristics of that person. No definitions for these target words were provided, and the time for this activity was about 15 minutes for every participant. To prevent order biases, the order of these terms were counterbalanced. Subsequently, reviewing the 90 sheets of paper, we eliminated redundancies and created a measure with 28 items that included those characteristics that had at least two endorsements in the first phase (i.e. at least two of our participants had listed that characteristic for leader or boss).

After the responses were collected, we asked most of the respondents for their feedback regarding what they thought and how they felt about the target words. This provided an insight in recognizing the best words (terms) to be used in place of *leader* in Persian. Their comments substantiated that the terms *raiis* and *modir* seemed to activate similar images in their minds. Also the term *raahbar* captured the generic equivalent to the term *leader* used in the North American and Western European literature. This was further ascertained with the analysis of the list of the characteristics we had obtained from them. The findings addressed two issues. One, it identified whether these terms are context-specific or synonymous. Also, we were able to find a general term similar to the word *leader* used in the English language. Two, the descriptions of these terms established the potentially unique implicit leadership theories of the participants in Iran. For the second phase, our main study, we chose *raahbar* (which is part of the daily news language) to represent the term *leader* and the word *raiis to* refer to the *boss/manager/supervisor.*

Main study

Measures. To further substantiate our preliminary findings and expand them, in this comparative study, a scale was developed that included both items based on the descriptors collected in the pilot study. Participants expressed their level of agreement with each item as it depicted – on two separate, labelled sheets – a *leader* and a *boss* on a 7-point Likert-type (1=very highly agree, 7=very highly disagree) scale. This arrangement of the agreement continuum adapted the typical US orientation so that it was convenient for the Persian participants who read right-to-left. During analysis, we reverse-coded these responses so that 7.0 represented greatest agreement.

Participants and data collection procedure

We recruited a total of 420 participants from Tehran and other cities. Although most of the participants resided in Tehran, their places of origin included different parts of Iran. Due to special conditions in Iran and limitations on the researchers, we engaged ten data-collection assistants to find qualified participants all over Tehran. Participants were given ten minutes to complete the questionnaire. Each question- naire was kept in a sealed envelope and delivered to us by the selected assistant.

Half of the respondents in each subgroup for the *leader* or *boss* scale were men and half women, all between 25 and 65 years old. Demographic data such as age, gender, education, occupation, experi- ence at being a leader or boss, place of origin and place of residence were collected from them. We also conducted a Chi-square test for gender on various demographics. The only meaningful differences were observed in two variables: *occupation,* where more men were employed than were women; and *experience at being a leader or boss,* where men had more managerial/supervisory experience.

Results

Descriptive statistics

Table 8.1 contains descriptive statistics for item responses in the *leader* and *boss* conditions. Few responses were missing in either condition. Mean item response on a 7-point scale (where 7.0 was 'very highly agree') ranged from 4.58 to 6.35 for *leader* and between 4.56 and 6.33 for *boss*. The responses tended to be skewed towards agreeing that the trait characterized leaders and bosses, which is unsurprising given that all 28 characteristics were provided by at least two of the participants in the initial stage.

Exploratory factor analysis

Bassari and Ayman (2009) conducted exploratory factor analyses (EFAs) on this dataset. They found that models for the two conditions of *leader* and *boss* had similarities and differences. In both conditions, they found four-factor models; and the first three factors (confident; goal oriented and considerate) were similar across conditions. However, the *leader* group and the *boss* group disagreed on the fourth factor (severe versus sentimental), and some item loadings on the similar factors were apparently different between the two conditions.

Table 8.1 Descriptive statistics for items under *Boss* and *Leader* conditions

	Boss			Leader		
	Mean	**SD**	**Skewness**	**Mean**	**SD**	**Skewness**
Loveable	4.88	1.13	0.45	5.25	1.17	–0.16
Goal oriented	6.25	0.96	–1.46	6.35	0.92	–2.07
With perseverance	6.16	0.95	–0.98	6.30	0.94	–1.64
Responsible	6.33	0.92	–1.96	6.50	0.85	–2.31
Sincere	4.56	1.37	0.13	5.06	1.10	0.22
Able to work with groups	5.88	1.12	–1.24	5.95	1.09	–1.09
Coach or guide	5.93	1.04	–0.92	6.19	1.06	–1.51
Experienced	5.85	1.07	–0.68	5.93	1.08	–0.57
Reliable	6.22	1.02	–1.25	6.31	0.90	–1.37
Future oriented	5.98	1.00	–0.84	5.75	1.15	–0.73
Kind	4.70	1.27	0.09	4.79	1.12	0.21
Just, fair	6.06	1.15	–1.53	5.75	1.15	–0.67
Powerful	5.88	1.05	–0.71	5.83	1.12	–0.84
Energetic	5.97	0.98	–0.80	5.95	1.08	–1.13
Rational, logical, sound mind	6.30	0.98	–1.82	6.26	0.92	–1.23
Planner	5.98	1.00	–1.15	6.12	1.01	–1.29
Eloquent	5.62	1.12	–0.53	5.81	1.15	–0.76

	Mean	**SD**	**Skewness**	**Mean**	**SD**	**Skewness**
Witty and ingenious	5.38	1.15	–0.44	5.44	1.07	–0.03
Encourager	5.64	1.03	–0.34	5.42	1.07	–0.53
Informed	5.93	1.05	–1.08	5.91	1.02	–0.98
Self-confident	5.97	1.03	–0.91	5.98	1.10	–1.17
Progressive	5.62	1.05	–0.42	5.70	1.14	–0.77
Patient	5.55	1.26	–0.63	5.62	1.22	–0.99
Aware of others	5.64	1.09	–0.40	5.64	1.10	–0.85
Open to criticism	5.62	1.20	–0.60	5.62	1.19	–0.88
Intelligent	5.89	0.91	–0.44	5.85	1.08	–0.76
Decisive	5.79	1.02	–0.60	5.83	1.19	–0.74
Severe	4.63	1.09	0.27	4.58	1.24	0.07

Note: N=204–206 for *boss*; N=200–203 for *leader*.

We chose to re-analyse the data using EFA for three reasons. First, in the former study, the authors used orthogonal rotation to determine the number of factors. From a psychometric perspective, we feel that oblique rotation is more appropriate than orthogonal rotation because dimensions of psychological models are unlikely to be uncorrelated and orthogonal rotation includes an implausible assumption.

Table 8.2   Exploratory Factor Analysis (EFA) factor loadings for *Leader* and *Boss* conditions

	Leader			Boss		
	F1	F2	F3	F1	F2	F3
Loveable	0.25				0.47	
Goal oriented	0.68			0.45		
With perseverance	0.61			0.47		
Responsible	0.63			0.76		
Sincere		0.75			0.57	
Able to work with groups	0.50			0.52		
Coach or guide	0.71			0.36		
Experienced	0.44					0.18
Reliable	0.57			0.50		
Future oriented	0.63			0.37		
Kind		0.84			0.83	
Just, fair	0.35			0.65		
Powerful	0.68					0.55
Energetic	0.64					0.36
Rational, logical, sound mind	0.74			0.62		
Planner	0.62			0.42		
Eloquent	0.62					0.48
Witty and ingenious	0.57					0.49
Encourager		0.39				0.51
Informed	0.62					0.46
Self-confident	0.67					0.55
Progressive	0.67					0.47
Patient			−.40	0.49		
Aware of others		0.47		0.38		
Open to criticism			−.50	0.55		
Intelligent	0.70					0.30
Decisive	0.64					0.78
Severe			0.65			0.43

Note: Loadings with magnitude below 0.20 are not presented.

Second, determining the number of factors to extract and rotate is a sensitive judgment call in any EFA analysis, and we wished to use parallel analysis to determine the number of factors to retain. Parallel analysis has been shown to recover dimensions better than alternatives (Franklin et al., 1995).

Third, we also hoped that we might find a baseline model for confirmatory factor analyses (CFA) that fits both *leader* and *boss* responses using the same structure. We actually analysed the entire sample as well as each condition separately.

Two separate EFAs were conducted using all 28 items, with maximum likelihood as the extraction method and direct oblimin as the rotation method. Besides examining the screen plot, eigenvalues and percentage of variance explained, parallel analysis (PA) was also involved in determining the number of factors. Parallel analysis can be thought of as an improvement upon Kaiser's rule: the situation in which all the factors are uncorrelated is simulated, and those eigenvalues are overplotted on the real-data screen plot. Only factors that have eigenvalues greater than the simulated 'noise' factor analysis are retained.

In both conditions, the parallel analysis supported a three-factor model because the fourth eigenvalues of EFA were less than their respective PA eigenvalues. Table 8.2 shows the pattern of each model and item loadings on each factor for the two conditions. These results paint a picture of fairly different results for the two conditions. The *leader* EFA results seem to have a strong first factor, whereas the *boss* EFA results show more multidimensionality. The solutions would be most similar if one assumed that factor one (F1) of the *leader* condition broke into two factors, F1 and F3, in the *boss* condition while F2 was shared between both conditions.

For the *leader* condition, the items loaded on F1 represent a charismatic leader: one who brings hope, is knowledgeable and eloquent, and is visionary and just. F2 is primarily representative of other directed qualities: awareness of others, openness to criticism and kindness. For the *boss* condition, F1 shows an image of being conscientious, goal oriented, and skilled at working with others. F2 characterizes a person who gives primarily affective support. F3 represents a mover, one who is strong, knowledgeable, energetic, ingenious, self-confident, decisive and an encourager.

Confirmatory factor analysis

We prepared a covariance matrix for analysis by estimating polychoric correlations of the (pairwise) available data and then converting to covariances. Although the indicator variables were frequently skewed, Maximum Likelihood (ML) estimation has been found to be robust to this type of skew (Hau & Marsh, 2004). LISREL 8.80 was used for all analyses.

Our strategy was to build up a model from leader responses and then apply it to *boss* condition to test its fitness. If there was no difference, the model would fit both samples equally well. Alternatively, if the structures of *leader* and *boss* images were truly different, then a model developed from responses in either the *boss* or *leader* conditions would not fit the data from the other condition. Instead, an independent model would be needed for both the *leader* and the *boss* conditions.

Model 1 shown in Figure 8.1 was established based on the EFA results of *leader* responses; thus, it was a 'leader model'. After an initial model was fit, modification indices indicated a curious pattern: uniquenesses between items 1 and 2, 2 and 3, 3 and 4, and so on should be freed. This indicates that there was a response bias in which respondents had a tendency to repeat their response on subsequent items (without regard to the content of the item). Table 8.3 shows the improvement in fit due to this model change. Thus, freeing all the theta-delta values below the diagonal (i.e. allowing sequentially contiguous items to have shared unique variance – beyond the shared variance implied by the latent variable structure) significantly increased fit and was readily explainable as a response bias; so this feature was included in all CFA models.

After freeing the subdiagonal covariations, modification indices strongly suggested three additional modifications that we felt were theoretically justified: item 28 cross-loaded on F2; item 24 cross-loaded on F3; and uniquenesses of items 5 and 11 correlated. Although some other changes were also suggested, they were not interpretable conceptually. Thus Model 1, the *leader* model, has three factors:

- F1 – items 1, 3, 4, 6, 7, 8, 9, 10, 12, 13, 14, 15, 16, 17, 18, 20, 21, 22, 26, 27
- F2 – items 5, 11, 19, 28
- F3 – items 23, 24, 25, 28

Model 2, the *boss* model, was built according to the EFA results of the *boss* sample. It is shown in Figure 8.2. As in the *leader* model, the uniquenesses of consecutive items were allowed to covary, and additional modifications were made where conceptually interpretable. Our final *boss* model also had three factors:

- F1 – items 2, 3, 4, 6, 7, 9, 10, 12, 15, 16, 23, 24, 25
- F2 – items 1, 5, 11
- F3 – items 8, 13, 14, 17, 18, 19, 20, 21, 22, 26, 27, 28

Table 8.4 presents goodness-of-fit statistics for both models, which showed moderately good fit but not very good fit. For the *leader* model (Model 1), CFI=0.96, GFI=0.81 and RMSEA=0.073. Fitting the *leader* model to responses in the *boss* condition produced acceptable fit: CFI=0.93,

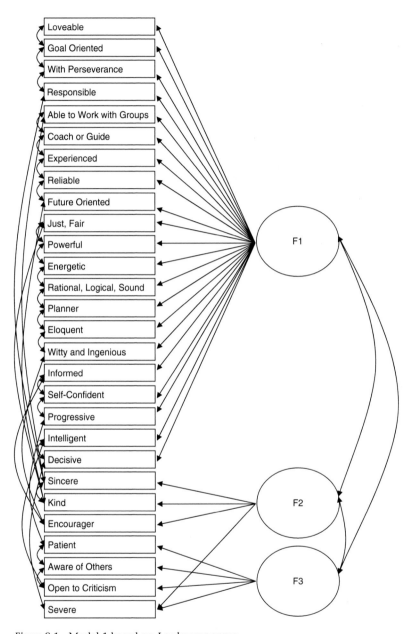

Figure 8.1 Model 1 based on *Leader* responses

Table 8.3   Goodness-of-fit evidence for a 'consecutive item' response bias

Model	Fixed (zero) subdiagonal uniquenesses						Freely estimated uniquenesses					
	X^2	df	X^2/df	CFI	GFI	RMSEA	X^2	df	X^2/df	CFI	GFI	RMSEA
1	916.94	347	2.64	0.93	0.75	0.093	719.35	320	2.25	0.95	0.80	0.079
2	773.10	347	2.23	0.92	0.79	0.076	574.65	320	1.80	0.95	0.84	0.060

Note: Fixed (zero) subdiagonal uniquenesses indicates models that ignore response bias. Freely estimated uniquenesses indicates models that allow consecutive items to have correlated errors. Model 1 was the *leader* model (developed from *leader* responses); Model 2 was the *boss* model (developed from *boss* responses).

GFI=0.80 and RMSEA=0.077. However, the *boss* model (Model 2) fit *boss* responses better: CFI=0.95, GFI=0.84 and RMSEA=0.060. Similarly, the fit of the *boss* model to responses from the *leader* condition was barely adequate, while the *leader* model fit these data well (see Table 8.4, bottom row). These results suggest that a hypothesis of shared structure across the *leader* and boss samples is not completely rejected (because the *leader* model fits the *boss* data moderately well), but an even better fit was obtained using different *leader* and *boss* models (Model 1, developed on the *leader* data, fits the *leader* data better; Model 2, developed on the *boss* data, fits the *boss* data better).

In terms of item loadings on factors, each condition seemed to have different patterns, as shown in Table 8.5. For the 'leader' model, *leader* and *boss* responses showed different loadings on the same item. All item loadings of the *leader* sample were moderate (between 0.30 and 0.70) or above. However, for the *boss* responses, most loadings were moderate, and some were below 0.30. Item loadings of the *boss* group on the *boss* model followed the same trend as on the *leader* model.

Mean comparison for each item on gender

In order to test whether gender differences existed in perceptions of *leader* and *boss*, independent group t-tests were performed for each item. As shown in Table 8.6, there were few significant gender differences. Men's expectation of leaders, as compared to women's, were higher for 'future oriented' and 'just, fair' and lower for 'eloquent' and 'informed'. Women's expectations of a typical boss were significantly higher than men's on 'able to work with groups', 'reliable' and 'open to criticism' and lower on 'severe'.

Discussion and conclusion

This study's main goal was to examine the content of Iranians' ILT and to test if this content is universal or if it is context-specific based

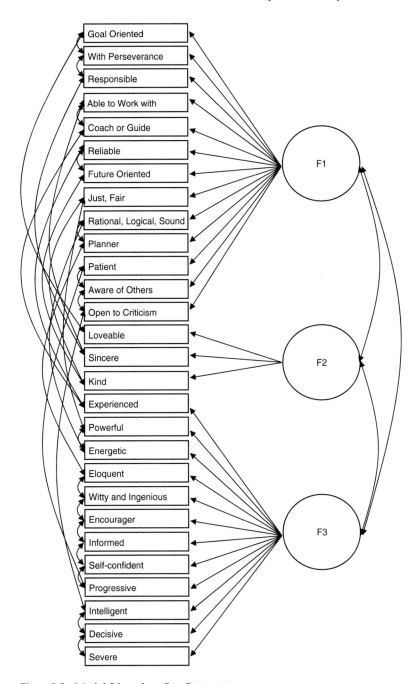

Figure 8.2 Model 2 based on *Boss* Responses

Table 8.4 Goodness-of-fit statistics for models applied to same and other samples

Model	Sample	X^2	df	X^2/df	CFI	GFI	RMSEA
Model 1	Leader	662.34	318	2.08	0.96	0.81	0.073
Model 1	Boss	676.65	318	2.11	0.93	0.80	0.077
Model 2	Boss	574.65	320	1.80	0.95	0.84	0.060
Model 2	Leader	725.74	320	2.27	0.95	0.78	0.090

Note: Model 1 was the *leader* model (developed from *leader* responses); Model 2 was the *boss* model (developed from *boss* responses).

Table 8.5 Factor loadings for *Leader* and *Boss* models applied to *Leader* and *Boss* conditions

	Leader Model in Leader Condition			Leader Model in Boss Condition			Boss Model in Boss Condition			Boss Model in Leader Condition		
	F1	F2	F3	F1	F2	F3	F1	F2	F3	F1	F2	F3
Loveable	0.33			0.19				0.64			0.42	
Goal oriented	0.60			0.57			0.58			0.60		
With perseverance	0.58			0.56			0.55			0.61		
Responsible	0.59			0.58			0.67			0.61		
Sincere		0.42			0.19			0.66			0.81	
Able to work with groups	0.60			0.45			0.50			0.63		
Coach or guide	0.71			0.48			0.46			0.72		
Experienced	0.50			0.31					0.29			0.50
Reliable	0.56			0.52			0.52			0.58		
Future oriented	0.63			0.57			0.56			0.63		
Kind		0.31			0.32			0.68			0.67	
Just, fair	0.45			0.60			0.62			0.48		
Powerful	0.68			0.65					0.68			0.69
Energetic	0.65			0.59					0.63			0.66
Rational, logical, sound mind	0.66			0.53			0.58			0.67		
Planner	0.63			0.64			0.65			0.62		
Eloquent	0.64			0.52				0.55				0.66
Witty and ingenious	0.57			0.59				0.63				0.58
Encourager		0.63			0.59			0.61				0.50

Continued

Table 8.5 Continued

	Leader Model in Leader Condition			Leader Model in Boss Condition			Boss Model in Boss Condition			Boss Model in Leader Condition		
	F1	F2	F3	F1	F2	F3	F1	F2	F3	F1	F2	F3
Informed	0.66			0.56					0.57			0.68
Self-confident	0.59			0.43					0.51			0.61
Progressive	0.64			0.62					0.65			0.66
Patient			0.74			0.55	0.45					0.43
Aware of others			0.84			0.59	0.44					0.52
Open to criticism			0.75			0.78	0.60					0.51
Intelligent	0.67			0.40					0.40			0.69
Decisive	0.56			0.50					0.58			0.59
Severe		1.00	–.89		0.54	–.42			0.24			0.28

Table 8.6 Results of T-test for each item between gender groups

	Leader			Boss		
	Female	Male	prob	Female	Male	prob
Loveable	5.17	5.33	ns	4.78	4.98	ns
Goal oriented	6.33	6.37	ns	6.24	6.27	ns
With perseverance	6.29	6.30	ns	6.11	6.21	ns
Responsible	6.46	6.54	ns	6.38	6.29	ns
Sincere	5.04	5.08	ns	4.58	4.55	ns
Able to work with groups	6.09	5.8	ns	6.01	5.75	<.01
Coach or guide	6.23	6.15	ns	5.85	6.02	ns
Experienced	5.94	5.91	ns	5.85	5.86	ns
Reliable	6.30	6.31	ns	6.31	6.12	<.05
Future oriented	5.59	5.91	<.05	5.98	5.97	ns
Kind	4.8	4.79	ns	4.76	4.64	ns
Just, fair	5.70	5.80	<.05	6.14	5.97	ns
Powerful	5.83	5.83	ns	5.81	5.95	ns
Energetic	5.99	5.90	ns	6.01	5.93	ns
Rational, logical, sound mind	6.3	6.22	ns	6.31	6.29	ns

Continued

Table 8.6   Continued

	Leader			Boss		
	Female	Male	prob	Female	Male	prob
Planner	6.2	6.04	ns	6.01	5.95	ns
Eloquent	5.95	5.66	<.01	5.72	5.51	ns
Witty and ingenious	5.44	5.44	ns	5.45	5.31	ns
Encourager	5.31	5.53	ns	5.68	5.60	ns
Informed	6.01	5.81	<.05	5.95	5.90	ns
Self-confident	5.83	6.13	ns	5.93	6.01	ns
Progressive	5.71	5.69	ns	5.62	5.63	ns
Patient	5.67	5.58	ns	5.67	5.43	ns
Aware of others	5.5	5.78	ns	5.76	5.51	ns
Open to criticism	5.58	5.65	ns	5.75	5.48	<.05
Intelligent	5.75	5.95	ns	5.90	5.89	ns
Decisive	5.84	5.82	ns	5.73	5.85	ns
Severe	4.53	4.63	ns	4.58	4.68	<.05

on the role of the leader or the gender of the respondent. The results of the confirmatory factor analysis (CFA) and t-tests demonstrated that these contextual factors did contribute both in the structure of the ILT content and in the endorsement of one characteristic more than another.

Some studies in the past have used a form of factor analysis to examine similarity or difference between factors related to leaders' roles (e.g. Foti et al., 1982); however, other studies (Ling et al., 2000; Offermann et al., 1994; Gerstner & Day, 1994) examined mean differences. In this study, we tested the effect of leader's role using a stringent statistical tool of CFA. Based on this analysis and subsequent follow-ups, it became clear that the attributes did not cluster similarly for the two conditions: *leader* and *boss*. The *leader* condition had two distinct factors where, in F1, the leader is charismatic and in F2, other-directed. However, when examining the factors in the *boss* condition, the concept of being an encourager and loveable is no longer on FI; F1 represents a strong leader, F2 a loveable one and F3 a mover.

These findings further elaborate on the findings of Offermann et al. (1994), because they did not do a comparison on the structure of the ILT content but rather examined mean differences. This study shows that the differences found in that study, at least in the Iranian sample, are not just endorsement but that the two roles are distinct. Similar to studies like Foti et al., the distinction between the image of a typical leader and that of a boss is based on fundamentally different characteristics. The leader is expected to incorporate more of the potentially present attributes at the same time whether they are other-directed or not, whereas the boss can be more focused on the job, fairness, caring about people, or being a mover.

The results for perceiver's gender difference effect on the endorsement of the attributes for each condition showed that, overall, there are some similarities. But these finding also showed some differences. This study shows a different result from the studies conducted in China (Ling et al., 2000) and the United States (Offermann et al., 1994) where no gender difference was found. It is possible that if these studies had also examined gender difference at attribute level, they would have found some differences. In their studies, the mean difference was conducted at the factor level.

Methodologically, this study shows how CFA can be used in an exploratory mode. Although the model fit here must be confirmed in independent samples, the use of CFA offered us two primary advantages over EFA. First, CFA models have a well-developed literature on model-data fit that allowed us to carefully review the fit of competing models and to determine which models fit the data best, and thus which models describe the data best. In contrast, in EFA all models are assumed to fit well. Furthermore, CFA models provide a more rigorous comparison between groups than can be achieved using EFA.

Also, finding the contiguous-item response bias is interesting, and highlights the flexibility of CFA models to fit data that violate the assumptions of EFA and might therefore cause inaccurate findings. We know of no prior work that found these response biases, and it is unclear whether it is unique to Iranians or can be found more widely. Although we modelled the bias by allowing all contiguous items to share unique variance, some item pairs were more affected, which would make perfect sense for unlike characteristics that happen to be contiguous. It was necessary in this study to use paper measures, but future research using computerized measures might ameliorate this problem by randomizing the presentation order of the items for each respondent.

Finally, in reviewing the results of this study in comparison with the two other emic studies on ILT, some similarities emerge. There seems to be some validity to the concept of a charismatic leader, but the meaning of it is very different from one culture to another, which makes the use of the term uninformative. In addition, similar to Ayman and Chemers' 1983 findings and different from the 1994 findings of Offermann et al., Iranians today seem to expect that attributes representing dedication, attractiveness, masculinity, intelligence and strength are all on one factor, not on separate factors. Interestingly in this study, unlike that of Offermann et al., *tyranny* and *male* were not part of this list of characteristics generated for the leader or the supervisor by the Iranians in the sample.

This study's results also did not show much resemblance to the Chinese findings (Ling et al., 2000) where *issue of morality* and *interpersonal competence* had distinct factors. In the Iranian list of attributes, the presence of individual morality and interpersonal competence was not as strongly represented, but they were included within other factors. This shows, perhaps, that Iranians are culturally bridging the Eastern and Western cultures.

Comparing these findings with other studies that were conducted in Iran, the similarity between the two sets of factors is not high. Of course, the charismatic leadership seems to be present; but it is important to point out the several key differences between the two studies. In the Dastmalchian et al. (2001) study, the measure was an etic measure that was universally agreed upon by the GLOBE scholars. Also, they only used managers and executives in the study; they used the term *leaders in organizations*; and they did not report if any women were part of their study. This study used a generic term for *leader* and a second term that reflected an organizational position of leadership. It also used a snowball method of sampling; and it included laypeople with various levels of work and education experience, as well as men and women. Considering the social conditions in Iran, it is possible the sample in the earlier study focused on only those who have or are associated with political power and are privileged in Iran, that is, Shiite Muslim men. This could be part of the reason for the differences in the findings. Also, it is important to be mindful of terms used for the concept of leadership when cross-cultural studies on leadership are conducted. In some cultures, it is very hard to find a generic term for leader, which could be indicative of that culture's contextualization of leadership based on role. This may remind us of Misumi's PM model (1985) in Japan, where he emphasized that the behaviours be embedded in the role of the leader.

While the sample of this study was sufficient for the purposes of this study, it was not based on a random sample of the population of Tehran. Though the sample did represent some individuals from various ethnic groups, it is not representative of all Iranians. Future research can expand and better understand similarities and differences that may exist between rural and urban populations and different ethnic and religious groups within Iran.

The findings in this study reaffirmed that the concept of leadership and the expectations of a leader are not universal, and that it is important for expatriate managers to be more attentive to cultural norms. In addition, these findings also supported the notion that, in Iran, focusing on the *people* aspect or the *task* aspect of the leader's role will contradict the cultural expectations. Iranians expect their leaders to be both cognitively and interpersonally competent. There is an old saying in Iran that 'To be learned is easy but to be a true human being is very difficult'.

References

Amuzegar, J. 2010. The Rial Problem: While All Eyes are Focused on the Streets of Tehran, the Real Cracking may be Occurring in Iran's Banking Sector, *Rahavard* 91–92: E34–E36.

Ayman, R. 2004. Leadership and Culture. In C. Spielberger (ed.) *Encyclopedia of Applied Psychology*, vol. 2. San Diego, CA: Elsevier, pp. 507–19.

Ayman R. and Chemers, M. 1983. Relationship of Supervisory Behavior Ratings to Work Group Effectiveness and Subordinate Satisfaction Among Iranian Managers, *Journal of Applied Psychology* 68(2): 338–41.

Ayman R. and Korabik, K. 2010. Leadership: Why Gender and Culture Matter, *American Psychologist* 65(3): 157–70.

Bassari, A. and Ayman, R. 2009. The Implicit Leadership Theory in Iranians, conference paper presented at *From Global to Worldly Leadership*, symposium, The Leadership Trust. Weston Under Penyard, England (May).

Central Intelligence Agency 2010. *The World Factbook* [https://www.cia.gov/library/publications/the-world-factbook/geos/ir.html, accessed 4th November 2010].

Chemers, M. M. 1969. Cross-cultural Training as a Means for Improving Situation Favorableness, *Human Relations* 22: 531–46.

Dastmalchian, A., Javidan, M. and Alam, K. 2001. Effective Leadership and Culture in Iran: An Empirical Study, *An International Review* 50(4): 532–58.

Duehr, E. E. and Bono, J. E. 2006. Men, Women, and Managers: Are Stereotypes Finally Changing?, *Personnel Psychology* 59: 815–46.

Eden, D. and Leviatan, U. 2005. From Implicit Personality Theory to Implicit Leadership Theory: A Side-trip on the Way to Organization Theory. In B. Schyns and J. R. Meindl (eds) *Implicit Leadership Theories: Essays and Explorations*. Greenwich, CT: Information Age, pp. 3–14.

Epitropaki, O. and Martin, R. 2005. From Ideal to Real: A Longitudinal Study of the Role of Implicit Leadership Theories on Leader-member Exchanges and Employee Outcomes, *Journal of Applied Psychology* 90(4): 659.

Franklin, S. B., Gibson, D. J., Robertson, P. A., Pohlmann, J. T. and Fralish, J. S. 1995. Parallel Analysis: A Method for Determining Significant Principal Components, *Journal of Vegetation Science* 6: 99–106.

Foti, R., Fraser, S. and Lord, R. 1982. Effects of Leadership Labels and Prototypes on Perceptions of Political Leaders, *Journal of Applied Psychology* 67(3): 326–33.

Foti, R. and Luch, C. 1992. The Influence of Individual Differences on the Perception and Categorization of Leaders, *Leadership Quarterly* 3: 55–66.

Gerstner, C. R. and Day, D. V. 1994. Cross-Cultural Comparison of Leadership Prototypes, *Leadership Quarterly* 5(2): 121–34

Hall, R. J. and Lord, R. G. 1995. Multi-level Information Processing Explanation of Follower's Leadership Perception, *Leadership Quarterly* 6: 265–87.

Hanges, P., Lord, R. and Dickson, M. 2000. An Information-processing Perspective on Leadership and Culture: A Case for Connectionist Architecture. *Applied Psychology: An International Review* 49(1): 133–61.

Hau, K. and Marsh, H. W. 2004. The Use of Item Parcels in Structural Equation Modeling: Non-normal Data and Small Sample Sizes, *British Journal of Mathematical Statistical Psychology* 57: 327–51.

House, R., Javidan, M., Hanges, P. and Dorfman, P. 2002. Understanding Cultures and Implicit Leadership Theories Across the Globe: An Introduction to Project GLOBE, *Journal of World Business* 37(1): 3–10.

House, R. J., Hanges, P. J., Javidan, M., Dorfman, P. W. and Gupta, V. 2004. *Cultures, Leadership, and Organizations: The GLOBE Study of 62 Societies.* Thousand Oaks, CA: Sage.

Heilman, M. E., Block, C. J., Martell, R. F. and Simon, M. C. 1989. Has Anything Changed? Current Characterizations of Men, Women, and Managers, *Journal of Applied Psychology* 74: 935–42.

Jepson, D. 2009. Studying Leadership Across Countries: A Critical Analysis, *Leadership* 5: 61–80.

Ling, W., Chia, R. and Fang, L. 2000. Chinese Implicit Leadership Theory, *The Journal of Social Psychology* 140(6): 729–39.

Lord, R. G. 2005. Implicit Leadership Theory. In B. Schyns and J. R. Meindl (eds) *Implicit Leadership Theories: Essays and Explorations.* Greenwich, CT: Information Age, pp. ix–xiv.

Lord, R. G., De Vader, C., & Alliger, G. M. (1986). A meta-analysis of the relation between personality traits and leadership perceptions: An application of validity generalization procedures. *Journal of Applied Psychology, 71,* 402–410.

Lord, R. G. and Emrich, C. G. 2001. Thinking Outside the Box by Thinking Inside the Box: Extending the Cognitive Revolution in Leadership Research, *Leadership Quarterly* 11(4): 551–79.

Lord, R. G. and Maher, K. J. 1991. *Leadership and Information Processing: Linking Perceptions and Performance (Vol.1).* Cambridge, MA: Unwin Hyman.

Lord, R. G., Foti, R. J. and de Vader, C. L. 1986. A Test of Leadership Categorization Theory: Internal Structure, Information Processing, and Leadership Perceptions, *Organizational Behavior & Human Performance* 34(3): 343–78.

Lord, R.G., Brown, D. J, Harvey, J. L. and Hall, R. J. 2001. Contextual Constraints on Prototype Generation and their Multilevel Consequences for Leadership Perception, *Leadership Quarterly* 12: 311–38.

Majidi, A. 2010. Considerations about the Islamic Revolution [original in Persian], *Rahavard* 91/92, Fall: 63–74.

Meindl, J. R. 1995. The Romance of Leadership as a Follower-centric Theory: A Social Constructionist Approach, *Leadership Quarterly* 6: 329–41.

Misumi, J. 1985. *The Behavior Science of Leadership: An Interdisciplinary Japanese Research Program.* Ann Arbor, MI: University of Michigan Press.

Offermann, L., Kennedy, J. and Wirtz, P. 1994. Implicit Leadership Theories: Content, Structure, and Generalizability, *Leadership Quarterly* 5(1): 43–55.

Runkle, J. and Ayman, R. 1997. Relationships Between Ethnic Stereotypes and Requisite Management Characteristics: The Role of Respondents Ethnicity, paper presented at the Society of Industrial and Organizational Psychology annual conference in St Louis, MO, USA (April).

Schein, V. E. 1973. The Relationship Between Sex Role Stereotypes and Requisite Management Characteristics, *Journal of Applied Psychology* 57: 95–100.

Schein, V. E. 2001. A Global Look at Psychological Barriers to Women's Progress in Management, *Journal of Social Issues* 57: 675–88.

Schein, V. E., Mueller, R. and Jacobson, C. 1989. The Relationship Between Sex Role Stereotypes and Requisite Management Characteristics Among College Students, *Sex Role* 20: 103–10.

Schein, V. E., Mueller, R., Lituchy, T. and Liu, J. 1996. Think Manager–Think Male: A Global Phenomenon?, *Journal of Organizational Behavior* 17: 33–41.

Schyns, B. and Meindl, J. R. 2005. An Overview of Implicit Leadership Theories and their Application in Organization Practice. In B. Schyns and J. R. Meindl (eds) *Implicit Leadership Theories: Essays and Explorations*. Greenwich, CT: Information Age, pp.15–36.

Turnbull, S. 2009. 'Worldly' Leadership for a Global World. In M. Harvey and J. D. Barbour (eds) *Global Leadership: Portraits of the Past, Visions of the Future*. Maryland, MD: ILA, pp. 82–94.

Zandian, M. 2010. An Interview with Dr Shaheen Fatemi Regarding the Iranian Green Movement and the Political and Economic Upheavals Preceding it [original in Persian], *Rahavand* 91/92, Fall: 31–47.

Zonis, M. 1971. *The Political Elite of Iran*. Princeton, NJ: Princeton University Press.

9
Leadership in the Arab Middle East: Does the Islamic Tradition Provide a Basis for 'Worldly Leadership'?

David Weir

Introduction

The premise of this chapter is that an effective model of 'worldly leadership' will not necessarily come from the uni-linear expansion of the Western model but may depend on the successful harmonizing of these practices with other cultural traditions (see Mangaliso, 1991). But if one model of 'worldly leadership' is to prevail, arguably the Muslim traditions offer alternative models to the largely Western paradigms of organization and enterprise that have dominated research in leadership studies hitherto. Undoubtedly the world economy is becoming more globalized, but because markets do not entail cultures, for markets can inhabit and co-exist with a diversity of cultures, there are increasing intimations that the Western approach may be time-expired. Moreover there are strong grounds for doubting that globalization must necessarily imply the homogenization of leadership cultures in some postmodern melting-pot mélange. So it may make more sense now to look forward to competing versions of what is implied in adjectives like 'worldly'.

Consequently, this chapter seeks to enlarge the discourse of leadership by drawing attention to leadership styles in the largely Muslim countries of Northern Africa and the Middle East (the MENA region) as well as in the Muslim countries of Pakistan, Indonesia and Malaysia. Together these regions comprise the 'Middle World'. The chapter will also point to some aspects of the leadership styles preferred in the Middle World as offering competing advantages in terms of alternative paradigms of 'worldliness'.

Many economists claim that developing countries can speed up their process of development by promoting the transfer of knowledge from developed countries, often through the medium of multinational firms (Baranson, 1970; Caves, 1974; Wu & Miao, 2009). Defenders of this claim presuppose that if developing countries adapt themselves to the knowledge available in more 'advanced' or 'developed' societies like those of the Western world, their economies will improve (Karsten & Illa, 2001). To a considerable extent the discourse of 'leadership' has followed this pattern, and the discourses of 'traditionalism' and 'conservatism' are used to privilege Western discourse and disqualify or devalue those of other origins. The learning is implicitly assumed to be one way, from the west to the east or from north to south.

There are several reasons for proposing that the Islamic traditions can provide a basis for a globalized 'worldly' leadership.

First, because of the favourable demography, the widespread location of Muslims in practically every part of the world and the increasing solidity of Muslim presence in the heartlands of the Middle World.

Second, because Islam is also, like Christianity, but unlike Judaism or Shinto, for example, a religion that claims universal application: it is in fact a *Unicist* religion, in the sense that it tends towards an end-state of unity and these concepts are at the core of its belief systems. This word Unicity is not, as is sometimes claimed, a neologism, but has a precise connotation in this context. The OED gives the definition of 'Unicity' as 'the fact of being or consisting of one, or of being united as a whole' and this is a very precise summary of the intrinsic nature of Islam as a cultural force. This is not the place for a theological discourse but it is impossible to understand the concepts of 'Tawhid' or of 'Ummah', for instance, without comprehending that in Islam there is a strongly integrative meme around the one-ness of all creation. Ummah denotes the whole collectivity of believers. Leaders in this tradition have a special responsibility to protect the Ummah by their decisions. One theological commentator notes 'Tawhid is the realization that God is One, is the Creator and Master of creation. He alone is the ultimate cause of all that is, as well as the ultimate end of all that was, is or will be' (Al Faruqi, 1985).

Third, because Islam is a belief system that perceives itself historically as incorporative of other competing traditions and is theoretically simple (Tripp, 2006).

Finally, because the leadership styles of this region are by no means incompatible with the postmodern realities of 'worldly leadership'.

Islam is the dominant mode of thought in the Middle World, and is a growing force throughout Africa. But this is by no means a static situation implying the persistence of archaic or 'traditional' patterns that must over time become eroded in favour of some more contemporary model of agnosticism, secularity, diversity or multiculturalism. Per contra, there is evidence that the influence of Islam is becoming in many ways more pronounced and emphatic and that it is the previous cultural diversity of this region that is becoming attenuated. Fisk claims '... across the Middle East, it is the same story of despairing – sometimes frightened – Christian minorities, and of an exodus that reaches almost Biblical proportions ...' (Fisk, 2010) and Fisk's claims are echoed by other researchers.

In principle Islam is a pattern of behaviours and beliefs that affect the whole of human life, and business and management are not regarded as exempt domains within which normal communal obligations do not apply; economic activity is subject to the same moral frameworks as those regulating society at large. The practical obligations of the five pillars of Islam (Testimony of Faith, Duty of Prayer, Provision of Zakat, Self-mortification and Purification – including the Duty of Fasting during Ramadan, and Obligation to make the Hajj to Mecca) comprise the foundations of the ethical behaviour of any believer and behaviours which are incompatible with these understandings are Haram or unworthy and will not survive.

Islamic regulation is a continually evolving set of principles, interpreted in the light of contemporary experience, not a fixed and unalterable set of dogmas. The community of believers, the Ummah, represents the totality of those who accept the principles of Islam and to whom, therefore this regulation applies. It represents also a massive internal market for goods and services of all kinds and we are currently studying the implications of 'halal' as a brand with intimations of universality (Ijaz & Weir, 2010).

The discourse of 'traditionalism' is often used to implicate the Muslim world in a discourse seen as somehow pre-modern or anti-modern, but this is misleading. Muslim societies are no more nor less 'traditional' than other societies, and Islam itself is a diverse, evolving and dynamic set of belief systems with many emergent aspects. These are societies where change is endemic, rather than ones of unquestioned and unexamined societal stasis. But it is important also not to fall into the trap of adopting the discredited discourse of 'orientalism' as trenchantly critiqued by Said and characterize this region in terms of irrelevant but presumed universal models (Said, 1978). Islam has been considered by Geertz (1968) as a universalizing culture and Redfield (1956) distinguished between world religions in terms of 'great tradition' and 'little tradition'. It is realistic to conceive of Islam as a 'great tradition' that comprises many local, even subaltern 'little traditions' with powerful integrating features (Asad, 1986, 1993).

The annual rates of increase of Christianity and Islam in terms of demography and population growth rates are similar but Huntington predicts that Islam will overtake Christianity by the year 2025 (Huntington, 1993). Christianity's total number of adherents is growing at about 2.3 per cent annually, approximately equal to the growth rate of the world's population. Islam is growing faster: about 2.9 per cent (Barrett, 2001).

The impact of Islam on business and management, including Islamic finance, is increasing in the global economy. As recently as 1988 Ariff was able to claim that 'Islamic banking is a new phenomenon that has taken many observers by surprise' (Ariff, 1988) but now Islamic finance is growing very strongly, not merely in Muslim countries but also around the world, for '... banks are building up their Islamic finance units in the wake of the global credit crisis, tapping into a nascent industry estimated at $700 billion to $1 trillion in asset size and a 15–20 percent annual growth rate' (Reuters, 2009). The introduction of broad macroeconomic and structural reforms in financial systems, the liberalization of capital movements, privatization and the global integration of financial markets did not, as predicted, favour only the existing Western-oriented finance and banking institutions but also Islamic finance, with the introduction of innovative and new Islamic products for non-traditional markets creating new levels of sophistication (Zaher & Hassan, 2001).

Management philosophies in the Middle World

Every major economic system re-creates in its business activity and management practices a recognizable pattern of beliefs and processes that relates in a functional and supportive way to the generic culture in which it is embedded. In previous writing we coined the term 'the fourth paradigm' to characterize the leadership practices of the Middle World (Weir, 1998). It may be precisely in the relative strengths of this tradition that a comparative advantage in the global world of the twenty-first century may lie.

First, it is networking rather than hierarchy that represents the dominant model of business organization in this tradition; this is probably the first aspect of leadership that Westerners typically come into contact with when they do business in the Middle World. This networking is often characterized as 'wasta' and like 'guanxi' in the Chinese world, this involves a social network of interpersonal connections rooted in family and kinship ties, but generating power, influence and information-sharing through social and politico-business networks. Wasta is central to leadership. Just as guanxi has positive connotations of networking and negative ones of corruption, so too does wasta as the creation of opportunity for others (Hutchings & Weir, 2005). Many younger leaders are critical of wasta, but admit nonetheless that it will continue to form the basis of organizational leadership for the foreseeable future.

The basic rule of leadership in this model is to establish a relationship first, build connections and only actually come to the heart of the intended business at later meetings. This process is very time-consuming, yet once a relationship has been established verbal contracts are often treated as absolute and an individual's word is regarded as his/her bond so that failure to meet verbally agreed obligations will certainly lead to a termination of a business relationship. Leaders are supposed to be able to profit from wasta connections: a leader without good wasta is in this culture practically inconceivable.

Traditionally, the head of a family or shaykh performed wasta services and more recently the term has also generalized, to comprise the seeking of benefits from government (Cunningham & Sarayrah, 1993, p. 9). The title of 'shaykh' embodies both implications of seniority and leadership and also of possession of personal ethical standing qualifying the holder to act as mediator or intercessory. The role of wasta has mutated from being the expected duties of a tribal shaykh to implying some special interpersonal competences of the leader. Though wasta pervades the culture in all significant decision-making throughout the Middle World, it is not usually mentioned by most academic writers, nor is it often openly discussed by leaders in these cultures themselves. Partly this is because wasta has come to be a focus of criticism among Western expatriates and some younger indigenous Westernized leaders because it is presumed to imply 'traditional' and pre-rational norms.

It is important to disentangle these more recent, corrupted uses of the terminology from the essential underpinnings of the concept based in belief systems supporting leadership claims, rooted in wider networks of social reciprocation and sustained by deep-rooted patterns of belief and psychic strength in the community. 'Wasta is not practised only because it is socially advantageous but because it is perceived to be right and to reinforce community standards of ethical behaviour, because "family ties are perceived to imply mandatory obligations to help"' (Cunningham & Sarayrah, 1993, p. 114).

Wasta leadership requires a supportive framework of generally hon-ourable dealing to be effective in terms of spiritual assumptions and behavioural practices, and this framework and its discourse is rooted in Islam.

Among other qualities of leadership, experience and seniority are especially venerated but ascent to a leadership position does not occur by the operation of simplistic formulae, even that of overt seniority. The over-riding criterion is that of the best-qualified person to undertake the duties of leadership. The choice is made by the senior representa-tives of those who will be most affected by the outcome. The principle applies even to Kings and Emirs, where the method of primogeniture used in Western monarchies does not strictly apply. Even in royal fami-lies, therefore, it is not necessarily the eldest who will be chosen, but the one who in the judgement of the responsible elders is perceived as the most likely to succeed as a leader.

The third major dimension of leadership is that of the family structures underpinning the matrix of social relationships and business organi-zation. As the leadership culture is primarily verbal, great importance attaches to the correct positioning of individuals in terms of such famil-ial designations as 'father' and 'uncle' and when these terms are met with in organizational contexts they invariably carry quite specific connota-tions. To be a leader is to be in some sense a 'father' to followers.

Leadership attributes are sometimes explained in terms of 'stories' that at first hearing appear to carry no definite organizational mean-ings but may turn out to have important significance in placing the story-teller or the listener in a social situation where obligations may be implicit.

Although originally based upon family loyalty, wasta relationships expand to encompass the broader community of friends and acquaint-ances and reinforce family ties, thereby connecting the individual to the wider economy and polity. Thus where a close family member appears at the office of even quite a senior leader, it is regarded as improper for the demands of organizational hierarchy to take precedence over the obligations due to family. The role-models of business leadership are found in family structures where the opportunity of personal contact prevails. Leaders are meant to be sometimes directly accessible rather than always distant. Accessibility is supported by diwan styles of deci-sion making and diwan-like wasta is a master interpretative category of discourse with powerful symbolic implications (Weir, 2009).

The diwan is a room with low seats around the walls, found in one guise or other in every Arab home but also well-known under other titles throughout Iran, Indonesia and many parts of the Indian subcontinent as a place of decision as well as of social intercourse. In diwan, decisions are the outcome of processes of information exchange, practised listening, questioning and the interpretation and confirmation of informal as well as formal meanings. While decisions of the diwan are enacted by the leader, they need to be owned by all, ensuring commitment based on respect for both position and process. While seniority and effectiveness are significant, to be a powerful leader the concurrent consent of those involved has to be sought, and symbolized in the process of the diwan (Weir, 2011).

In diwan leaders are expected to take decisions, taking time to consult those whose views need to be heard and those who may not otherwise have been heard because of their low hierarchical positions. Leaders may use the model of diwan as a virtual structure enabling them to tailor decision-outcomes to constituencies of power and influence and to assure all relevant parties that there has been an opportunity for their voices to be heard (Weir, 2008).

Leaders do not have to be clear and direct to be effective, for ambiguity may be celebrated rather than avoided, delay is as much an art-form as a tactic, and words are important for their sonority as much as for their denotative meaning. Poetry and the magic of language are perceived as essential aspects of performance, rather than as unnecessary and misleading frills. Poets like Mahmoud Darwish are superstars in the Middle World with enormous influence on political and business leaders. Leaders who are also poets and artists with words are especially respected. Metaphor and implication mediate abstracted, positivistic rationality, so the giving of overt reasons for decision outcomes may be avoided even where seemingly obvious. Causality is not insistently sought after in explanations of leadership decisions, for the linear logics central to Western analysis are regarded as only one of the appropriate modalities for establishing truth.

A central concept of leadership embodied in and practised throughout the cultures is that of 'the just ruler' (Sachedina, 1988). The association of authority with justice stems directly from the Quran and several hadiths that are well-known and quoted. Thus one hadith states 'the just will be seated upon pulpits of light ... those who are fair with regards to their judgement and their family and those who are under them ... a *just* successful ruler'.

The classic statements of the qualities expected of the 'just ruler' can be found in the writings of Ibn Khaldun who stated that the office of the Caliph 'demands perfection in attributes and manners' but the relationship between leader and follower is a reciprocal one because 'only the community which can recognize and give allegiance to a man of this description is worthy of living under the regime of Law' (Mahdi, 1964). This ideal of just rulership is derived from the first system of government established in Islam, representing the political unity of the Muslim Ummah; it is by no means a dead concept but may be referred to as a template of appropriate standards of contemporary leadership.

The precise qualifications for a perfect leader are that he must have knowledge of the Law to the extent of being able to make appropriate interpretations personally, but more than this his decisions must be just in themselves and in their effect so that those appointed by the leader must also meet these criteria. The leader must be personally courageous and be able to create the solidarity necessary for engaging in combat among his followers and must be competent in the administration of the organization. It is this competence which leads to the ability to protect religion and manage collective interests.

Thus there are elements of what we could describe as transactional leadership at the heart of this depiction and it is clearly on the mastery of the transactional duties that the display of the transformational performances rest. Combining the notions of justice, authority and diwan enables a characterization of these styles of leadership as 'consultative autocracy' with both elements necessary for the fulfilment of just rulership. It is in diwan that the individual social action becomes the collective responsibility and the personal option becomes the networked opportunity. For while diwan is a highly ordered interactional event, it is also a model for virtual bonding and extension because in diwan, we observe a characteristic pattern of social networking that reinforces existing strong bonds of family and kinship and draws trusted newcomers into a pre-existing network.

Of course the idea of the 'just ruler' is not unique to the Muslim world and Leach points out that it is also central in the Confucian tradition (Leach, 1960). The concept can be traced back at least as far as Plato. But it is a meme that is very widespread in Islam and it is commonly met with for instance as a justification for opposition to a regime, for example that of Saddam Hussein, that the ruler has acted *unjustly*. The interpretative traditions of Islam tend to err on the side of authority and usually concur that even when rulers behave in unjust ways overt rebellion is rarely justified, unless the ruler acts in ways that transgress the laws of God. The dangers of civil unrest (fitna) are usually held to outweigh the importance of general rights like those for example guaranteed by democracy. But these interpretations fall short of Machiavelli's position that all acts of the ruler are in principle legitimate if the ruler acts to protect the state, because in Islamic thinking the state is only legitimate if justly governed in line with God's principles.

Western leadership style compared with the Middle World

Table 9.1 indicates how some of these similarities and differences are organized.

Table 9.1   Core aspects of leadership cultures in the Western and middle worlds

Element	Western	Middle World
Relationship with others	Relationships are instrumental, contractual. The centre of focus is individual. Collective virtues predicated on individual qualities. Nuclear family important.	Reciprocal, family-based models. Individual has value in relation to family/clan. The Ummah transcends all personal obligations. Guests are sacred; because they are 'Angels come to dwell among us'.
Language	Written transmission of folklore. Words have precise meanings. Brevity is the soul of wit.	Universal language of revelation is Arabic. Poetry and music highly valued. Implication and metaphor highly prized.
Decision making	Usually by majority. Winner takes all. The most efficient processes are linear. Unity of vision is ensured by leadership's clarity. Monocular. Justice takes precedence over harmony. Leaders must be decisive even if wrong, or they will lose authority and credibility.	Autocratic-consultative. The decision-making principles of the Diwan ensure all relevant voices can be heard. Justice of God ensures harmony for we must submit to it. The prime unifying force in organizations is solidarity. Leaders must be wise over the long term, and should eschew short-term popularity among the unwise.
Time	Time is money, a strategic commodity to be used frugally. The present is paramount for 'there is no time like the present'. But through scientific technique and analysis of risks it is possible to plan and to forecast future events on a probabilistic basis.	Cyclical and evolving. Who knows where it leads? The right decision will emerge in the right time when the leader is prepared. Time past and time future are equally important because God resides in all domains and is the only Being to perceive how they are interconnected.

Continued

Table 9.1 Continued

Element	Western	Middle World
Productivity	Must be maximized. Denominator management. Individual rewards, benefits, suffering (lay-offs) can be justified because economic motives are most significant.	The right decision is that which maximizes and preserves wealth. But the poor may be equally significant because leaders have special responsibilities towards those who are less fortunate.
Leadership and Age	Age beyond a certain point becomes a negative. Aging is seen as slowing down. Senior citizens regarded as 'dead wood'.	Seniority is highly regarded. Knowledge is respected. Older leaders are presumed to be wise and worthy of respect.
Belief systems	Judaeo-Christian belief system dominant. Belief that economic, political and social virtue coalesce in the evidence of the fruits of economic performance. Possibility of a personal relationship with God.	Universal applicability of Islam as a religion of practice not of dogma. Subordination of the economic to the spiritual and religious domains. Leaders are no better or worse than other people because only God alone understands how economic rewards relate to individual virtue. God cannot be interrogated.
Leadership	Tension between 'autocratic', 'democratic' and 'participative' models.	The 'Just Ruler' who is consultative but autocratic. Familial model of relation to followers. Opposition is justified if the leader transgresses laws of God.

Some implications for 'Worldly Leadership'

The economies of the Muslim world are sometimes characterized in such terms as 'conservative' or 'traditional' but this is far from accurate and may often mislead the Western manager or scholar, for these are dynamic societies which have known much change in the past fifty years.

If the global economy moves from an industry-based to an information-based format and enterprise structures in the information society segue from the prevailing command organizations with their persistent and obstructive hierarchies to networked organizations, with latent, virtual and active elements, then the familial models prevalent in the

Middle World may seem more appropriate (Cogburn, 2003) than juridical composites linked by shareholder and stakeholder obligations that generate purely legal obligations and support an army of corporate lawyers to soak up the intermittent profit streams.

Decision-making follows different rules in the network economy of the Information Society. Certainly research in leadership studies needs to take account of cultural variations and the changes introduced by the postmodern technologies of the internet (Weir & Hutchings, 2006).

Maybe informed consent as in the model of the family diwan with its balance of consultative and autocratic phases can provide a better guide than the corporate boardroom to the 'loose-tight' properties of effective worldly leadership in the organizations of the future.

To be effective, leadership principles and practices must be compatible with the core values and practices of deeply rooted cultures; globalization does not necessarily bring the assurance that any one model will survive, but the Middle World model seems as possible as the Western paradigm. This has recently suffered a deep shock, not merely to the technical operations of its financial systems but to the underlying success values of its culture. Consequently the Western model is not perceived as universally successful and paramount in the global world at present. This is a question not just of the Western world learning with difficulty to accommodate other paradigms of organizational culture but of an emerging diversity in the business systems of the world. As academics we warn managers to be aware of the need for change, to be responsive and receptive and to develop personal skills and creative competences that permit them to embrace change and profit from its opportunities. It is important for us as scholars to act as if these lessons also applied to our scholarly pursuits. It is time for Western scholarship to look more broadly and with greater understanding at the bases of culture and belief systems that exist inside as well as outside its traditional home. The need to re-engage with other cultures of leadership is urgent. There is a special responsibility for European managers and scholars of leadership to sensitize themselves to this emerging diversity.

Middle World philosophies of behaviour based directly or indirectly on the cultures of Muslim society may provide alternative glosses on worldly leadership. In particular the claims of Western religions based on Judaeo-Christian belief systems for universal application are matched by similar but possibly more strongly based claims on behalf of Islam. For if there is to be a convergence to any single paradigm of organizational leadership, it is no longer clear that this will be in the direction of what is conventional in the models preferred in the liberal, capitalist market economies of the West. Even the introduction of Western-style democratic political institutions will not necessarily imply the adoption of Western varieties of leadership, when the underpinning values deriving from deeply rooted belief systems and spiritual assumptions are differently based.

For leadership studies in the international context, the challenge is to become familiar with these values and, whenever possible, incorporate them in organizational policies about leadership selection and development. For leadership researchers, the challenge is to chart a new research agenda on a more inclusive and less Western-centred basis. Whatever happens over the next period in the global economy, it will not necessarily evolve in ways that conform to our western models of leadership (Bauman, 2005). The world economy is entering a period of seriously hard times and it is not obvious that the existing paradigms of leadership that have prevailed in the Western discourses have the best chances of survival.

References

Al-Faruqi, I. 1985. Tawhid: The Quintessence of Islam, *Journal of South Asian and Middle Eastern Studies* VIII (Summer).

Ariff, M. 1988. Islamic Banking, *Asia-Pacific Economic Literature* 2(2): 48–64.

Asad, T. 1986. *The Idea of an Anthropology of Islam*. Occasional Papers Washington, DC: Center for Contemporary Arab Studies, Georgetown University.

Asad, T. 1993. *Genealogies of Religion: Discipline and Reasons of Power in Christianity and Islam*. Baltimore: Johns Hopkins University Press.

Baranson, J. 1970. Technology Transfer Through the International Firm, *American Economic Review* 60: 435–40.

Barrett, D. et al. 2001. *World Christian Encyclopedia: A Comparative Survey of Churches and Religions – AD 30 to 2200*. Oxford: Oxford University Press

Bauman, Z. 2005. *Liquid Life*. London: Polity Press.

Caves, R. E. 1974. Multinational Firms, Competition, and Productivity in Host-Country Markets, *Economica New Series* 41(162): 176–93.

Cogburn, D. L. 2003. *Globalization, Knowledge, Education and Training in the Information Age*. Paris: UNESCO.

Cunningham, R. B. and Sarayrah, Y. K. 1993. *Wasta: the Hidden Force in Middle Eastern Society*. Westport, CT: Praeger.

Fisk, R. 2010. Exodus, the Changing Map of the Middle East, *The Independent*, Tuesday 26th October.

Geertz, C. 1971 [1968]. *Islam Observed*. Chicago: University of Chicago Press.

Huntington, S. 1993. The Clash of Civilizations?, *Foreign Affairs* 72(3): 22–49.

Hutchings, K. and Weir, D. T. H. 2005. Cultural Embeddedness and Contextual Constraints: Knowledge Sharing in Chinese and Arab Cultures, *Journal of Knowledge and Process Management* 2: 89–98.

Ijaz, A. and Weir, D. T. H. 2010. Muslim Buying Behavioural Challenges in UK Product Selection, British Academy of Management Conference, Sheffield University.

Karsten, L. and Illa, H. 2001. Ubuntu as a Management Concept. *Quest* 15: 111–34.

Leach, E. 1960. The Frontiers of 'Burma', *Comparative Studies in Society and History* 3: 49–68.

Mahdi, M. 1964. *Ibn Khaldun's Philosophy of History.* Chicago: University of Chicago Press.

Mangaliso, M. P. 1991. Whose Knowledge Matters? The Case for Developing Multicultural Theories of Management. In J. D. Jansen (ed.) *Knowledge and Power in South Africa: Critical Perspectives Across the Disciplines.* Johannesburg: Skotaville.

Redfield, R. 1956. *Peasant Society and Culture.* Chicago: University of Chicago Press.

Reuters 2009. *UBS Sees Growth in Islamic Finance,* News release dated DUBAI Thu 16th April, 4:22am EDT.

Sachedina, A. A. 1988. *The Just Ruler (al-sultan al-adil) in Shiite Islam: The Comprehensive Authority of the Jurist in Imamite Jurisprudence.* New York: Oxford University Press.

Said, E. 1978. *Orientalism.* London: Vintage.

Tripp, C. 2006. *Islam and the Moral Economy.* London: Cambridge University Press.

Weir, D. T. H. 1998. The Fourth Paradigm. In A.A. Shamali and J. Denton (eds) *Management in the*

Weir, D. T. H. 2008. Cultural Theory and the Diwan, *Innovation: the European Journal of Social Science Research* 21(3): 253–65.

Weir, D. T. H. 2009. Liminality, Sacred Space and the Diwan. In S. Brie, J. Daggers and D. Torevell (eds) *Sacred Space: Interdisciplinary Perspectives within Contemporary Contexts.* Newcastle: Cambridge Scholars.

Weir, D. T. H. 2011. Space as Context and Content: Diwan as a Frame and a Structure for Decision-making. In D. Yanow and A. Van Marrewijk (eds) *Space and Social Organization.* New York: Sage.

Weir, D. T. H. and Hutchings, K. 2006. Cultural Filtering in the Arab World and China: Exploring the Interrelationship of the Technological Knowledge Age, Traditional Cultural Networking and Interpersonal Connections. In S. Van De Bunt-Kokhuis (ed.) *World Wide Work: Filtering of Online Content in a Globalized World.* Amsterdam: VU University Press, pp.129–42.

Wu Jie, S. Q. and Jiang Miao, Z. 2009. Study on Dynamical Mechanism and Gambling of University Knowledge Transfer, *Information Science and Engineering (ICISE)*, 1st International Conference: 5146–9.

Zaher, T. S. and Hassan, M. K. 2001. A Comparative Literature Survey of Islamic Finance and Banking, *Financial Markets, Institutions and Instruments* 10(4): 155–9.

10
Worldly Leadership through Local Knowledge: Discovering Voices of Emirati Women Business Leaders

Lynda L. Moore

Introduction

While there is a growing body of research on global studies of management and leadership, more recently scholars have expressed concern about the underlying cultural bias of social science models and the resulting leadership research. Most of the management and leadership knowledge to date is a product of North American and Western European scholars (Tsui, 2004; Thomas 2008). Universal definitions of leadership have been called into question as differences across national and cultural boundaries emerge. Given the Western orientation of dominant management and leadership research paradigms contextual knowledge is essential to generate global knowledge, especially in contexts that differ greatly from North American and Western European contexts in their economic, political and sociocultural systems (Tsui, 2004). Thus the uncovering of worldly leadership requires a local sensitivity best explained by 'think global, research local'.

This exploratory study of Emirati women business leaders investigates leader identity and behaviour in a previously under-researched part of the world, the Middle East, and with a historically marginalized group, women business leaders of the UAE.[1] The worldly research stance adopted here

* This research was originally funded through a Fulbright fellowship to the United Arab Emirates (UAE); additional funding was provided through the Simmons College Presidents Fund for Research and the Simmons School of Management's Swahnberg Novotny Fund. The author wishes to thank Alison Koegler, Aparna Lahiri and especially Michelle Kweder for their assistance in research and manuscript preparation.

does not assume similarity among women but rather captures the voices of women as emerging leaders within one specific country and cultural context. This is particularly important in light of the dearth of research on the experience of women in leadership positions at a time when the global focus on gender issues in Arab and Middle Eastern countries[2] is particularly visible and the pressures on those societies to become more equitable and gender-inclusive societies is dominant (Al-Lamky, 2006).

From a scholarship perspective, normative models of leadership and leadership success result in monolithic and hegemonic studies of women leaders. This research captures unique experiences and challenges of successful women leaders, acknowledging multiple aspects of their identity (Betters-Reed & Moore, 2007). Using case-based research as grounded theory to inform a conceptual framework influences research design and methodology for culturally sensitive studies of women leaders (Betters-Reed et al., 2007). The larger research question is what factors do we need to consider if we are trying to conduct culturally sensitive and contextualized studies of women business leaders? This current work builds upon the author's prior research that identified several major factors: awareness of the researcher's ethnocentric bias, importance of interdisciplinary knowledge, and use of qualitative, ethnographic and narrative research methodologies.

Context: culture

To better understand the challenges and opportunities of Emeriti women leaders, it is necessary to understand the role of culture in the UAE. Situating research findings within the historical, socio-economic, political and religious context of the state was essential in understanding the unique voice and characteristics of these leaders and the embedded context necessary for interpreting leadership narratives.

The UAE's economy has shifted from a seafaring and pearling to an oil- and trade-based economy to a re-exporting and knowledge-based economy; these changes have been supported by a government-driven strategy of innovation, investment in infrastructure and penetration of the knowledge space. The discovery of oil in the 1930s led to the first signs of the development of affluent society and later, post-unification in 1971, to the education of women (Randeree, 2008). However, the absence of economic necessity meant households continued to be supported by men and women were denied participation in the workforce outside of healthcare and educational services (Randeree, 2008). More recently, Emiratization, combined with an emphasis on human capital development has created new career opportunities for women and growth and development in the region (Randeree, 2008).

Similar to the GCC countries, the UAE lacks an educated and experienced local workforce necessary to maintain and grow its new economy; the private sector[3], in particular, has had to look outside of the country for qualified workers (Randeree, 2008). The UAE has a need for local labour to reduce its dependence on foreign labourers (Al Rostamani, 2004; Hijab, 1994) who comprised 75 per cent of the population and in 2004 held 91 per cent of the jobs in the country (Al Rostamani, 2004). In addition, the level of unemployed nationals has been rising.

While foreigners occupy positions at all levels, from unskilled workers to top management, the current focus of the nationalization programme has been to employ nationals, both male and female, at the middle to upper management levels (Gallant & Pounder, 2008). The resulting policy of Emiratization, coupled with relatively progressive policies of educating girls and women, creating career opportunities for women and encouraging the public lives of women, continues to contribute to the trend of Emirati women entering formal, private-sector workspaces and taking on leadership positions. In fact, in the area of education, nearly half the students registered in over 1250 schools across the UAE were girls; about 75 per cent of all students in the UAE University were women; and three out of every five students in the public higher education system were women (UAE Yearbook, 2009). In the public policy area, the teaching of English in schools, political quotas, policies that encourage a knowledge economy, and leadership that calls for the full participation of women in the country support the advancement of women (Randeree, 2008).

The last decade's rise of women into private sector leadership, while statistically insignificant, signifies a major social and political transition. Women are succeeding in positions of leadership, power and authority previously held exclusively by men within a society best described as traditionally patriarchal. In light of this important historical transition it is important to document the experiences, views, challenges and key career issues of women who have 'made it' in UAE businesses.

According to the government-sponsored UAE Yearbook and not validated by reliable independent research, women now enjoy equality of opportunity in the workplace, including pay equity with men. Sources reported that women accounted for 27.95 per cent of the national labour force, marking an annual growth rate of 3.5 per cent between 1985 and 2005.

Significant gains are also documented in the political and public spheres. Four women ministers were appointed to the Cabinet in 2007 by the president; women occupied 22 per cent of the seats in the Federal National Council; and women accounted for 20 per cent of the diplomatic corps with two women appointed as ambassadors in 2008 (UAE Yearbook, 2009). Representation is better at lower levels with data showing that women occupied 66 per cent of public-sector jobs; 30 per cent of those were leadership and decision-making posts (UAE Yearbook, 2009). Women were present in both traditional (healthcare, education) and non-traditional (military, police) occupations. However, only 4 per cent of women work in the private sector and women are still underrepresented at the highest levels with women filling just 0.8 per cent of seats at the level of Board of Director (UAE Yearbook, 2009).

In the UAE where the state religion is Islam and 96 per cent of the population of the UAE are Muslim, religion is embedded in Emirati culture at the individual, organizational and societal levels and influences the economic, political, academic and domestic lives of all Emiratis (Metcalf, 2008). To make a distinction between religious norms and cultural norms would be arbitrary and not adequately reflect the complexity of the cultural context.

For example, gender norms that influence Emirati's views and enactment of leadership may have their origins in Islam but are now deeply embedded in the culture of the UAE and its workplaces. Scholars have identified four of these norms as pervasive: First, the family is the central unit of society. Second, the man is recognized as the sole breadwinner of the family. Third, it is largely women who must adhere to a code of modesty to uphold a family's dignity. Finally, family laws uphold an unequal balance of power in society. These norms result in barriers including childcare and household duties remaining the almost exclusive responsibility of women, a lack of affordable childcare facilities, narrow interpretations of Islam restricting the full participation of women in the workplace, and men holding most management positions (Chamlou, 2004; UNDP, 2003). This seamless union of state and religious tradition is seen in the workplace where labour laws are partial to custom (*urf*) and Islamic law (Metcalfe, 2008). Specifically, the Islamic value of *Quiwama* is translated as protection and care of employees and *Hadith* as learning, knowledge and development; both factor heavily into the roles of women leaders. *Surah*, meaning humility and benevolence, is a factor in both how women are protected in business and how attire and workspaces are regulated. Moreover, *wasta* determines power or authority secured and sustained by personal relationships with powerful others, and limits access to important business networks for many women (Neal et al., 2007; Metcalfe, 2008; Maremount, 2009).

Understanding leadership in the Arab world

In their discussion of the GLOBE studies, House et al. (2004) argued that in order to understand people's ideas about leadership, one must appreciate how these ideas are embedded in indigenous sociocultural systems and institutions. In approaching the specific issue of leadership in the Arab world, Muna (1980), Ali (1995, 2005) and Weir (2000, 2003) emphasized the influence of tribal and familial systems on leadership concepts (Neal et al., 2007).

According to prior research the dominant secular leadership prototype in Arab culture is the sheik (Neal et al., 2007; Weir, 2000). While there have been celebrated female leaders throughout Arab history, their status and impact have been embedded within the patriarchal sociopolitical and wasta systems of the time (Guthrie, 2001; Mernissi, 1997). Historically, most female leaders rose to power and influence by leveraging family connection (usually male connections) and wealth (Guthrie, 2001; Mernissi, 1997). This does not diminish women's achievements. Rather, as identified by Metcalfe (2008), this points to the skill, creativity and sustained effort of exceptional women in succeeding in such male-dominated circumstances. Furthermore, as Al-Lamky (2007) has pointed out, those who are part of the recent 'feminization' of leadership positions in the Arab region face many of the same problems as their predecessors: they operate in conditions that are still influenced and shaped by family, tribe, religion and wasta; and in order to succeed, they often have to act in this manner (see Shaheed, 1999 cited in Metcalfe, 2008). Wasta relates to the recognition that power in society is related to tribal and familial structures, and that business is conducted through these power networks in the Arab world. The national business system is largely characterized by an interlocking structure that stretches across, and between, networks in families, organizations and political life (Edwards & Kruvilla, 2005 quoted in Metcalfe). In their discussion of the GLOBE studies of cultural values and leadership, Kabasakal and Bodur (2002) identified an 'Arab' cluster of countries consisting of Egypt, Morocco, Turkey, Kuwait and Qatar; leaders in these countries scored low on future orientation, and high on group-orientation, masculinity and power distance. Within the cluster, outstanding leadership was associated with charisma and with team attribution. While the GLOBE studies did not research UAE, the findings for other Gulf

States, Kuwait and Qatar, discussed by Abdalla and Al-Homoud (2001), are relevant and highlight the importance of consultation in Gulf Arab leadership (Neal et al., 2007). Weir (2000) emphasizes business relationships as guided by *diwan* and wasta. Diwan is a style of decision-making, which represents a process of achieving balance (*adl*) and justice or equilibrium (*adalah*). Rooted in Islamic traditions, and emphasized in the Qur'an, is that those who conduct their affairs through consultation are among the ones who will receive heavenly rewards. This diwan process is commonly referred to as shura and emphasizes personalism, although autocratic relationships are respected (Tayeb, 1997).

Overall, leadership and management relies on the importance of informal relations, family networks and patronage, and on building trusting, open relations. Employer – employee relationships are based on consensus and unity (*itihad*), balance or equilibrium (*adl*); and high trust exchanges facilitated through extended family networks (*naseeb*), which are quite different from the organizational and managerial cultures in many European and US corporations (Metcalfe, 2007).

Although the policies of educating girls and women, creating career opportunities for women and encouraging the public lives of women mark the UAE as progressive in the region, the UAE does not compare as well globally. The UAE ranks 103 out of 134 economies according to the World Economic Forum's 2010 Gender Gap Index. The UAE remains a traditional Muslim society, retaining its implicit assumptions about the public and private roles of Emirati women and their responsibilities to their community, their extended families and their children (Mostafa, 2005; Metcalfe, 2006). In some organizations, including all of the country's leading indigenous banks, it is still common to find men-only and female-only working areas. Inevitably, such deeply ingrained cultural beliefs continue to influence women's advancement into leadership positions (Moore & Forster, 2009).

Context: scholarship

An ongoing in-depth literature revealed a paucity of worldly research that connects the interwoven issues of women, leadership and culture in geographic localities in the Middle East and, for the purposes of this scholarship, the UAE. While studies of gendered workspaces and female experience of leadership inclusive of the traits, styles, challenges and contribution of women leaders are on the rise (Fels, 2004; Rhode, 2003; Acker, 1990; Kanter, 1993; Moss, 1994), most of these studies are conducted in Western societies that are not generalizable to other cultures. For the most part, scholarship persists in a siloed state, imparting incomplete knowledge about the complex leadership narratives of women leading in the Middle East.

Over the past three decades, mainstream management literature focused on women managers in the United States identified individual and organizational factors that facilitate and impede success. Despite the fact that these factors are based on extant literature and have persisted over time it is not assumed that the research that has been conducted on US women managers holds true in other cultures (Adler & Izraeli, 1988; Adler, 2002; Berthoin & Izraeli, 1993) nor that the dominant organizational cultures in the UAE are similar (Ali, 2005). Early research (Adler & Izraeli, 1988) suggests there are several similar factors that shape women's entrance into managerial positions worldwide, including their career patterns and access to organizational power although the relative impact of each factor varies from culture to culture (Adler & Izraeli 1994; Omar & Davison, 2001). It should be noted that none of the earlier studies included women in the Middle East or Islamic societies.

Most leadership scholarship, whether global or local, fails to address the development of Turnbull's conception of worldly leadership (2009), where questions of integrity, ethics, dispersed or shared leadership, networks, boundary-crossing, stewardship, sustainability and notions of the common good are central to leaders across all sectors. A challenge in creating more inclusive gender, race and ethnicity studies in leadership is the need to develop culturally sensitive frameworks that go beyond the dominant model of leadership. Several scholarly projects have contributed new knowledge and conceptual models to allow for more multidisciplinary and global, cross-cultural analyses of gender, diversity and leadership. These methods, best described as feminist and relational, critique the dominant discourse of leadership scholarship and organizational practices as exclusionary and ethnocentric (Betters-Reed & Moore, 2007; Betters-Reed et al., 2007; Moore & Betters-Reed, 2009). This leadership inquiry framework challenges dominant models of organizational leadership and legitimizes new ways of knowing and diverse leadership voices. As an exploratory study, this supports previous research that identifies the authentic voices of women (Gilligan, 1993) and a socially responsible ethic of care infused through leadership (Block, 1993; Greenleaf, 2001; Spears & Lawrence, 2002).

Moreover, scholarship has not adequately documented the overall increase in women's employment, one of the most significant cultural, economic and political changes of contemporary times globally. The significant labour market advances made by women in the Middle East (Salloum, 2003) has been considered statistically insignificant in the eyes of dominant Western academics (Al-Lamky, 2006). The resulting scarce research highlights both the challenges of being a female manager, as well as the factors that facilitate a woman's leadership progression (Ali, 2005; Greiss-Miller, 1995; Kattara, 2005; Sakalli-Ugurlu & Beydogan, 2002) and shows overall challenges including the patriarchal societal attitude and gender discrimination (Sakalli-Ugurlu & Beydogan, 2002) which limit women's recruitment, hiring, advancement (Greiss-Miller, 1995), relationships at work, mentor support and network access (Kattara, 2005). Additional research explores the biographical backgrounds of women (Al-Ajmi, 2001; Greiss-Miller, 1995).

More recently, Middle Eastern scholars have investigated the status of women in society and a small body of literature has emerged that begins to examine the issues related to gender and management in the Middle East (Metcalfe, 2006; Al-Lamky, 2006). Just as recently as 2010, the Dubai Women's Establishment and Price Waterhouse Coopers published the first Outlook on Arab Women Leaders, which identifies leadership attributes and makes recommendations for Arab women's leadership advancement (Dubai Women's Establishment, 2009).

At this time, not only do we know very little about women leaders in the region, but also research on business leadership in the Middle East has invariably been subsumed under generic analyses of the 'Arab World' (Eden & Leviatan, 1975; Lord et al., 1978; Kenney et al., 1996; Javidan & Carl, 2004). In turn, this has characterized the Gulf region as a homogenous economic, cultural and social bloc (e.g. Hofstede, 1980, 1984; Ronen, 1986). While such meta-research has led to a greater understanding of how culture shapes assumptions about business leadership in the region, it is necessary to refine the notion of 'Arab' leadership by including three additional categories: women leaders, individual leaders of Arab states and Arab leaders leading in their home culture. There is a clear need to understand women's views of leadership and effective leadership styles, the implicit cultural values that underpin their leadership beliefs and practices, and the cultural, attitudinal and cultural barriers they encounter in business and organizational life.

Research: purpose and methodology

The purpose of this research was threefold: to develop a baseline of understanding of contemporary women leaders in the UAE inclusive of their leadership identity and practices, to generate knowledge to build leadership theory that reflects regional context and gender perspectives and to identify a research agenda by using grounded theory (Glaser & Strauss, 1967) for conceptual development.

This study of nine first-generation Emirati women investigated the leaders' backgrounds; education; career experiences and path; and perceived individual and organizational challenges and solutions. The study of UAE's most senior female business executives contributes to our understanding of women's empowerment in the UAE and attempts to capture their traits, experiences and challenges as women leaders in male-dominated work environments. At a time of great economic and social transition in a country barely 40 years old these narratives should generate more scholarly interest regarding the unique challenges and experiences of Emirati leading women and the factors that may have assisted their advancement to leadership positions.

The research methodology consisted of an up-to-date in-depth interdisciplinary literature review, the development of cases through interviews of women business leaders and an analysis that was context sensitive. This carefully chosen cross-cultural methodology was selected to yield rich insights into the personal characteristics of the participants as well as the social, cultural, political and economic factors that influenced the participants' experiences; to affirm or deny pre-existing assumptions; and to capture local knowledge within an Islamic framework (Cox, 2005; Hjorth & Steyaert, 2005; Dechant & Al-Lamky, 2005; Betters-Reed & Moore, 2007; Betters-Reed et al., 2007). The interview methodology can be described as narrative-based, discursive and ethnographic. This intentional exploratory qualitative research design yielded short cases as a source of grounded research and theory development considered an appropriate first-stage approach in nascent research areas (Glaser & Strauss, 1967).

Following the literature review, a two-hour interview format with guiding questions was developed. Open-ended questions focused on background and upbringing, career and leadership profile. These research questions were designed to examine the top factors of success and top barriers to women's advancement identified in the literature review. Questions also ascertained the interviewees' perceptions of women's changing roles in business and the connection with social and political advancement.

Over a one-year period in 2007 nine women were identified opportunistically; initial contacts were made through the two dominant professional businesswomen's associations in the country. In-depth, videotaped interviews with these nine first generation women business leaders generated data for short cases. All were Arab with eight of nine being Emirati; all were Muslim; most were married; all had undergraduate degrees with three of nine having Master's degrees; and all were Managing Directors, Presidents or CEOs. Semi-structured interviews allowed for the audibility of women's voices embedded with the influences of cultural heritage; by-products of the interviews included the discovery of contextualized life journeys and the testing of the perceptions of prior research on individual and organizational challenges. The totality of the cases was useful in the descriptive analysis, which revealed thematic responses across leadership narratives.

This study is based on a small, select sample and exploratory in nature. Findings should not be generalized to the entire populations of MENA, GCC or Emirati women leaders.

Results: leadership journeys

Previous studies show that early socialization can shape personal characteristics that, in turn, can facilitate or hinder one's role as a leader (Fels, 2004; Rhode, 2003; Karsten, 1994). Consistent with Al-Lamky's earlier research of leaders in emerging economies, the subjects' narratives revealed that family influences were strong, positive and began early in their lives. Most first credited the support of their fathers as key to their success as young learners, then in school and finally in the workplace; further, they credited their mothers for taking roles that bolstered their father's determination in having educated and successful working daughters. They described home environments where sons and daughters were treated equally in their upbringing and where educational attainment was highly valued. Many benefited from siblings and extended family members endorsement and approval of their career choices. Additionally, the women shared a common background of being raised in privileged, business-owning families. Similar to the findings of prior research on Omani women leaders (Al-Lamky 2006), the majority identified the benefits from travelling, living in Western, developed nations and/or obtaining tertiary degrees in the United States or United Kingdom. As one woman said: 'One of the advantages I always think that being a UAE and studying abroad. You are having two spins of thinking. You can think as the UAE what they want, what they need and you can also think as somebody who lived abroad, of how Arabs are thinking and what you can give them, which sometimes if I am an ex-pat I only would be thinking one direction, but not both. If you are a UAE, you can think both, [be] multicultural'.

All described being raised in religious families, continuing in the Muslim tradition as adult women, and feeling that Islam was a point of strength. As one noted, 'The influence of Islam in my life has been integral to everything I achieved'. Several other external influences were experienced by all or many of the women: all immediately went from college to work; all of the married women described their husbands as supportive of their careers; many started in their family businesses and many returned to their family businesses; and many also described their childhood homes as a place where creativity was nurtured. Further, all described operating in a contemporary context where they experienced the simultaneity of their roles as women living in the economic, political, academic, religious and domestic spheres.

Characteristics of leaders

Study participants described themselves as highly motivated, dedicated and self-confident. These leaders characterized themselves as democratic and participative, yet decisive in approach. These qualities led them to portray themselves as forward thinking with action-oriented strategies. Each leader worked internationally and described concrete skills that allowed them to succeed cross-culturally and globally.

One woman elaborated on her motivation: 'My legacy will be that I would like people in my society to remember me as a person who worked for the society and spent a lot of effort to build an image for women in this society and to change the misperception of the West to Eastern Women specially the Arab and Muslim women in this part of the world'. Another spoke of a vision shaped by sense of role and responsibility in family and business, sense of faith and ability to give back: 'Every woman is a leader in her own way, raising a family is much more difficult than making a business work'. And 'I don't think of myself as a leader...it is my responsibility, to my family, my country'. For most a philanthropic dual agenda of giving back to the UAE and of advancing the roles of women and the perception of those roles was more important than personal financial gain.

Concurrently, Islamic values permeated their stories. Islam was described as a support system and critical to developing a sense of self-efficacy and integrated roles and identity as a Muslim woman. Women stated that Islam was both a key to their success and contributed to their very definition of success. It follows that success factors included long-term, non-monetary factors such as reputation; peace with one's self; and giving back to the UAE. Moreover, their day-to-day management styles and leadership activities supported their inclusive definitions of success. One leader remarked: 'It isn't about how much you earn but about how comfortable and peaceful your life is'. The Islamic values of kindness, simplicity, and generosity are congruous with women's leadership practices and religious observance.

When the leaders spoke of interacting with employees within the workplace, they commented on the necessity to prove oneself to others, to be democratic and to accept the ideas of others. They described being able to delegate work and empower employees to make decisions. All described treating employees like family and showed a strong collectivist orientation, focusing more on the 'we' and less on the 'I'.

When defining leadership, the women shared their passion for their work. For example, one leader stated: 'I think one of the leader's main functions...is to inspire people. I don't think you can inspire people, if you are not passionate about [the work] yourself...so if you are passionate about something then you can convey that passion and that translates into motivation and inspiration'. The previously mentioned philanthropic agenda was embedded in their notion of leadership.

Some described their leadership as a unique combination of traditional feminine qualities and highly entrepreneurial skills. Feminine qualities including dress and demeanour in business settings were described as comfortable, authentic and demanding of respect of all colleagues. These qualities were often paired with entrepreneurial skills, adaptability and an innate ability to respond to opportunities and challenges. Several mentioned the historical legacy of trade in the region as fundamental to their cultural heritage and identity as businesswomen, supporting a historical context for their business acumen.

Communication, collaboration, 'listening to and accepting ideas of others', family support, the gaining of respect and having the right team were identified as key factors of success. They further emphasized an evaluation of their leadership and success through indirect and external indicators: 'It's what you hear people say about you'. On a macro level, all identified the support of the UAE government as an essential ingredient in providing an encouraging environment in which women are urged to pursue leadership positions in all levels of society.

Barriers to success

Study participants identified a small group of internal and external barriers to success that they had encountered on their leadership journeys. One participant talked of internal factors as paramount: 'I think women have to live to expectations and to be very ambitious, because now everything is here, the challenge is in women themselves, it is not in the regulations [nor] is it in the support or the families, it is in them. I think that self-confidence, goals, these are the issues that they have to tackle by themselves; they have to really be self-confident and work towards their objectives.'

To a very small degree, women mentioned the external issue of stereotyping. Some said that senior men in the workplace had assumptions about their leadership and achievement possibilities based on their gender; these assumptions had or could have had a negative effect on their advancement.

Another issue mentioned was the difficulty of balancing work and family .One of the major factors that influences women's participation in the workforce is the difficulty of balancing family and work responsibilities (Aryee et al., 1999; Hijab, 1994; Rugh, 1985; Sha'aban, 1996). These issues surface in two areas: the lack of childcare and long working hours in the private sector. Global research has reported that as a result of potential family – work conflict, many adolescent women, especially in Middle Eastern society where family ties are strong, eliminate from consideration high-prestige careers requiring a high degree of commitment (Looker, 2000, quoted in Gallant & Pounder, 2008).

Many commented that hijab was not a barrier to their leadership effectiveness. All but one of the women interviewed wore hijab. (It is tempting to note that this may be due to the fact that she was the youngest and the only non-Emirati in the study.) Prior research on women in Bahrain identified that women who wore hijab considered it an important aspect of their social identity and that those who wear hijab were given more status and respect as well as work opportunities. Hijab was associated with the image of a devout professional Muslim woman (Metcalfe, 2006). Several participants also commented that an important motivation for wearing hijab in their current role was to dispel the western stereotype of them as disempowered and oppressed women. One observed: 'When you are in business you realize after a while that people pay attention to what you are selling and what you're saying and not at your appearance. So you are dealt with much more as a human being rather than an object that is sitting there, using her appearance.'

Conclusions

As previously described, these women leaders are influenced by the Islamic values of team attribution, consultation, personal attention and familial organizational cultures. For these women leaders, socio-economic privilege provided networks that facilitated a rapid rise to leadership positions; their wasta was invisible yet operated to provide power and privilege in a manner not available to all women. Their leadership narratives convey a strong sense of organizational culture and value of close personal relationships: all described their organizations as familial cultures characterized by trust, openness and team development.

While western research has identified the participative and consultative nature of women's leadership styles (Eagly & Carli, 2007), in this context the intersection of gender and religious values are difficult to disentangle. Moreover, leading feminist scholars cite the importance of acknowledging the simultaneity or intersectionality of women's identity in order to ensure a more complete, culturally sensitive and holistic view of women's lives (Holvino, 2006). For these women, leadership effectiveness is intertwined with their integrated identities as Muslim women leaders. Weir's (2000) characterization of Arab management as consultative, open-system, networked and personalized also meshes well with current definitions of leadership as a networked process (Turnbull, 2009) and with current calls for more consultative approaches to managing employees, often portrayed as a 'female advantage' and described elsewhere as relational leadership (Fletcher, 2001).

Thus the participative nature and team orientation expressed in these women's leadership styles are consistent with family and in-group oriented societal culture, and some believe also common to Asian, Arab and African cultures. Prior research points to the fact that some non-western cultures share conformity, loyalty, kindness, tolerance, forgiveness, consideration and face-saving as valued leadership traits (Mellahi, 2000, cited in Thomas).

For these Emirati women, definitions of success and use of power as intertwined with notions of giving back and doing for others also reflects a more universal set of attributes assigned to women leaders (Gilligan, 1993; Merrill Sands et al., 2005). Likewise, their definitions of leadership, motivations, decision-making styles and definitions of success can simultaneously be attributed to Arab, tribal, Muslim and female influences as portrayed above. This confluence of integrated identities makes the 'unpacking' of their leadership identity particularly complex. Yet as women in the sheikhocractic tradition, they bring a distinctive female influence to consultation and relational leadership intelligence.

Study limitations and future research

Given the very small sample size, this study cannot be generalized to all Emirati businesswomen or leaders, much less all women in the region, or Arab women. As a very small subset of women in the country, these pioneering women are the first generation female business leaders. Their backgrounds, leadership identities and behaviours are simultaneously shaped by their unique individual histories, their shared experiences and cultural legacy as Muslim Emirati women.

Future research must expand the sample size and use other research methodologies to complement this qualitative exploratory study. Specifically, these women leaders hailed from a powerful socioeconomic elite; we cannot assume that women of other economic status would experience the same leadership journeys. Future research needs to address the different economic and social status as they shape women leaders' experiences and perceptions of leadership.

Additionally, this research took place at a particular yet dynamic point in the UAE and the wider region's economic and political life cycle. The UAE is considered the most progressive and 'westernized' among the GCC countries, setting a cultural tone for more progressive policies for women. Researchers may want to explore the challenges and opportunities for the next generation of leaders, as the study participants and their peers advance to visible public service roles. Others may want to explore the relationships among women across issues of generation and social class; the study participant's acute awareness of being a female business leader at this time coupled with the Islamic value of 'zukat' (the responsibility of giving to those less fortunate) and a government mandate creates an atmosphere ready for change.

Structural and cultural barriers persist and future research could identify and suggest implementation of barrier reduction and policy change. The social construction of gender and leadership in the UAE is influenced by Islamic and tribal notions of leadership within a traditionally patriarchal and Sheikocractic leadership legacy. An important interpretative factor involves gaining familiarity with the construction of gender relations and the equality agenda through an Islamic philosophy of gender separation signifying respect rather than subordination. For example, what may appear as a western relational 'female' style of leadership focused on team development is also embedded in Islamic religious values. Researchers have identified the need to 'unpack' deeply held beliefs regarding women, which are often confused with misinterpreted religious beliefs. It is beyond the scope of this research to do so yet this broader contextual analysis would yield additional data as it impacts women's leadership advancement. Investigation of women leaders' identity and behaviour in different sectors and industries would test assumptions of assumed similarity and the perpetuation of a monolithic category of 'UAE businesswomen' or UAE women leaders.

Very little research exists that documents women's voices and leadership within a global context. Very recently scholars have pointed to the importance of generating local knowledge to further delineate gender and diversity topics across cultures. Leading feminist organizational scholars have also identified the importance of using interdisciplinary literature and qualitative approaches to uncover more indigenous paradigms, considered next generation research in the field of gender and diversity (Calas & Smircich, 2009). Further research will enable the development of cases that bring visibility to these women leaders, within a country-specific context. These cases will point to the leadership contribution of Emirati women with their integrated Islamic female leadership identity and empowered action counteracting popular portrayals of Arab and Muslim women.

A culturally nuanced global perspective to the study of women business leaders also raises questions about how to create more cross-cultural and inclusive perspectives in management education and development. Given the problematical nature of importing western models of leadership, this research approach holds potential to inform less ethnocentric and parochial approaches to management education.

Given the lack of instructional materials and methodologies to deconstruct dominant western leadership theory, related research may create appreciation of the importance of educating the thought leaders in management research and education, and identifying the contributions of other leadership voices (Betters-Reed, Davitt and Moore 2005), bringing visibility to women's roles and contributions to business and society around the globe. Complete cases would provide examples of successful Emirati women business leaders, a void in the management and organizational literature. Case-based research provides the opportunity to explore how leadership reflects culturally embedded values and practices to document the voices of women leaders in other parts of the world.

This research reveals a complex set of religious and cultural influences on the identity of an Emirati woman business leader. The combination of Islamic values combined with their pioneering female status created team-oriented, ambitious, well-educated leaders with multiple definitions of success. Importantly, these cases create local and contextualized knowledge, which challenge earlier essentialist leadership attributes. This research on Emirati women business leaders profiles the contribution of their integrated Islamic female leadership identity to leadership effectiveness. Worldly leadership cannot be considered truly inclusive or global without hearing these previously silenced and undocumented voices.

Endnotes

1. The UAE (United Arab Emirates) is a constitutional federation of seven emirates: Abu Dhabi, Dubai, Sharjah, Ajman, Umm al-Qaiwain, Ra's al-Khaimah and Fujairah.
2. Although diverse in economies, politics and social conditions, Arab states are often grouped in two ways. The GCC Cooperation Council for the Arab States of the Gulf (GCC) includes The United Arab Emirates, the State of Bahrain, the Kingdom of Saudi Arabia, the Sultanate of Oman, the State of Qatar and the State of Kuwait. The Middle East and North Africa (MENA) is an economically diverse region that includes both the oil-rich economies in the Gulf and countries that are resource-scarce in relation to population; the MENA Region includes: Algeria, Bahrain, Djibouti, Egypt, Iran, Iraq, Israel, Jordan, Kuwait, Lebanon, Libya, Malta, Morocco, Oman, Qatar, Saudi Arabia, Syria, Tunisia, United Arab Emirates, West Bank and Gaza, Yemen. Whereas some might see the term Arab world as an externally imposed etic category it is actually an indigenous emic category commonly used in Arab discourse. The term incorporates 22 countries in the Middle East and North Africa, broadly united by a common language and religion. The region is highly important to the West strategically and economically, not just as a supplier of oil but increasingly as a huge and growing market, with a population of more than 280 million.
3. For the most part, Emiratis prefer government sector jobs to private sector jobs. Government jobs come with higher salaries, better non-monetary benefits and shorter work hours (Randeree, 2008). Specifically, the government sector operates on a single-shift, eight-hour-day and five-day-week system; many private sector establishments operate on 10-hour days, six days per week, with a split shift day. However, given an oversaturated public sector and rapidly globalized knowledge economy the need for private sector workers is paramount.

References

Abdalla, I. A. and Al-Homoud, M. A. 2001. Exploring the Implicit Leadership Theory in the Arabian Gulf Stattes. *Applied Psychology: An International Review* 50(4): 506–31.

Acker, J. 1990. Hierarchies, Job, Bodies: A Theory of Gendered Organizations, *Gender & Society* 4(2): 139–58.

Adler, N. 2002. Global Managers: No Longer Men Alone, *International Journal of Human Resource Management* 13(5): 743–60.

Adler, N. and Izraeli, D. (eds) 1988. *Women in Management Worldwide*. Armonk, NY: ME Sharpe.

Adler, N. and Izraeli, D. 1994. Where in the World are the Women Executives?, *Business Quarterly* 59(1): 89–94.

Al-Ajmi, R. 2001. The Effect of Personal Characteristics on Job Satisfaction: A Study Among Male Managers in the Kuwait Oil Industry, *International Journal of Commerce and Management* 11(3/4): 91–110.

Al-Lamky, A. 2007. Feminizing Leadership in Arab societies: The Perspectives of Omani Female Leaders, *Women in Management Review* 22(1): 46–67.

Al-Lamky, S. 2006. The Development of Human Resources in the Sultanate of Oman:

Omanization and the Role of Women, *unpublished presentation at the Sultan Qaboos Cultural Center*, Summer Institute on Oman and the Gulf, Washington, DC.

Al Rostamani, N. (2004). Call for strong push towards emiratisation. *Gulf News*, 12 March: 34.

Ali, A. 1995. Cultural Discontinuity in Arab Management Thought, *International Studies in Management and Organization* 25(3): 7–30.

Ali, A. J. 2005. *Islamic Perspectives on Management and Organization*. Cheltenham: Edward Elgar.

Aryee, S., Fields, D. and Luk, V. 1999. A Cross-Cultural Test of a Model of the Work-Family Interface, *Journal of Management* 25(4): 491–511.

Berthoin, A. A. and Izraeli, D. N. 1993. A Global Comparison of Women in Management: Women Managers in their Homelands and as Expatriates. In E. Fagenson (ed.) *Women in Management: Trends, Issues and Challenges in Managerial Diversity*. Newbury Park, CA: Sage, pp. 52–96.

Betters-Reed, B., Davitt, M., and Moore, L. 2005. Lessons learned about the cultural impact on leadership: Case of Kija Kim and Harvard Design and Mapping, Inc. *Proceedings of the International Eastern Academy of Management*, Cape Town, S. Africa, June 2005.

Betters-Reed, B. L. and Moore, L. L. 1995. Shifting the Management Development Paradigm for Women, *Journal of Management Development* 14: 24–38.

Betters-Reed, B. L. and Moore, L. L. 2007. Integrating an Authentic Cultural Lens in Case

Dialogue, *Proceedings of the International Eastern Academy of Management*, Amsterdam: The Netherlands .

Betters-Reed, B. L., Moore, L.. and Hunt, L. 2007. Toward a Conceptual Approach to Better Diagnosis and Resolution of Cross-Cultural and Gender Challenges in Entrepreneurial Research. In A. Fayolle (ed.) *Handbook of Research in Entrepreneurship Education*. Cheltenham: Edward Elgar.

Block, P. 1993. *Stewardship: Choosing Service Over Self-interest*. San Francisco, CA: Berrett-Koehler.

Calas, M. B. and Smircich, L. 2006. Feminist Perspectives on Gender and Organizational Research: What Is and Yet to Be. In D. A. Buchanan and A. Bryman (eds) *The Sage Handbook of Organizational Research Methods*. London: Sage, pp. 246–69.

Chamlou, N. 2004. *Gender and Development in the Middle East and North Africa: Women in the Public Sphere*. World Bank.

Cox, T. Jr 2005. Problems with Research by Organizational Scholars on Issues of Race and Ethnicity, *The Journal Of Applied Behavioral Science* 40: 124–45.

Dechant, K. and Al Lamky, A. 2005. Toward an Understanding of Arab Women Entrepreneurs in Bahrain and Oman, *Journal of Developmental Entrepreneurship* 10(2): 123–40.

Dubai Women's Establishment 2009. *Arab Women Leadership Outlook 2009–2011.* Dubai: DWE.

Eagly, A. H and Carli, L. L. 2007. Women and the Labyrinth of Leadership, *Harvard Business Review* September: 63–71.

Eden, D. and Leviatan, U. 1975. Implicit Leadership Theory as a Determinant of the Factor Structure Underlying Supervisory Behavior Scales, *Journal of Applied Psychology* 60: 736–41.

Fels, A. 2004. Do Women Lack Ambition?, *Harvard Business Review* 82(4): 50–60.

Fletcher, J. K. 2001. *Invisible Work: The Disappearing of Relational Practice at Work. CGO Insights.* Retrieved from Center for Gender in Organizations, Simmons Graduate School of Management.

Gallant, M and Pounder, S. 2008. The Employment of Female Nationals in the United Arab Emirates (UAE): An Analysis of Opportunities and Barriers to Education, *Business and Society: Contemporary Middle Eastern Issues* 1(1): 26–33.

Gilligan, C. 1993. *In A Different Voice.* Cambridge, MA: Harvard University Press.

Glaser, B. and Strauss, A. 1967. *The Discovery of Grounded Theory: Strategies for Qualitative Research.* New York: Aldine de Gruyter.

Greenleaf, R. K. 2001. Servant Leadership: A Journey into the Nature of Legitimate Power and

Greatness. In L. C. Spears (ed.) Mahwah, NJ: Paulist.

Greiss-Miller, N. 1995. *Egyptian Women Leaders: Societal Factors that Helped or Hindered them in their Development as Leaders and Decision Makers,* doctoral dissertation, Seattle University [Accessed 25th July 2006 from Dissertations & Theses database].

Guthrie, S. 2001. *Arab Women in the Middle Ages: Private Lives and Public Roles.* London: Saqi Books.

Hijab, N. 1994. *Womanpower: The Arab Debate on Women at Work.* New York: Cambridge University Press.

Hjorth, D. and Steyaert, C. 2005. *Narrative and Discursive Approaches in Entrepreneurship.* Cheltenham: Edward Elgar.

Hofstede, G. 1980. *Culture's Consequences: International Differences in Work Related Values.* London: Sage.

Hofstede, G. 1984. *Culture's Consequences: International Differences in Work-related Values.* Beverly Hills, CA: Sage.

Holvino, E. 2006. *Tired of Choosing: Working with the Simultaneity of Race, Gender, and Class in Organizations.* CGO Briefing Note number 24 [Retrieved from CGO, Simmons School of Management].

House, R. J., Hanges, P. J., Javidan, M., Dorfman, P. W., Gupta, V. and GLOBE Associates, 2004. *Leadership, Culture and Organizations: The GLOBE Study of 62 societies.* Thousand Oaks, CA: Sage.

Javidan, M. and Carl, D. 2004. East Meets West: Searching for the Ethics in Leadership, *Journal of Management Studies* 41(4): 665–91.

Kabasakal, H. and Bodur, M. 2002. Arabic Cluster: A Bridge between East and West, *Journal of World Business* 37: 40–54.

Kanter, R. 1993. *Men and Women of the Corporation.* 2nd edn. New York: Basic Books.

Karsten, M. G. 1994. *Management and Gender: Issues and Attitude.* London: Quorum Books.

Kattara, H. 2005. Career Challenges for Female Managers in Egyptian Hotels, *International Journal of Contemporary Hospitality Management* (17)3: 238–51.

Kenney, R., Schwartz-Kenney, B. and Blascovich, J. 1996. Implicit Leadership Theories: Defining Leaders Described as Worthy of Influence, *Personality and Social Psychology Bulletin* 22(11): 1128–43.

Looker, E. D. 2000. Gender and Work: The Occupational Expectations of Young Women and Men in the 1990's, *Gender Issues* 18(2): 74–89.

Lord, R., De Vader, C. and Alliger, G. 1978. The Effects of Performance Cues on Leader Behavior on Questionnaires Ratings of Leadership Behavior, *Organizational Behavior and Human Performance* 21(1): 27–39.

Maremount, K. 2009. Women-Focused Leadership Development in the Middle East: Generating Local Knowledge, *INSEAD Working Paper No. 2009/25/IGLC.*

Mellahi, K. 2000. The Teaching of Leadership on UK MBA Programmes: A Critical Analysis from an International Perspective, *Journal of Management Development* 19(3/4): 297–308.

Mernissi, F. 1997. *The Forgotten Queens of Islam.* Minneapolis: University of Minnesota Press.

Merrill-Sands, D., Kickul, J. and Ingols, C. 2005. Women Pursuing Leadership and Power: Challenging the Myth of the Opt Out Revolution, *CGO Insights no 20*, Boston, MA: Center for Gender in Organizations, Simmons School of Management.

Metcalfe, B. D. 2006. Exploring Cultural Dimensions of Gender and Management in the Middle East, *Thunderbird International Business Review* 48(1): 93–107.

Metcalfe, B. D. 2007. Gender and Human Resource Management in the Middle East, *International Journal of Human Resource Management* 18(1): 54–74.

Metcalfe, B. D. 2008. Women, Management and Globalization in the Middle East, *Journal of Business Ethics* 83: 85–100.

Moore, L. and Forster, N. 2009. An Exploratory Analysis of Cross-Cultural Differences in Sex-Typing and the Emergence of Androgynous Leadership Traits, *Vidwat: The Indian Journal of Management* 2(2): 4–15.

Moore,L. and Betters-Reed, B. 2009. Kija Kim and Harvard Design and Mapping, *The CASE Journal,* 5(2): 66–81.

Moss, S. 1994. Effects of Sex and Gender Role on Leader Emergence, *Academy of Management Journal* 37(5): 13–35.

Mostafa, M. M. 2005. Attitudes Towards Women Managers in the United Arab Emirates: The Effects of Patriarchy, Age and Sex, *Journal of Managerial Psychology* 20: 522–40.

Muna, F. A. 1980. *The Arab Executive.* New York: St. Martin's Press.

Neal, M., Catana, G. A., Finlay, J. L. and Catana, D. 2007. A Comparison of Leadership Prototypes of Arab and European Females, *International Journal of Cross Cultural Management* 7(3): 291–316.

Omar, A. and Davison, M. 2001. Women in Management: A Comparative Cross-Cultural Overview, *Cross Cultural Management* 8(3/4): 35–67.

Randeree, K. 2008. Challenges in Human Resource Management and Organisational Development in the Arabian Gulf: An Analysis of National Identity and Diversity, *The International Journal of Interdisciplinary Social Sciences* 2(5).

Rhode, D. 2003. The Difference 'Difference' Makes: Women and Leadership. In D. Rhode (ed.) *The Difference 'Difference' Makes: Women and Leadership.* Stanford, CA: Stanford University Press, pp. 159–80.

Ronen, S. 1986. *Comparative and Multinational Management.* New York: Wiley.

Rugh, A. B. 1985. Women and Work: Strategies and Choices in a Lower-class Quarter of Cairo. In E.W. Fernea (ed.) *Women and the Family in the Middle East: New Voices of Change.* Austin, TX: University of Texas Press, pp. 273–88.

Sakalli-Ugurlu, N. and Beydogan, B. 2002. Turkish College Students' Attitudes Toward Women Managers: The Effects of Patriarchy, Sexism, and Gender Differences, *The Journal of Psychology: Interdisciplinary and Applied* 136(6): 647–56.

Salloum, H. 2003. *Women in the United Arab Emirates.* London: Contemporary Review.

Sha'aban, B. 1996. The Status of Women in Syria. In S. Sabbagh (ed.) *Arab Women: Between Defiance and Restraint.* New York, NY: Olive Branch Press, pp. 54–61.

Spears, L. C. and Lawrence, M. 2002. *Focus on Leadership: Servant-Leadership for the 21st Century.* New York, NY: John Wiley & Sons.

Tayeb, M. 1997 Islamic Revival in Asia and Human Resource Management, *Employee Relations* 19(4): 352–64.

Thomas, D. C. 2008. *Cross Cultural Management: Essential Concepts.* Thousand Oaks, CA: Sage.

Tsui, A. S. 2004. Contributing to Global Management Knowledge: A Case for High Quality Indigenous Research, *Asia Pacific Journal of Management* 21: 491–513.

Turnbull, S. 2009. 'Worldly' Leadership for a Global World. In M. Harvey and J. D. Barbour (eds) *Global Leadership: Portraits of the Past, Visions of the Future.* College Park, MD: ILA, pp. 82–94.

UAE Yearbook 2009. Dubai: Trident Press.

Weir, D. T. H. 2000. Management in the Arab World. In M. Warner (ed.) *Management in Emerging Countries: Regional Encyclopedia of Business and Management.* London: Business Press/Thomson Learning, pp. 291–300.

Weir, D. T. H. 2003. Human Resource Development in the Arab Middle East: A Fourth Paradigm. In M. Lee (ed.) *HRD in a Complex World.* London: Routledge.

World's Economic Forum 2010. *Gender Gap Index: United Arab Emirates 2010.*

United Nations Development Programme 2003. *Arab Human Development Report,* New York: United Nations Publications.

United Nations Development Programme 2005. *Human Development Report: Aid, Trade and Security in an Unequal World.* New York: United Nations Publications.

11
Worldly Leadership in Pakistan *Seth* Organizations: An Empirical Challenge to the Concept of Global Leadership

Shakoor Khakwani and Peter Case

Introduction

In the introduction to this volume, it was suggested that one way of differentiating between global and *worldly* leadership would be to be more appreciative of indigenous leadership constructs and narratives. By way of making a modest contribution to research and scholarship that engages with worldly leadership in this sense, we report on preliminary findings from an empirical study of indigenous organizations in Pakistan. We attempt to elicit both continuities and discontinuities between Anglo-American forms of organization and large-scale family-run firms in Pakistan. It is important to acknowledge from the outset the influence which Anglo-American organizational thinking and practice has had in Pakistan. Both the British colonial legacy and contemporary management education in Pakistan result in hybrid organizational cultures which display distinct signs of modernity while, simultaneously, preserving traditional ways of leading and organizing that are rooted in kinship relationships. Our empirical enquiry is thus intended to shed critical light on the question of global versus worldly leadership by exploring the admixture of modern and local cultural practices which characterize what we shall shortly define as the Pakistan *Seth* organization.

To this end we present empirical evidence from a small-scale study of leadership and management practices in the Pakistan textile industry. Using an interpretative approach we have analysed an initial data set comprising 14 semi-structured interviews with senior executives employed in two companies which we designate O1 and O2 respectively. O1 is a producer and exporter of yarn and fabric based in Multan (a city with a primarily agrarian economy relying on cotton, wheat, sugar cane and mango production) while O2 is a producer of highly specialized and value added textile products situated in Karachi (an industrial and commercial hub of the country). O2's family is small, nuclear, relatively modern and foreign-educated while in the case of O1 the family is large, extended, traditional and locally educated.

O1 started business in 1935 as a leather tanning unit. The group grew rapidly between the mid-1980s and 1990s and moved to a vertically integrated model of production, which includes cotton ginning, spinning and weaving activities. The group possesses its own vast cotton farms in the area of Multan, a region of Punjab province. The cotton ginning, seed oil extraction, spinning and weaving units are located at strategic locations to enhance efficiency of its various production processes. The group owns and operates with seven companies, incorporating twelve modern production units, which are located in various parts of the country. It is one of the fastest growing groups in Pakistan with an annual turnover in 2010 of about 200M USD.

At present O2 is headed by a second generation family CEO who graduated from Boston College in the mid-1990s. The organization has seven manufacturing operations and markets its products in Australia, South Africa, China and Russia. It has three divisions: two in Pakistan and one in Colombo, Sri Lanka. The organization is run by a production team of about 30 managers with each factory having three senior managers who report directly to a General Manager (GM) Production. O2 is a vertically integrated company with its own spinning unit for yarn production and power generation unit. It produces a huge variety of gloves – around 200 styles – manufactured from a range of raw materials. It is an unlisted company with a turnover of approximately 200M USD in 2010.

Many themes and attributes can be identified in the data but we shall focus exclusively on two dominant features of organizational praxis that we denote 'informational politics' and 'unwritten leadership'. We have selected these two themes as they seem to offer evidence that highlights the kinds of relational leadership practices which typify Pakistani *Seth* organizations. This evidence also supports the theoretical challenge to the notion of global leadership that was mounted in Chapter 1 of this collection.

Leadership through informational politics

In attempting to understand leadership processes in the Pakistan context it is essential to adopt an explicitly political perspective. The view that complex organizations, in general, can be viewed as constituted by political processes is supported by Pfeffer (1992) who considers organizations to be political arenas oriented around the display of power (see also Morgan, 1986; Smircich, 1983). In fact, Mintzberg and Quinn (1991) have suggested that professional organizations are more political than other types and from the Critical Management Studies perspective organizations can never be considered politically neutral. However, presumptions of political neutrality and rationality in modern organizations serve a very important ideological function. They help privilege managers over subordinates and invest the former with the prerogative *to manage*.

The managerial prerogative has its own history. Djelic (quoted in Czarniawska, 2006), for example, has traced a genealogy back to workplace conflicts in US history where, he asserts, 'by redefining industrial conflict as a mechanical problem rather than as a result of political struggles engineers were able to universalize their particularistic interests to depoliticize the conflict-ridden nature of their rationality and eventually to monopolize industrial discourse and almost completely silence alternative ideological voices' (p. 333). It is this dehumanizing process of rationalization which is attacked robustly by postmodernist and critical management theorists.

It is commonly observed by academic observers that politics implicitly dominates organization processes (Feldman, 1999). This manifests in the maintenance of the focus of organizational theory on control phenomenon within organizations in multifarious ways. Rational control seems to be the focus point in mainstream organization literature whether viewed in terms of decision-making, objective-setting, motivation or leadership/management performance (Nirenberg, 1998). However, the suppression of politics and non-normalized knowledge results in management theory becoming more complicated, indirect and at times *irrelevant* in practical terms as it seeks to compensate for the absence of the core political process. The sheer ignorance of the political perspective results in the emergence of a theory/practice gap.

The tendency for leaders to be political outwardly, if seen in combination with House's (2005) 'humane orientation', offers a more comprehensive framework for understanding the Pakistani context. House's data and analyses revealed that organization and society in South Asia and the Middle East were in fact more humane than those of the so-called developed North. The descriptor 'humane orientation' runs contrary to the image of cutthroat professionalism that eventually culminates in political behaviour. Instead, it has been a dominant inclination in modern Anglo-American management literature to treat people, relationship-orientation or any other collective attitude with suspicion if not outright contempt. As such, the workplace collective carries the managerially negative connotations of social loafing and labour activism.

What one can see in the Pakistani organizational context as outwardly political, however, differs significantly from conceptions found, for instance, in Europe and the United States. In contrast with rational approaches which deny politics, organizational leadership in Pakistan is outwardly and explicitly political on two counts: first, there are internal aspects of leading and managing people and the formally driven professional-bureaucratic component of organization, and, second, politics arises from the exogenous factors of managing in relation to government institutions and bureaucracies.

Before we introduce some data to illustrate the nature of organizational politics in Pakistan, we need to define some indigenous terms that we refer to in our account: *Seth-Sahab* or *Sahb*, and *Mian Sahb*. In common parlance, *Seth* refers to an entrepreneur or rich man in South Asia (India and Pakistan), and is someone who knows the art of money making, or is a leader in economic and organizational terms. The word is widely used in the same sense in India, as it originates etymologically from the Hindu *mahajan* or moneylenders. In the Karachi region, *Seth* is commonly used to refer to business and industrial tycoons but can also be used to characterize a mode of organizing. The word *Sahab* or *Sahb* contains an element of respect and esteem that can be considered linguistically equivalent to 'Mr' in English. However, in the province of Punjab, the popular term for business entrepreneur or tycoon is *Mian Sahb*. Interestingly, it is commonly held among industrialists, as confided by one of the leading textile industrialists, that unless one is an owner of a textile mill one is not culturally qualified or entitled to be considered a 'genuine *Mian Sahb*'.

An interview with a top decision-maker in a *Seth* organization is instructive in terms of shedding light on the Pakistani attitude towards organizational politics. This purchasing director offered the following autobiographical narrative:

> I joined this organization in 1997 as Chief Accountant in the power plant, then became Chief Accountant of the Weaving unit and

eventually, in 2005, became GM Commercial & Purchase, owing to honesty, professional competence and family background – only then did I experience and learn how to deal [politically] with *Mian Sahiban*; previously I worked under only one *Mian Sahb*. Now I know what to say and what not to. When to be silent and just listen. When to speak out so that you are not held responsible for anomalies. To what extent you have to listen to others. When to interrupt and when not to. This is just to listen continuously so that one can reply at apt times and with appropriate answers. When to let someone talk and then wait for an opportunity to reply. And finally when you have to speak incessantly so as not to give others a chance to talk meaningfully. This sort of training and experience I have received by virtue of being in the purchase department...now I command 13 units [all units of the group]...I joined the organization with a starting salary of Rupees 18000/- and now getting 10 times more.

The above interview extract is indicative of the political nature of *Seth* organizing and managing. This manager was promoted not only owing to his professional qualifications (CA and CMA training) but also because of his family connections. His father, a FCMA, had worked for the same organization and was still acting as a consultant in the textile industry. The narrative also points to the importance of understanding and crafting political skills so as to engage in contextually appropriate, acceptable and trust-inducing communication with superiors and subordinates. Moreover, as far as career development is concerned in this kind of organization, professional qualifications are often secondary to political adeptness, family connections and ethnic identity.

This same purchasing director was also asked about decision-making on the part of the owners and offered the following commentary:

The way they decide? Very soon we come to know, say in six months, that they [leaders] took the right decision. It is collective decision-making...all directors consult their father and discuss with each other...think of backup plans and have done their homework. And even for loans they make sure they have adequate backup ready. They listen to everybody from a peon sweeper [*sic*] to accountants and general managers. They are well aware of what is happening, and they know who is satisfied with his job and who is not and intends to leave. There is a kind of competition between employees as to who is going to provide directors with information first; good or bad. In such a situation people cannot hide themselves for very long. Therefore owners can lead and manage very effectively even if they have been away from the organization for a long spell ... say for six months. Within the context of official meetings, *who* is speaking is more important rather than *what* is said.

One of the key questions arising from this preliminary study is how do owner-leaders exercise control over, lead, or carry with them a wide range of employees – from technologists, engineers, supervisors and financial experts to manual workers and administrators? However well technically qualified, managers need to learn the *Seth* family's way of doing things if they are to gain power and influence in the organization. The above interview extract goes some way towards answering this question and reveals the primary importance of informal conversation strategies and political sensibility. The political dexterity of *Seth* leaders is dependent on up-to-the-minute access to 'word on the ground', as it were. A perpetual and reliable flow of information enables them to make timely political judgements and interventions as demanded by a given context.

Recruitment and retention practices in the *Seth* organization also speak to the importance of political relationships. Unlike MNCs in Pakistan who have generally imported the openly competitive appointment processes and qualification criteria typical of modern organizations, *Seth* organizations place far greater emphasis on family connection, identity, personal performance and loyalty. As this purchasing director stated:

> Educational qualification is not the main criterion of appointment and promotion in this organization. *Mian sahiban* are more concerned to retain old and loyal people who are not even graduates rather than to hire young and qualified people.

There is a certain degree of tolerance for incompetence which might be explained, in part, by the sensitivity to pragmatic and emergent considerations rather a concern for abstract, rationalist principles or transcendental ideals. This is in marked contrast to modern Western organizations where, for instance, educational qualification is given more explicit weight than certain other tacit personal features. In another *Seth* organization (O2) a general manager with expertise in project and production management differentiates his organization from other local organizations in the following ways:

> Our firm is different from others in this sector as professionals have greater voice and influence here in this organization. It is a

professionally led company with owners in the background. The culture of this organization depends much on the individual general manager's personality and leadership style as against that of owners since they are least involved in day-to-day operations. But certainly they [owners] are there as they get reflected in the overall culture of the organization [to the extent that] a certain form of dynamism and openness, focus and a certain vision comes from them. However as far as implementation, project management and operations and organizing is concerned it is more around the individual general manager's cultural and leadership orientation. By vision I mean direction, plans, new markets and openness in organizing always comes from the owners.

As can be seen from the above interview extract, the *Seth* owners in this particular case delegate operational management to qualified and professional managers by and large, with little intervention from them. Strategic decision-making concerning major investment or expansion, however, still rests with the owners. In this instance, top leaders delegate to such an extent that managers experience, feel and *interpret* the organization as being professionally led. This in itself is an example of political sophistication on the part of the owners who still pull the important strings.

When asked about his role and position, the following owner (of O1) reveals a scenario that contrasts with the preceding one:

As I am sitting in the director's seat all I am faced with is responsibility. I am not sure whether I would have been here in this position had I not been the son of the K family. I am here by being the son of the owner of the firm whereas much more competent colleagues of mine still wander around [in more junior positions]. So I keep taking knowledge from my father, uncles and grandfather, throughout the day, right from the beginning of the day till the end. He is into buying and selling decisions and we keep asking 'why this' and 'why that'? However, to run the organization I should have such knowledge. I do differentiate my knowledge from that of my family as my knowledge is more oriented along systemic and integrated lines – something based on theory and books. But the knowledge of my father and grandfather is based on the philosophy that 'no one can do anything unless we do or say something'. We have to give them [the workforce] guidance... everything should revolve around me and they need my guidance.

Here one observes tension between the younger and older generation of the family. This younger director, in his late twenties, holding an MBA and with the organization for no more than two years, is critical of his predecessors' ways of doing things. The thoughts and practices espoused in the above extract appear to have been influenced by the principles of Western business education, an increasing trend that can be discerned more widely in Pakistani industrial and corporate life. The newer generation of leaders is exposed simultaneously to two streams of education: (1) a conventional or *traditional* one coming informally from the mentoring of family elders and driven by emergent and practical considerations, and (2) a modern form deriving from Anglo-American influenced schooling and exposure to Western managerial literature.

When questioned about the successful attributes of leaders, the same young director said:

> The beauty of leadership and management in Pakistani organizations lies in 'the blindness' created by the leadership all around the company. Everybody [in the company] knows *what* he has to do but none *why* he has to do it. For example, if a production manager knows how much to produce but he never knows the accurate and very specific costing of that production – and in this case if he wants to know about impact of change in production process in some manner that would benefit the company – the owners and directors of the company would never allow him to access the finance manager directly... rather both, finance and production managers will be restricted to their own spheres. The information will be mediated and channeled by *Mian sahb*. As a result, nobody will get the overall or true picture of the organization, even people in top managerial positions. This is the beauty of the system driven by family-based organizations and it prevails all across the textile sector in Pakistan... This has some weaknesses, innovation and R&D suffers most, but has the benefit of streamlining and stabilizing the process, especially that all organization politics are confined to, and revolve around, *Mian sahb* as he becomes the linchpin for holding information and the complete picture, and everybody comes to him for answers. An added benefit he receives is developing and portraying himself as an invincible and enigmatic person who is always able to take better decisions than technocrats and professionals.

One sees in the above extract a frank and honest admission by one of the more vocal and critical directors that leaders have to act as intermediaries between top level managers. A certain degree of 'blindness' or ambiguity is deliberately created by *Mian sahb*, thereby controlling the 'flow of information' and 'interaction amongst senior decision-makers'. This is not only to establish the centrality of *Mian sahb* but also to demonstrate his (in Pakistani society this is exclusively a male role) eminence and invincibility as a successful leader; he is the one who has the full picture. What we observe is the institutionalization of leadership in local *Seth* organizations through the formation of a business leaders' identity – *Mian sahb*. This identity is established through the management and manipulation of organizational politics which, in turn, entails building up authenticity and credibility through the gathering, control and mobilization of high quality information. It is a matter of creating the 'myth' of the *Mian sahb*, that is, the *Mian sahb* who knows the whole picture when nobody else does and who never allows others to obtain the fuller picture.

Unwritten leadership

One can discriminate between leadership and management process in Pakistani organizations in ways that parallel the differences between 'technical' and 'adaptive work' identified by Heifetz and Laurie (1997). As we tried to demonstrate in the previous section, according to our respondents, leadership is highly informal, family-based and political while management is construed to be bureaucratic, professional, technical and technologically driven. However, although the 'technical work' of management exhibits modern Anglo-American cultural traits, the 'adaptive work' of leaders seems to have distinctive Asiatic qualities. Organizations in the textile industry appear to achieve an appropriate mix of these leadership and managerial elements *for the context they operate in*. For instance, a typical textile company would be led managerially by a highly experienced and professionally qualified textile engineer as its director of production. In addition, there would probably be a chartered or cost accountant as director of finance and an MBA-qualified director of marketing. The job of an HR director is often somewhat less specialized and most of the time managed by the director of finance. The organization structure in these departments is traditionally hierarchical. Leaders (owners) respect, trust and delegate much of their authority to functional heads, especially the production and financial directors, while they tend to be involved and intervene more in marketing and HR-related decisions. Consequently, functional heads tend to enjoy greater autonomy – albeit subject to relative 'blindness' and ambiguity cultivated by the *Seth sahb* – and stay loyal to the leadership. Over the functional hierarchy there remains a hierarchy of owners who identify themselves using the modern formal nomenclature of 'Board of Directors', but operate more informally than this designation might imply. As discussed above, the common term for this kind of organizing within and outside the organization is '*Seth sahb*' in Karachi (Sindh province) while it is '*Mian sahb*' in Lahore (Punjab province).

It is interesting to note that leaders who consider themselves more progressive and educated abhor the idea of being identified as *Seth* or *Mian sahb* as it is commonly perceived to have highly negative connotations, for example, being considered as miserly and cost- or penny-conscious. The *Seth sahb* is also caricatured as something of a 'control freak' in common English parlance. Leadership in the case of large family-based organizations is not simple, unitary or particularly coherent; rather, it manifests in complex and multiple ways. For instance, studying one of the leading textile giants (O1) there were eight family members occupying positions in a nine-member Board of Directors (BOD). The only non-family member, head of production, was granted membership of the BOD because of his loyalty and technical competency. The other eight family members consisted of the grandfather, his four sons and three grandsons. These members kept closely in touch with management, actively seeking information and also meeting each other frequently. Such meetings were easily facilitated as they were all a part of a joint family system and living together in one big compound. So practically speaking, board meetings could be convened any time from breakfast until late at night and, as a consequence, organization and organizing went on perpetually. It is not a typical nine-to-five organization of the sort familiar in Europe and the United States. In our view, it is this strong and vibrant informal component of leadership fused with formal organizational structure which helps to account for the productivity of traditional Pakistani organizations. In such organizations, the normative dividing line between family relationships, work- and organizational-relationships cease to exist.

Even within the forms of modern management found in MNCs operating in Pakistan, managers and leaders exhibit an 'Asiatic spirit' of holistic attitudes towards work and organization, family and professionalism. For instance Shaukat Mirza, one of the legendary corporate leaders of Pakistan, and someone who might seem to embody the global leadership ethic, exhibits peculiarly local views and behaviours. While narrating the successful buyout of Exxon in his autobiography, *From Exxon to Engro*, Mirza attributed his business success to the supplications and prayers of his family members and wife in particular (Mirza, 2005). More evidence can be sought from one of the world's leading Fast Moving Consumer Goods companies in which, despite having one global policy for the company worldwide, follows practices of *'glocalisation'* (Ritzer, 2004). For example, during the last decade or so the company's CEOs have always hired from Pakistan. An interview with one of the company's directors established that earlier CEOs hailed from the home country or were of European origin. This change in appointment policy is evidence of adjustment and adaptation to local culture. One might conjecture that global leaders and managers (of Western origin) have, through experience, been seen to have limited capacities relative to locally groomed leaders and managers.

The peculiarly informal processes of organization and leadership are further illustrated in the following scenario drawn from our interview data. This depicts the case of another leading successful export-based organization in Karachi (O2) which has been performing well financially for nearly two decades in the absence of formal and tightly developed job descriptions. The informant – a senior manager responsible for coordinating operations, sales and quality across company divisions – has the experience of working in both Western-influenced MNCs and the *Seth* organization. He states:

> There is no formal or written job description, though the organization is primarily being developed by professionals and owners, who have by and large delegated authority to professional managers. We are realizing this now and moving more towards greater formalization in our organization as we intend to have a foreign HR consultant for this. Nonetheless, personally I have some apprehensions in going too much along this direction as I believe the organization culture here is more flexible and it is certainly not compartmentalised. For instance, you can quite easily change your job or department if you want to do so. And this is what attracted me to stay here in this organization as sometime back I was offered a job at EN which you know is a very prestigious [MNC] to work with, and I joined that for some time in 2001, in a permanent position as senior commercial and contract officer. The job was very well defined with clear cut job responsibilities but in a compartmentalised way. Well this type of job has its own benefit but the type of job enrichment and satisfaction I was getting here was not there. So the job with the MNC never appealed to me for its challenges as targets were set up on an annual or quarterly basis and I achieved those quite easily and received a

very good performance report as well – nonetheless I never enjoyed that job entirely. I know in such types of organization there is the possibility of job rotation in due course but somehow it was not that challenging for me. So it was a surprise for people when you just leave EN for this local organization, and even today I cherish my decision to return to this organization.

This account indicates that even managers who might have an ability to work with greater levels of formalization of control in certain contexts prefer the indigenous informality of the *Seth* context. Furthermore what is revealed here, interestingly, is that the informality of this large local organization is a source of attraction and retention to senior and experienced Pakistani managers. The lack of job definition and more formalized contract is not off-putting.

The informality of organizational processes is also demonstrated through a comment made by this organization's highly charismatic general manager (GM). While discussing leadership practices he observed that:

> We encourage interaction-, conversation- and discussion-based decision-making amongst managers, and do not believe in written correspondence and communication, and if I see two managers perpetually engaged in writing or exchanging even e-mails I will give them very tough time for doing this.

This interview revealed a number of interesting phenomena relating to the *Seth* organization. Leadership is exercised more through *relational* – as opposed to 'professional' or 'technical' – modes of conversation and of face-to-face interaction. Written communication, even if it is faster and more rationally efficient, can be seen and interpreted as a sign of *distrust* and *avoidance*. During the same interview with this GM it became clear that he is not moved by the written communication of his subordinate managers but, rather, uses intuitive judgement to read their political intentions. Moreover, within this *Seth* organization, traditional values were not completely supplanted by modern, Western-influenced management thought and practices, even if some of the production and project management techniques are adapted and implemented in this local production context.

When asked about the extent of formal and informal organizing, a marketing General Manager in O1 responded:

> If I have to quantify leadership and organizing on the scale of 100, it is 60% informal and 40% formal. I think the problem with our

organizational setting is that policies and procedures are not well defined, and are marked by ambiguity and variation. In the absence of well-defined procedures we either tend to have charismatic leadership or no leadership at all.

This is an interesting extract insofar as it demonstrates how managers in *Seth* organizations often do not like to admit that the non-rational approaches are effective. If educated and trained in Western management methods (as many of them are), when questioned they tend to want to distance themselves from or deny the efficacy of these culturally local practices.

Conclusion

Chapter 1 of this volume argued that since leadership processes are inherently ambiguous, contextual and complex, the drive to discover and establish principles of 'global leadership' is misplaced. Studies of leadership should be far more sensitive to differing indigenous contexts – national, cultural and organizational – and be prepared to think through the ramifications of this diversity. In this chapter we have sought to take this message to heart and reported on a small-scale study of indigenous leadership and organization practices in Pakistan. Two thematic attributes of Pakistani leadership discovered through our study of *Seth* organizations is the role of 'informational politics' and 'unwritten leadership'. We compared and contrasted interview data from senior managers and owner-leaders in two such organizations, O1 and O2.

Whereas O1 appeared to prioritize the traditional criteria of ethnic identity, family connections and loyalty in recruiting and retaining senior staff, in O2 we saw more reliance on professionally qualified managers and delegated authority. There seems to be more open interaction and information sharing in O2 while communication channels in O1 are set up and used strategically by owners to create forms of organizational commitment over which they exert direct control. The latter organizing strategy entails propounding the *Mian sahb* myth; perpetuating ambiguity and, where expedient, casting a strategic 'blindness' or cloud over affairs. It is important to note that even within the large *Seth* organizations in Pakistan there are different shades of leadership and different levels of adherence to traditional, local cultural or modern managerial and leadership practices. Despite these differences, however, both organizations are considered highly successful, as evidenced by strong and consistent financial performances, together with healthy growth in sales and capacity in recent years.

When it comes to examining the detailed practices that make up leadership and management processes within indigenous Pakistani organizations, it seems to be fallacious to think in terms of the kinds of universal pattern implied by the term 'global leadership'. If there are complex and subtle inter-organizational differences in the *Seth* sector alone, then it would follow that further geographical and anthropological distance will entail even greater diversity. Rather than neglect such differences or paste over them with such misplaced and ubiquitous ideas as 'global leadership', the research agendas of leadership studies would do well to accommodate, investigate and, where appropriate, celebrate such worldly differences.

References

Czarniawska, B. 2006. The Quiet Europeans, *Journal of Management Inquiry* 15(3): 332–34.

Feldman, S. P. 1999. The Levelling of Organization Culture. *The Journal of Applied Behavioural Sciences* 35(2): 230.

Heifetz, R. A. and Laurie D. L. 1997. The Work of Leadership. *Harvard Business Review*, Jan/Feb, 75(1): 124–34.

House, R. 2005. *Culture, Leadership and Organizations: The GLOBE Study of 62 Societies*. London: Sage.

Mirza, S. 2005. *From Exxon to Engro*. Karachi: Oxford University Press.

Mintzberg, H. and Quinn, J. B. 1991. *The Strategy Process: Concepts and Cases*. 2nd edn. London: Prentice Hall.

Morgan, G. 1986. *Images of Organization*. London: Sage.

Nirenberg, J. 1998. Myths We Teach, Realities We Ignore: Leadership Education in Business Schools, *Journal of Leadership Studies* 5(1): 82–99.

Pfeffer, J. 1992. *Managing With Power: Politics and Influence in Organizations*. Cambridge MA: Harvard Business School Press.

Ritzer, G. 2004. *The Globalization of Nothing*. London: Pine Forge Press.

Smircich, L. 1983. Concepts of Culture and Organization Analysis. *Administrative Science Quarterly* 28: 339–58.

12
Linking the Worldly Mindset with an Authentic Leadership Approach: An Exploratory Study in a Middle Eastern Context

Behice Ertenu Saracer, Gaye Karacay-Aydin, Çigdem Asarkaya and Hayat Kabasakal

Introduction

In recent years, there has been a loss of trust towards the leaders in social life, politics and the business world. This loss of trust has directed researchers to focus their studies on new leadership approaches that can rebuild trust. One of the promising results of these studies is the introduction of an 'authentic leadership' approach (Avolio et al., 2004; Avolio & Gardner, 2005; Bass & Steidlmeier, 1999; Price, 2003; Walumbwa et al., 2008).

Authenticity can be defined as knowing oneself through personal experiences, thoughts and beliefs and behaving in accordance with the true self (Harter, 2002, p. 382). This definition of authenticity requires thoughts and feelings to be consistent with actions. Authenticity, as a concept, dates back to ancient times and is deep rooted in every civilization. For instance,

- *'The superior man acts before he speaks, and afterwards speaks according to his action'* Confucius (China's most famous teacher, philosopher and political theorist, 551–479 BC)
- *'Be as you wish to seem'* Socrates (Ancient Greek philosopher, 470 BC–399 BC)
- *'Either seem as you are or be as you seem'* Mevlana Celaleddin Rumi (Anatolian philosopher and poet, 1207–73)
- *'Say as you think and speak it from your souls'* William Shakespeare (English dramatist, playwright and poet, 1564–1616)

In line with the value congruence theory of leadership, it might be expected that authentic leadership, although quite universal as a concept, would be manifested in different ways when the cultural context changes (House et al., 2004, p. 5). This study aims to highlight the extent to which the universal characteristics of authentic leadership are valid in a region covering Turkey, Iran, Jordan, Syria and Lebanon, and also to gain an insight about its emic manifestations in these countries. A qualitative methodology is used in this research in order to explore the antecedents, dimensions and outcomes of authentic leadership. This approach fits the concept of 'worldly mindset', since it proposes the consideration of contextual characteristics, as opposed to the universalistic 'global mindset'.

Authentic leadership

Luthans and Avolio (2003) defined authentic leadership as a process, resulting in greater self-awareness and fostering positive development. In parallel Kernis (2003) defined authenticity as operating as one's true or core self in daily life. Authenticity actually is not an either/or condition; people can be described as being more or less authentic or inauthentic (Erickson, 1995). This gives room for leaders and followers as people to have an opportunity for self-development.

In recent studies several researchers (Gardner et al., 2005; Walumbwa et al., 2008) have proposed that authentic leadership can be analysed as composed of four main dimensions: self-awareness, relational transparency, balanced processing and internalized moral perspective.

In these studies *self-awareness* was explained as being aware of one's own strengths and weaknesses, being able to make self-criticism and being cognizant of others' perceptions of self. *Relational transparency* was referred to as presenting one's authentic self to others, as opposed to presenting a fake or distorted self, and encouraging others to be transparent. *Balanced processing* was identified as objectively analysing all relevant data and opinions before coming to a decision. *Internalized moral perspective* was referred to as an integrated form of self-regulation guided by internalized moral standards and values, and results in expressed decision-making and behaviour that is consistent with these inner values.

Cultural context

Previous studies have pointed out that while national cultures have their unique attributes, geographic location serves as the basis of the cluster (Ronen & Shenkar, 1985). Kabasakal and Dastmalchian (2001) argue that geography precedes some important variables like language, ethnicity, climate and religion, which in turn have impact on some cultural dimensions (p. 481).

In this study, we have collected data from Turkey, Iran, Jordan, Syria and Lebanon, five countries that are geographically located in the Middle East. Although in previous studies these five countries have not been grouped together in the same cluster, the societies in these countries are found to share similar cultural values like large power distance and low individualism (Hofstede, 2001). Similarly, Kabasakal and Bodur (2002) point out that the Middle Eastern cluster consisting of Egypt, Morocco, Turkey, Kuwait and Qatar are highly group-oriented, hierarchical, masculine and low on future orientation. These highly collectivist cultural aspects merge with significance attached to family and other in-group members and result in a hierarchy of relations where the father figure is the most respected one (Kagitcibasi, 1994).

The underlying similarities for the cultural clustering of countries also have implications for defining outstanding leadership attributes in these countries. Kabasakal and Dastmalchian (2001) point out that effective leader attributes in Middle Eastern societies were found to be team-orientation and charisma. The most noteworthy culture-specific leadership practices in this area are 'consulting the followers' and 'asking their participation as a sign of respect' and 'creating a family atmosphere' (Kabasakal & Bodur, 2002). Further, these leader characteristics hold regardless of the subcultures in societies. Kuzulugil's (2009) research in different geographic regions of Turkey identified preferred leadership attributes in three subcultural groups based on their value orientations. Activism was found to be the preferred leadership attribute, followed by diplomacy and participative paternalism. Other researchers have also found paternalistic leadership to be a preferred leadership characteristic in Turkey and the Middle East (Aycan et al., 2000; Kabasakal & Bodur, 2002). Paternalistic leaders are authoritarian in a fatherly way and consider the welfare of their subordinates both at work and in their private lives and expect loyalty and commitment in return.

Theoretical background

Researchers who analysed the concept of authentic leadership attempted to differentiate it from other leadership approaches and showed that authentic leadership has some commonalities with ethical, transformational and charismatic leadership approaches on some of their dimensions (Bass & Steidlmeier, 1999; Walumbwa et al., 2008). According to another point of view, the point of differentiation is that authentic leadership is a 'root construct' constituting the basis of positive leadership (Gardner et al., 2005). In line with this reasoning, one can talk about authentic-transformational and pseudo-transformational leaders (Bass & Steidlmeier, 1999). In the present study we took authentic leadership as a root construct and attempted to analyse how individuals lead authentically while trying to act in line with local and culturally accepted ways of leading people.

In this framework the authentic leadership construct, as proposed by Walumbwa et al. (2008), can be regarded as universal. However, it can be assumed that every culture will define its own authenticity based on its values and local practices. Therefore, high power distance and in-group collectivism in the Middle East might lead to some differences in defining authentic leaders in this part of the world. This is in line with the 'worldly' mindset proposed by Mintzberg (2004, p. 304). Turnbull (2008) supports this view and argues that there is no such thing as a universal economic, psychological or cultural rationality, and therefore the defining of a universal set of global leadership competencies is inherently problematic. Gosling and Mintzberg (2003) recommend that today's managers should internalize a worldly mindset in order to manage the context which includes government relations, societal trends, legal climate, international developments among other areas. Mintzberg (2004, p. 304) argues that adopting a worldly mindset is not simply about observation; it is also about the way that someone is engaged with and acts within and across these worlds.

Turnbull (2008) believes that one of the essential elements for developing a deep understanding of worldly leadership in action is ethical leadership. It is explained as the kind of leadership that attempts to put ethical decision-making high on its agenda, recognizes the cultural difficulties associated with this and aims to put integrity and propriety at the heart of organizational governance. These characteristics of ethical leadership are completely in line with the internalized moral perspective dimension of authentic leadership (Brown & Trevino, 2006; Walumbwa et al., 2008).

The challenge of global leadership, on the other hand, is partly seen as how to blend a deep understanding of the immediate context with a broad understanding of the world. Turnbull (2008) mentions that instead of focusing on global leadership as being exclusively about top leaders it can more usefully be seen as a 'dispersed', 'distributed' or 'shared' process within and across organizations, and the interaction of people and ideas among and across cultures. As all dimensions of authentic leadership, through the participatory ingredient they have, support these points mentioned by Turnbull, authentic leaders might well be agents of this dispersion, distribution or sharing of leadership.

According to Mintzberg (2004, p. 307), our world covers political, social, economic dimensions in 'developing' as well as 'developed' worlds. Therefore, effective management requires the related competencies of networking, negotiating, working with different stakeholders and managing across cultural divides. All these competencies integrate internalized reflection with externalized analysis.

The internalized reflections of a person, in turn, lead to the development of that person on a continuous basis. In this respect, authentic leadership is regarded as a dynamic concept, which is open to lifelong development (Luthans & Avolio, 2003). At the core of authenticity lies the harmony of one's self and behaviour (Gardner et al., 2005; Luthans & Avolio, 2003). This implies that reflections of his/her own life experiences may help the individual to get closer to genuine self. The concept of 'worldly mindset', as put forward by Mintzberg (2004, p. 305) is quite close to authenticity because it is defined as a process of experiencing other people's worlds, their cultures and habits and reflecting on own experiences.

In consideration of this framework, this research is about inquiring into the conceptual and behavioural aspects of authentic leadership in the Middle East Region, as well as their antecedents. In other words, the study aims to understand how a leader is defined as authentic and to gain an insight about emic manifestation of authentic leadership in this unique part of the world.

Methodology

The study comprises three phases. In the first phase, the conceptual links between trust and authentic leadership are analysed as well as their importance. To that end, unstructured in-depth interviews were held in Turkey with seven people selected on the basis of convenience. The mean age was 38, four being mid-line managers, one retired state employee, one architect and one systems analyst. A similar survey was also carried in Jordan, Lebanon, Syria and Iran, via internet and telephone. The sample consisted of ten mid-line managers working in a large multinational company. The average age was 34. The responses are content analysed and a noticeable intersection between being authentic and being trustworthy is underlined.

The second phase aimed to get an understanding about the construct of authentic leadership in this region. Two focus group meetings are organized, each consisting of six people. The first meeting was held with doctorate students at Bogazici University; the second group was composed of mid-line managers working at different organizations. The participants were asked to give their definition of authentic leadership and their answers were explored in relation to the dimensions of the authentic leadership construct as defined by Walumba et al. (2008). The group discussions were tape-recorded and the minutes were content analysed.

The third phase aimed to gain an insight about the validity of universal dimensions of authentic leadership in the countries covered by this study and to determine the emic manifestations. For that purpose, 36 in-depth interviews were held: 21 in Turkey, 9 in Iran and 2 each in Lebanon, Syria and Jordan (Exhibit 1). These interviews also aimed to explore the anteceding factors for authentic leadership development. The sample in Iran and Middle Eastern countries consisted entirely of managers and directors working in the multinational company included in the first phase. The sample in Turkey was more varied; 60 per cent consisting of professionally employed mid-line managers/directors working in diverse organizations, the rest being self-employed people. The average age of the total group of 36 participants was 41 with an average of 18 years of work experience. Seventy-three per cent were male, consistent with the male dominance in the business sector in the region. The recordings from these interviews were tabulated on an excel sheet such that each verbatim/idea articulated by a participant was vertically listed whereas the horizontal lines were used for content analysis of these narratives.

Exhibit 1

List of Interviews

Codes	Age	Occupation	Gender
In Turkey			
T1	35	Marketing manager	f
T2	45	Architect	f
T3	36	Financial specialist	f
T4	34	Accountant	m
T5	33	Tourism officer	f
T6	62	Industrial engineer	f

Continued

Exhibit 1   Continued

List of Interviews

Codes	Age	Occupation	Gender
T7	34	Linguist	m
T8	35	Editor in chief	f
T9	37	Pharmaceutical com. Manager	m
T10	61	Retired executive	m
T11	64	Retired executive	m
T12	32	Informatics-executive	m
T13	56	Export executive – Glass industry	m
T14	33	HR manager – IT	m
T15	37	Sales manager – pharmaceuticals	m
T16	38	Marketing manager – telecom	m
T17	33	Public sector – specialist	f
T18	40	Sales manager	m
T19	45	Bank executive	f
T20	54	Managing director – sportswear	m
T21	42	Sales manager – chemicals	m
In Iran			
IR 1	32	Lawyer and translator	f
IR 2	56	General Manager	m
IR 3	35	Director marketing	f
IR 4	44	Director sales	m
IR 5	52	Key account manager	m
IR 6	43	Marketing Director	m
IR 7	42	Human Resource manager	m
IR 8	49	Managing partner	m
IR 9	31	Quality control manager	m
Lebanon			
L1	44	Sales director	m
L2	34	Marketing manager	m
Syria			
S1	42	Sales manager	m
S2	34	Technical & manufacturing manager	m
Jordan			
J1	34	Sales manager	m
J2	35	Marketing manager	m

In this research, an in-depth interview method was used to gather data because it is the most popular tool in qualitative leadership studies (Bryman, 2004) and recommended for 'exploratory' work. Content analysis is a well-established method in the analysis of qualitative data because it ultimately gives meaning to gathered information (Krippendorff, 2004, p. 18). According to the suggested steps of content analysis, 799 narratives or extracts from interviews, each representing at least one idea articulated in one or more phrases, were documented on an excel sheet and a perceptive clustering method was used to categorize them. The same process was followed in order to sort out the antecedents and classify them separately. Upon the completion of the categorization process, the frequencies of each category were tabulated to make the data accessible for further analysis.

In order to check the accuracy and reliability of the content analysis done, the inter-judge reliability method was used. For that purpose the two other authors, who were not involved in the in-depth interviews and the initial coding of narratives, independently re-coded all the reported cases according to the commonly agreed clustering criteria. Both independent evaluation of data and access to sources, where it was needed, provided the necessary conditions to ensure the reliability of the data (Krippendorff, 2004, p. 216). Consistency between judges was checked and the average inter-judge reliability score was calculated at 80 per cent, which is acceptable (Krippendorff, 2004, p. 242).

Following the reliability check, all researchers came together and made a final analysis of all the categories in order to eliminate repetitions and conclude the findings.

Findings

General

The findings reflect that authentic leadership is recognized as important and valuable in gaining the trust of followers in the Middle Eastern countries.

Analysis of the results confirmed that authentic leadership could be considered as a root construct. Being authentic is important but is not synonymous with 'ideal' leadership. The results of this study reveal that leaders are expected to be powerful, charismatic and ready to take charge; however, also humble and able to balance power with a humane and fair approach towards followers.

This study proposes that the four dimensions of authentic leadership (Walumba et al., 2008) are also valid in the geography covered in this

Table 12.1   Dimensions of authentic leadership

(SELF) AWARENESS	RELATIONAL TRANSPARENCY
Personal Mindset	**Personal Mindset**
Awareness of weaknesses and strengths	Open and honest communication
Self-disclosure	No lies
Self-development	Admitting mistakes
Self-critique	Sincerity in displaying emotions
Collaborative Mindset	**Collaborative Mindset**
Prioritization of collective interests and having a collective mission	Relational honesty and fairness
Awareness of followers' values	Two-way communication
Awareness of weaknesses and strengths of followers	Gentle and incremental feedback
Honest feedback	Empathic feedback
Recognition and appraisal of followers	Valuing ideas of followers
Mentoring, coaching and counselling	Creating group solidarity
Benevolence	Balancing social distance
Empowerment	
Protection of others	
Empathy and care for others	

BALANCED PROCESSING	INTERNALIZED MORAL PERSPECTIVE
Personal Mindset	**Personal Mindset**
Consulting others before reaching a decision	High values and ethics
Objectively analysing relevant data	Standing strong for ethical principles
Unbiased approach to other ideas	Internalized principles
	Consistency of thoughts, values, with conduct
Collaborative Mindset	**Collaborative Mindset**
Encouraging all parties to participate	Role-model for followers in terms of values, and life-style
Non-discriminative approach	Modesty
	Tolerance for others
	Respect followers

study. However, as demonstrated in Table 12.1, these dimensions can be subdivided further into 'personal mindset' and 'collaborative mindset' sub-categories, the latter addressing emic manifestations of authentic leadership and reflecting the collectivist rather than individualist cultural feature, which is typical of this region (House et Al., 2004; Kabasakal & Bodur, 2002).

Detailed results about the dimensions of authentic leadership
(Self)-awareness

- Although knowing the self is important, it became evident that awareness of the 'we' rather than the 'self' counts more. In other words, leaders should develop a sense of 'otherness' or minimize the self or the 'ego' so that they can be seen as authentic. Therefore, leaders are definitely expected to prioritize collective interests over their personal goals. Striving for a collective mission is perceived as respectful and trustworthy. *'The primary goal of the leader should not be making more profits or earning more money. He should have a spiritual mindset and set a moral mission in life and somehow give something to others than take more'* [Exhibit 1, T5].
- In addition to being aware of personal weaknesses and strengths, the leaders are expected to be more aware of the followers' qualities and values because that would lead to honest feedback, open communication and the distribution of welfare in an effective and fair manner.
- Appreciation and recognition are very powerful tools for developing the (generally missing) self-confidence of followers. However, most leaders refrain from offering this 'honour' because of their own fears, for example, of losing power and concerns that over-appreciation might lead to discontinuation of good behaviour. Therefore a leader who is confident in himself and in his relations with others is seen as an authentic one.
- The leader, being the ideal figure, the 'role model', the 'knowledgeable', is also expected to be a mentor and share knowledge and experiences with their followers: *'It is very important to let the followers develop self-confidence and self-awareness. That has a quantum effect on the whole organization'* [Exhibit 1, T6].

Empowerment of subordinates is a necessary tool within the process of their development. However, it is hard for leaders to delegate their power or authority to subordinates unless their fears about powerlessness are alleviated. This shift of power is perceived as a sign of confidence in the subordinate and reduced ego, or authenticity of the leader. In that context, mentoring, sharing, being the 'elder brother' or father, demonstrating empathy and benevolence are some of the basic characteristics associated with the authentic leadership.

Relational Transparency

- Transparency *'equals honesty, openness and reliability'* [Exhibit 1, L1] and it helps managerial effectiveness and efficiency. However, transparency is quite an issue because fear of losing control might put a barrier in being open towards oneself and towards others.
- Lack of transparency is a way to protect the power of the leaders and to keep their relational distance with their followers in balance. *'Transparency can be "used and abused" or misinterpreted! It can be used against the manager'* [Exhibit 1, IR5]. Therefore lack of transparency can be tolerated as long as the followers are convinced about the honesty of their leaders: *'The followers don't need to know the thinking process of the leader. One should not say everything but whatever he/she says should be true'* [Exhibit 1, T18].
- Communicating openly, accepting the blame and sharing emotions are not so common. However, giving feedback to the follower is welcome as long as it is fair, it is shared gently and on the spot. Negative feedback necessitates more care and should be given in private whereas positive feedback is an opportunity to boost the self-confidence of the follower and should be given in public. Valuing people and demonstrating are important.
- Listening to subordinates is a virtue and the landmark of valuing and respecting people. Therefore, a leader who shows the wisdom to listen to others for any good reason is the one who also deserves the respect and trust of followers.
- Personalized care is the opposite of power; social distance being a tool for balancing these two forces. *'The leader should have just enough power to give confidence without creating fear!'* [Exhibit 1, T11].

These findings are in parallel with the attributes of paternalistic leadership (Pellegrini & Scandura, 2008), which is quite common in many developing countries. The workplace is considered as the family surrounding and the leader keeps the rights of being authoritarian if it is for the 'common good'. Despite some limitations, relational transparency is still relevant and is considered as a highly important qualification of an authentic leader. However, in practice, transparency is conditional to the development level of the follower, the quality of leader–follower relationship or level of trust between them.

Internalized Moral Perspective

- Honesty and fairness are considered as necessary in the distribution of scarce resources evenly and equally among the followers. Both are unanimously mentioned as landmarks of authentic leadership.
- Consistency and keeping words are crucial for building trust. *'One loses respect and trust when he makes high promises and forgets later'* [Exhibit 1, T8].
- Leading by example is important and leaders are considered 'worth following' only if they give the impression that their morals and values are solid and 'real'. *'Any effort to disguise his strengths and weaknesses gives the impression that he is role playing and that reduces our respect. He would rather say so before we even notice so that we build more trust'* [Exhibit 1, T1].
- Internalization of values necessitates a certain degree of maturity and life experience. Age is highly respected in this geographical region because increased maturity is parallel to gaining wisdom and developing tolerance for others. Both respect and tolerance are found to be of paramount importance. *'One should know how to respect the followers and never break their pride so that this respect is reciprocated'* [Exhibit 1, J1]; *'People are intolerant and tough to each other. The leader should create a climate of tolerance for diverse opinions by being a role model himself'* [Exhibit 1, T13].

In sum, an authentic leader is the one who is humble and simple and does not need to demonstrate his power in a flamboyant manner. *'Be yourself: don't try to assume a different character because of the position. If a leader makes big manners he does not deserve the respect of others. We dislike a show-off; you need to speak the language of the street, be simple, plain and charismatic'* [Exhibit 1, S1].

Balanced processing

- In general, leaders are expected to decide, but only after consultation with followers. Listening to followers' opinions is a way to demonstrate personal care and respect.
- Authentic leaders are expected to be 'wise' people with 'balanced' attitudes and not be over reactive. *'An authentic, natural and intimate*

leader should separate professional life from friendship, he should be objective and fair so that one could build trust and respect' [Exhibit 1, T3].

- Authentic leaders are the ones who welcome different opinions and are not afraid of losing power. *'He/She should be able to show that he can be trusted and that the door is always open. He should not dismiss discussion or ideas without giving perspective or explanation'* [Exhibit 1, T19].

Leaders should refrain from presuming to 'know everything'; they should be tolerant, patient and keep a low profile towards others so that followers trust them more. *'An "I know everything" attitude is not appreciated. One should look humble. In general, Westerners and expatriates look at us from above'* [Exhibit 1, IR4].

In summary, the study confirmed that authentic leadership characteristics are tightly connected with respect and trust. Respect is defined in the literature as 'paying attention to and taking seriously another person' or as a way of 'subordinating one's ego for the greater good' (Reilly, 2002, p.132). In the Middle Eastern region, respect has a slightly different connotation compared to the West. It refers not only to subordinating but rather suppressing one's ego vis-à-vis someone who is perceived to be more powerful, such as respect for the elderly, for parents, for the 'boss'. Respect is not always by will, but mostly by fear or by admiration. In this study, it was found that respect for an authentic leader emerges out of admiration towards the leader rather than by fear. Another implication of this study is that respect is 'deserved' by being fair, considerate and consistent: *'He gets the respect of people by being consistent, communicating gently and not using his position'* [Exhibit 1, T10].

Antecedents to authentic leadership

In this study three factors appeared to be of prime value to the development and demonstration of authentic leadership in a work context. These are: life experience of the leader, readiness of the followers, and congruence of values of the followers and the leader.

Life experience: In line with the life story approach of Shamir and Eilam (2005), a unique life experience is considered an important precondition of being authentic. Authenticity is regarded as a process, also called authentic leadership development (Avolio & Gardner, 2005), according to which one cannot be entirely authentic or inauthentic (Erickson, 1995). *'Age is important in being and becoming yourself. As I age I am getting more and more myself and I am not pretending. I don't need anymore to impress people'* [Exhibit 1, IR2]. In line with the life experience approach, emotions and positive values like social justice, loyalty, honesty, responsibility are important in developing authenticity (Michie & Goody, 2005). This is in compliance with the worldly mindset since the experience that is meant by these authors is built on truly lived facts rather than sole observation: *'You don't become authentic just by saying so. Authentic leaders have a path to follow in their lives'* [Exhibit 1, T12].

Follower Readiness: The expectations of the followers determine the degree of transparency that the leader can effectively demonstrate towards them. In that respect, the education level of the followers, the socio-economic background, professional experience and personality determine their expectations from and reactions to a leader (Gardner et al., 2005). In that respect, the life experiences, values and emotional sensitivity of the followers may or may not support the authenticity of the leader, confirming the view that authenticity is mutually developed and influenced in line with the social exchange theory (Blau, 1964; Ilies et al., 2005).

Value congruence: The results of the study have confirmed the importance of value congruence between the followers and the leader so that the relationship as a whole becomes 'authentic'. The authenticity of the leader opens the way to the authenticity of the follower because the follower may identify himself/herself with the leader and take the leader as a role model. This finding is also supported by Avolio et al. (2004) who have proposed 'identification' as a mediator between authentic leadership and 'trust'. The social identity theory of leadership (Van Knippenberg, 2000) implies that the followers identify with the leader to the extent that the leader is prototypical of the group, that is to the extent he or she embodies and represents central group values and characteristics. This proposition gains high support in societies marked by high in-group collectivism because in such a context, people do not look with a critical eye to their group members, including their leaders: *'The leader should make us feel that he has the same genes as we do'* [Exhibit 1, T18]. In the absence of negative criticism, members and leaders might develop more authentic and open relationship which in turn might lead to even greater value congruence and follower reciprocation.

Discussion

The findings of the present study confirm previous research results as to how much leadership is contextual, especially in the Middle East where morals and values are of prime importance both in the social and work sphere. Although leading by authority is a more popular practice, leading by example is also quite common. However, the extent to which this may be effective is dependent upon the level of development of the follower and the harmony between the leader and subordinate(s). Paternalism and active leadership are among the more authoritarian leadership attributes that are perceived to be positive in this part of the world (Aycan et al., 2000; Kabasakal & Bodur, 2002; Kuzulugil, 2009). As one moves towards the East, a personal mindset is less important and a collaborative mindset becomes more dominant. In-group collectivism can be interpreted as a kind of support for people who have handed over their individual power to their leader for setting peace and order. In that respect, it is no surprise that this region shows high in-group collectivist characteristics and demonstrates a different pattern for leader–follower expectations and relations. For example, tightly knit in-group solidarity brings non-tolerance for others outside the group and feeds in-group favouritism. In line with the high power distance characteristics of these societies (Kabasakal & Bodur, 2002) respect and power go well together and respect is gained by caring for people's egos, emotions and sensitivities. Fear and admiration for the leaders may co-exist so that respect does not dissolve. *'A leader is to be loved and scared as well. He should put a distance because if too close they would not respect him but if the distance is too much they would try to harm him. Thus, a leader should be both fatherly kind and firm'* [Exhibit 1, IR1].

Given the cultural assumptions, leadership practices that favour more transparency and more authenticity may take some time to gain support. Still, authenticity is a highly desirable model because leaders who are authentic not only give directions but also have sound psychological capital and are able to give hope, demonstrate optimism, resilience and benevolence (Luthans & Avolio, 2003; Gillham & Seligman, 1999). These characteristics in turn are so much needed to resolve centuries-long conflicts and problems in this region. Thus, we expect that preserving group solidarity, harmony and interdependence by balancing power and social distance may be manifestations of authentic leadership in the Middle Eastern region.

References

Avolio, B. J., Gardner, W. L., Walumbwa, F. O., Luthans, F. and May, D. R. 2004. Unlocking the Mask: A Look at the Process by Which Authentic Leaders Impact Follower Attitudes and Behaviours, *The Leadership Quarterly* 15: 801–23.

Avolio, B. J. and Gardner, W. L. 2005. Authentic Leadership Development: Getting to the Root of Positive Forms of Leadership, *The Leadership Quarterly* 16: 315–38.

Aycan, Z., Kanungo, R. N., Mendonca, M., Yu, K., Deller, J., Stahl, G. and Kurshid, A. 2000. Impact of Culture on Human Resource Management Practices: A

10-Country Comparison, *Applied Psychology: An International Review* 49(1): 192–221.

Bass, B. M. and Steidlmeier, P. 1999. Ethics, Character, and Authentic Transformational Leadership Behaviour, *The Leadership Quarterly* 10(2):181–217.

Blau, P. 1964. *Exchange and Power in Social Life*. New York: Wiley.

Brown, M. E. and Treviño, L. K. 2006. Ethical Leadership: A Review and Future Directions, *The Leadership Quarterly* 17: 595–616.

Bryman, A. 2004. Review: Qualitative Research on Leadership: A Critical but Appreciative Review, *The Leadership Quarterly* 15: 729–69.

Erickson, R. J. 1995. The Importance of Authenticity for Self and Society, *Symbolic Interaction* 18: 121–44.

Gardner, W. L., Avolio, B. J., Luthans, F., May, D. R. and Walumbwa, F. O. 2005. Can You See the Real Me? A Self-based Model of Authentic Leader and Follower Development, *The Leadership Quarterly* 16: 343–72.

Gillham, J. E. and Seligman, M. E. P. 1999. Footsteps on the Road to a Positive Psychology, *Behaviour Research And Therapy* 37(7), Supplement 1: 163–73.

Gosling, J. and Mintzberg, H. 2003. The Five Minds of a Manager, *Harvard Business Review*, November: 54–63.

Harter, S. 2002. Authenticity. In C. R. Snyder and S. Lopez (eds) *Handbook of Positive Psychology*. Oxford: Oxford University Press, pp. 382–94.

Hofstede, G. 2001. *Culture's Consequences: Comparing Values, Behaviours, Institutions, and Organizations Across Nations*, 2nd edn. Thousand Oaks, CA: Sage.

House, R. J., Hanges, P. J., Javidan, M., Dorfman, P. W. and Gupta, V. 2004. *Culture, Leadership, and Organizations: The GLOBE Study of 62 Societies*. Stamford, CN: Jai Press.

Ilies, T., Morgeson, F. P. and Nahrgang, J. D. 2005. Authentic Leadership and Eudaemonic Well-being: Understanding Leader–follower Outcomes, *The Leadership Quarterly* 16: 373–94.

Kabasakal, H. And Dastmalchian, A. 2001. Introduction to the Special Issue on Leadership and Culture in the Middle East, *Applied Psychology: An International Review* 50(4): 479–88.

Kabasakal, H. and Bodur, M. 2002. Arabic Cluster: A Bridge Between East and West, *Journal of World Business* 37: 40–54.

Kagitcibasi, C. 1994. A Critical Appraisal of Individualism and Collectivism: Toward a New Formulation. In U. Kim, H. Triandis, C. Kagitcibasi, S. C. Choi and G. Yoon (eds) *Individualism and Collectivism: Theory, Method and Applications*. Thousand Oaks, CA: Sage, pp. 52–65.

Kernis, M. H. 2003. Toward a Conceptualization of Optimal Self-esteem, *Psychological Inquiry* 14: 1–26.

Krippendorff, K. 2004. *Content Analysis: An Introduction to Its Methodology*. London: Sage.

Kuzulugil, S. 2009. *Does One Size Fit All? Value-based Subcultures and Leadership Preferences in Turkey*. Unpublished doctoral dissertation. Istanbul, Turkey: Boğaziçi University.

Luthans, F. and Avolio, B. J. 2003. Authentic Leadership: A Positive Developmental Approach. In K. S. Cameron, J. E. Dutton, and R. E. Quinn (eds) *Positive Organizational Scholarship*. San Francisco: Barrett-Koehler, pp. 241–61.

Michie, S. and Goody, J. 2005. Values, Emotions, and Authenticity: Will the Real Leader Please Stand Up?, *The Leadership Quarterly* 16: 441–57.

Mintzberg, H. 2004. *Managers Not MBAs*. San Francisco: Berrett- Koehler.

Pellegrini, E. K. and Scandura, T. A. (2008). Paternalistic Leadership: A Review and Agenda for Future Research, *Journal of Management* 34(3): 566–93.

Price, T. L. 2003. The Ethics of Authentic Transformational Leadership, *The Leadership Quarterly* 14: 67–81.

Reilly, T. 2002. Respect Builds Trust, *Industrial Distribution* 91(8): 132.

Ronen, S. and Shenkar, O. 1985. Clustering Countries on Attitudinal Dimensions: A Review and Synthesis, *Academy of Management Review* 10(3): 435–54.

Shamir, B. and Eilam, ve G. 2005. What`s Your Story? A Life-Stories Approach to Authentic Leadership Development, *The Leadership Quarterly* 16: 395–417.

Turnbull, S. 2008. From Global Leadership to 'Worldly Leadership', *LT Focus* Autumn: 1–3.

Van Knippenberg, D. 2000. Work Motivation and Performance: A Social Identity Perspective, *Applied Psychology: An International Review* 49: 357–71.

Walumbwa, F. O., Avolio, B. J., Gardner, W. L., Wernsing, T. S. and Peterson, S. J. 2008. Authentic Leadership: Development and Validation of a Theory-based Measure, *Journal of Management* 34(1): 89–126.

13
The Modern Challenges Facing Traditional Igbo Village Leadership

Onyekachi Wambu

The (male) individual as leader

The traditional and classical culture of the Igbo people of West Africa reveals a fascinating approach to the issue of political leadership. Unlike many of their neighbours in Southern Nigeria, Igbo people did not, on the whole, maintain centralized polities run by a king or any other individual strongman. In fact a popular proverb and slogan, which has been handed down as an article of faith, reveals their contempt for kings. *Igbo Enwe Eze* (Igbo have no king), the Igbo chant whenever they feel they are being bossed around too much by their neighbours or others who would be 'king' over them.

The Igbo language, according to the leading Igbo novelist Chinua Achebe, contains many words for kings. So the Igbo clearly understood the concept, but chose deliberately not to have them (Achebe, 1988, p. 112). They would also have seen a version of kingship in action in the nearby, militarized kingdom of Benin, which has been one of Africa's most dominant empires during the last 500 years.

So why did they actively reject an institution that seemed to work so well among their neighbours? Why did they avoid importing the centralizing baggage that would have accompanied such an institution?

Achebe relates two popular tales about why most Igbo communities dispensed with the institution of kingship. The stories offer important insight into Igbo attitudes about leadership. In the first, he reveals comically that in the dim past the Igbo did have kings but the institution 'fell out of use because of the rigorous conditions it placed on the aspirant, requiring him to settle the debt owed by every man and every woman in the kingdom'(Achebe, 1988, p. 112). Individuals aspiring to be king in the end abandoned their ambitions, choosing liquidity and wealth rather than the onerous poverty inherent in assuming the community's potentially endless debts and liabilities.

The second story concerns the reason the chicken became the foremost sacrificial animal in this part of Africa. All the animals had become alarmed after hearing that man suddenly demanded animal blood to appease the gods. The village bell rang out, calling all animals to a meeting to respond to this new menace. As they converged on the village square, chicken was walking casually in the opposite direction, apparently on his way to attend to some important business of his own in another village. When confronted by his fellow animals over why he was not attending the critical village assembly, the breezy chicken, according to Achebe, did a remarkable thing: 'He asked them to convey his good wishes to the assembly and, for good measure, added his declaration to support and abide by its resolutions' (Achebe, 2000, p. 15). Chicken's nonchalant behaviour and his dereliction of his collective duty and social responsibilities was duly punished by the assembly: 'After a long heated debate the animals accepted, and passed unanimously, a resolution to offer the chicken to man as his primary sacrificial animal. And it has remained so to this day' (Achebe, 2000, p. 16).

A number of ideas stand out in these two funny, but deadly serious stories which offer a glimpse into how the Igbo traditionally organized their societies and viewed leadership. The first is their suspicion of those who would put themselves forward for leadership or power, and the burden that they immediately place on such aspirants to dissuade them from wanting to rule over others. The second is their abhorrence of individual males not wanting to assume the burden of their own leadership, if only to represent or defend their own interests in the popular assembly. What fully emerges is a preference for egalitarian and flat political structures, and the embrace of an almost republican form of direct democracy for male individuals.

In fact, traditional Igbo society overwhelmingly abhorred empires, standing armies and the paraphernalia that accompanied large states. The Igbo deliberately scaled the level of their political unit to no larger than a village that had 'a popular assembly that is small enough for everybody who wishes to be present to do so and to "speak his own mouth", as they like to phrase it' (Achebe, 2000, p. 16).

When the British colonized this area of Nigeria between 1900 and 1914, they found that they literally had to conquer the territory village by village, so decentralized was the system of organization in the Igbo culture area. Bringing order to thousands of such small-scale village societies, where each person could represent themselves was a remarkable achievement, given the size of the Igbo ethnic group which, at the turn of the last century, numbered in the millions. The British effectively had to introduce a state into what had been, up until that point, a well organized stateless arrangement characterized by village participative democracy.

Blood, land and collective political leadership

Although each male individual was his own political leader, the thousands of villages were also collective social and political units. The method of aggregating individual decisions into collective actions was through the legitimating principle at the heart of these villages – blood and land.

The villages were usually constituted by related male siblings (or blood-based relationships which were invented). This real or invented family would then establish control over a communally owned patch of land, highly important in a society based on an agricultural mode of production. Male heads maintained and had sovereignty over their own households, but would share collective sovereignty of communally owned land and responsibility for the institutions needed to manage it. This arrangement promoted and sustained peace and order in the wider village.

The overwhelming common purpose and motivation of the village, as understood by convention, was to provide security for the related siblings and their extended family, and to ensure that the land was passed intact, down the bloodline to the next generation. Because everybody in the village was related through the original founding siblings, a vigorous incest taboo was enforced, and exogamy practised. Wives were married into the villages, and daughters married out to other villages that did not share a bloodline. A patriarchal system consequently evolved to limit the transfer of communal lands only to the descendents of the original founding siblings. Thus daughters from the village were denied inheritance because it was feared they would take ownership of the land out of the village with them on their marriage.

The married male descendents of the original founding siblings became the trustees or custodians of the land for the next generation, and assumed the position of the most powerful political actors in the village. They formed the legislative council, with a smaller executive and judiciary also emerging from this group. Given that legitimacy was also linked to how close one's connections were to the original founding ancestors, those who were closer to them in time, the oldest members of the community and also of the legislative council were given the greatest powers in the village – the executive power to allocate land and make sovereign decisions regarding the village. Despite in theory being an ostensible direct democracy, where each married male represented his household at the assembly and had equal voting rights, the village actually deferred to a gerontocracy because they controlled the most important elements – the allocation of common land and the important interpretation of the orally handed down common law and rules *'Omenala'* that govern the village. Within this system it was important to understand that legislative, executive and judicial power and leadership was therefore *generational* – and young married men could wait sometimes until they were in their sixties before they began to exert executive or judicial power and make significant decisions.

So all married males, their wives and children (male and female) could attend the village assembly to argue and influence debates about common village matters, but only a proportion of the assembly, married males, could then legislate, and beyond that, only an even smaller proportion in reality had executive or judicial powers. Decision-making among the legislative community of married men, and among the executive and judiciary tended to be slow and time consuming, as the aim was to build consensus around major decisions rather than simply arrive at majority decisions.

Dispersed leadership and power centres

Beyond the display of power and leadership ritually enacted at the assembly, court and other hearings, there were several other loci of what could be identified as formal centres of power and leadership which inform and influence the legislature. The first centre was occupied by a group, 'Nwanyi alu aru' (or 'married in' wives). They derived all their power and authority through marriage, and depending on their relationship within the household, had the potential to shape their husband's behaviour in the legislature, the executive or judiciary. Outside the home, they were entitled to attend village assemblies and were able to shape discussions, particularly if they had taken chieftaincy titles, but had no voting rights because they do not own land independently. Talking without power means that in reality they tended to get on with practical business at home and rarely attended assembly meetings unless the matter directly impacted them or a very serious issue was under discussion. They did, however, provide an important element of the 'civil service' for implementing decisions made by the legislature and executive, and they wielded a considerable degree of *de facto* power as a result of actually doing the work.

The second centre of power was occupied by the sons of the 'married in' women. This is the age graded younger unmarried males in the village, officially called 'Nwa afo' (sons of the soil). As the next generation, their voices were important, especially as traditionally they provided internal policing and external military functions for the village on the orders of the elders; they provided an element of the 'civil service' for implementing executive decisions; and finally, they provided the music making, wrestling and masquerades that were the physically demanding parts of cultural entertainment.

The final centre of traditional power was occupied by the sisters of the above, 'Nwa ada' (or the daughters of the soil). Unlike their brothers they were not able to inherit land because they were expected to eventually marry out, which limits their political rights. Spinsters or divorced daughters were entitled to a parcel of land to live on in the home village, but access to this land was through the 'grace and favour' of their fathers or, later on, brothers, and did not entitle them to voting rights in the village. Convention did, however, allow them a massive space for leadership and power. As a collective, the daughters of the soil were seen by the village as the final arbiters of its affairs. They had the right to intervene if there was a dispute that could not be resolved in any of the other constituted forums and the village was on the brink of tearing itself apart. It is not clear why ultimately the buck stopped with them, and they were seen as the great healers and reconcilers. The fact perhaps that they were the only group in the village who did not have an axe to grind over land, and are seen to be neutral because they were expected to live outside the village with their husband, might have something to do with it. Although convention allowed space for this leadership intervention by the daughters of the soil, it was rarely activated.

As important as it has been to describe individuals and groups with formally recognized power and leadership functions, there were also people in these villages without any formal role, and who were powerless, and played no role in the affairs of the village. The first in this category of the powerless were the 'foreign' landless families living within the jurisdiction of the village but without a blood or marriage link to the descendants of the original founders. In time (after a generation or so) these families were eventually integrated into the village story. This was usually done through the invention of a familial link to the original founding siblings, which would then effectively convert them into full citizens of the village.

The second in the category of powerless people were the outcasts or people who had broken various religious and moral taboos. These people were frequently banished from the village for long periods, effectively revoking their citizenship. Or if their sentence allowed them to remain within the village, they had their rights severely curtailed by being considered non-citizens.

As can be seen, citizenship and other core political rights were fundamentally linked to land and blood. Inheritance to the land determined the gendered nature of rights and power for men and women. So linked to blood and land were all these rights that, in the Igbo language, the word *Amadi* – 'free person' – is understood to mean: 'a male with land who lives within a community of equal peers'. Everybody else, while not quite 'slaves', are certainly not considered to have full political, or human rights.

Transition to colonial rule and independence

Today the Igbo people are between 16 and 25 million strong, making them one of Africa's largest ethnic groups.[1] They are predominately concentrated in their culture area which is located in five states in the south east of Nigeria. Just over half the population continue to live in thousands of rural villages, but increasingly the population is becoming urbanized as people drift to the rapidly expanding Igbo cities and towns of Enugu, Onitsha, Owerri, Aba and Umahia.

Significant numbers also live outside the five states of the Igbo culture area – first, in neighbouring states; second, across the rest of Nigeria, where they are industrious traders and business people; third, throughout the West African region; and finally beyond Africa, mainly in the United Kingdom and United States. Defeat and colonization by the British, and then incorporation into the Nigerian state in 1914, provided the most profound break between classical Igbo political and leadership structures and what we have today, which is a hybrid system. The British brought in schools through the missionaries, and their laws and customs. But they did not really have the men on the ground to overhaul the traditional system entirely. Instead they co-opted the traditional structures to rule, also using them to channel their orders downwards and demands from the people upwards. In this set up, 'customary law' and governance continued to have the greatest impact on the majority of peoples' lives at the village level. It was only in the new colonial constructs, the urban centres that grew up around railways and which were used as administration centres, that British rule of law came into its own.

Since independence in 1960, the Nigerian state has proved as weak as the British in having an impact on governance at the village level. The Nigerian state has formalized this weakness, and allowed the village level leadership to remain the main arbitrating structure. The Nigerian constitution allows for the 'customary settlement of disputes'.

On paper, Nigeria's laws would be grouped in the following hierarchy (international conventions, pan-African conventions, Nigerian federal law, Nigerian state law and local law and finally, customary law) with what one would expect to be the most powerful at the top and weakest at the bottom. In reality, in the rural areas the customary law category is in fact the most powerful in peoples' lives because by using it: they enter into a legal and governance structure where they deal with people they know and trust; they can speak the language and understand the culture; know that they can get relatively quick justice (unlike the Nigerian courts where people have been known to be imprisoned on remand for ten years); and finally justice is inexpensive and within their means (usually resolved by the provision of livestock or food to the adjudicating officers).

Since the intervention of the British, this traditional system has sat uneasily with the modern bureaucratic state and its paraphernalia of functionaries, politicians and other religious and civic bodies. The modern structures dip in and out of village life, mostly around national and local elections when the modern structures harness the traditional structures to deliver votes in order to monopolize control of the security services and, through them, control the oil revenues.

Villages will occasionally organize to push their sons and daughters into that national space, so they can capture local, state and national power, in order to return resources to the village. This new hybrid leader, comprising both men and women, with one foot in the village and in national politics has been evolving since the British intervention, and is one of the most interesting developments of the last one hundred years. Adaptation has however been difficult. Blood and land has proved a difficult obstacle to surmount, especially when evolving the kind of accountability demanded of politicians in a large state. How do you select/elect people in this new structure, where they are operating without the sort of trust and social capital that exists at the village level to hold people accountable? Like the story of the chicken, the Igbo have found it tricky electing leadership that can represent them in the multi-ethnic Nigerian state. As with the chicken, they have found that once you delegate power, you frequently become the 'sacrificial lunch'. So at the national level, there is a sense of every man for himself. In the last Presidential elections in Nigeria, the Igbo threw up at least eight candidates for President, while most other big ethnic groups rallied around one candidate.

The churches are one element of the modern bureaucratic colonial state that has deep roots within the villages. In the early days of colonization, as well as having a church building in most villages, they also provided education through the mission schools. In the new evangelizing and 'born again' phenomenon that has been sweeping Nigeria since the 1980s, new groups of power brokers have emerged in most villages. These are educated young men and women, who have acquired authority and legitimacy as alumni of the church schools. Such schools have been important institutions in villages for the last seventy years.

Challenges and crisis in the modern world

Due to the weakness of the Nigeria state, in the rural areas traditional leadership structures, contrary to expectation, have continued to hold sway. Over the years Igbo village elders have continued to deliver justice and other services, usually with minimal resources from the state or federal government, while the state and federal government monopolizes resources while usually delivering minimal services (ECA, 2007, pp. 20–3; Okafor, 2000, pp. 503–28; Uwazie, 1991 pp. 87–103).

A new and growing force, rapid urbanization, is however threatening to totally undermine the way village governance operates. My own village, Uhuru Umu Ekweasu is at the centre of this new storm. Uhuru lies about 5 kilometres from Aba, an industrial city of over half a million people. Aba is a polluted, chaotic eyesore, but is an important manufacturing and trading centre in Nigeria. It is a place where you can buy well-made leather goods, including shoes and handbags, and also car spare parts. It has been growing at an exponential rate and my village is becoming a suburb of this new, thrusting metropolis.

The coming of Aba is having a dramatic impact on the village. Over the last 15 years, land has begun to attract a premium price, and villagers have begun illegally privatizing and selling communal lands to 'strangers' for development. The sales have led to increased tension and disputes within the village as communal lands shrink rapidly, and, against all common law, become privatized. Most of this privatization is driven by young men, members of the village assembly. These young men are abandoning farming and are selling communal village land so they can raise capital to enable them to set up new businesses in the town. They are also frustrated by their lack of executive and judicial powers in the village, which is preventing orderly reform. They are at least 30 years from power, and are frustrated that the elders on the executive and judicial committees are not responding quickly enough to the challenges confronting the village with the expansion of Aba. So generational leadership is under immense stress in a fast moving world – where the young have become impatient.

The old men, on the other hand, whose power and authority was dependent on trusteeship over common lands, and the authority this gave them to make law, appear powerless to do anything about the sales. Determined 'privatizers' of land are taking the arising legal disputes beyond the village into the Nigerian judicial system, a location where the old men have neither the education, language skills, or money to contest the privatizations. As their role as custodians and trustees of communal land is eroded, so their political authority and leadership role is also being challenged. In the short term, neither the Nigerian state functionaries nor other leadership groups within the village have filled the leadership vacuum that has been created. What is apparent is a kind of creeping chaos and anarchy which three years ago produced a situation where there was an unprecedented total breakdown in law and order in the village. The incident triggered violence and anguish that had not been seen in the village in living memory. It led indirectly to the deaths of at least two of the elders at the hands of the younger men (Wambu, 2007, pp. 112–33).

The forces unleashed by modernization have also led to other demands from different foci of leadership in the village. The born again alumni group from the church school are demanding a greater role in village life. The group who are making the greatest challenge are the women in the village, both wives and daughters. Changes in the mode of production, urbanization and migration have also led to women wanting reform of the denial of land rights. The denial of land inheritance rights to women (which was based on pragmatic reasons when the village was a universe unto itself and people lived and died within a five mile radius) is no longer practical. If land in the village is increasingly privatized, sold to 'strangers' and no longer part of a blood pact, why cannot women inherit from their husbands or fathers? However reversing the gender discrimination against women is proving difficult, as the defenders of the status quo wrongly argue that women were denied rights not for pragmatic reasons to do with inheritance and the land being taken out of the village, but because women's inferiority was always codified in the common law and rules, *'Menial'*, which literally translates as 'conduct and the land'. Incidentally Ala, the earth, is a female deity, so the position of the defenders of the status quo is even more peculiar.

Conclusion: Enduring principles

Urbanization and modernization are producing rapid changes in the village of Uhuru. The dispersed leadership and power centres in the village appear unable to respond. Blood linked to shared land, the basis for power and civic engagement and rights in the village, cannot cope when confronted with the half million strong urban entity of Aba with its privatized land and amorphous bureaucratic structures.

Meanwhile, the dispersed leadership and power centres in the village are not talking to each other about the common threats facing them. They are also not honestly discussing the different opportunities and disadvantages that confront them separately (liberation for the young and women from generational power and discrimination, and loss of power and authority for elders on the legislative and executive council). Instead, the community is fragmenting into chaos and facing crisis. Perhaps it is time for the daughters of the soil to intervene in the power and leadership space, allowed them by convention and, pull the community back from the brink. It would mean them turning a rarely used potential and theoretical space for leadership into an actual site of struggle that would facilitate meaningful and beneficial change for the village.

Despite the challenges that the classical Igbo leadership and governance structures are facing in modern Nigeria, there continue to be enduring principles from the tradition which are worthy of salvaging. First, direct or self-representation might become increasingly attractive as the crisis of representative leadership deepens in the West, Africa and elsewhere. Like the chicken, we do not want to become the sacrificial lunch, while corporations, their lobbyists and the rich fund our representatives in order to purchase, as journalist Greg Palast would say, 'the best democracy money can buy' (Palast, 2003. Technology will enable the kind of instant referenda that could facilitate the workings of a system of direct democracy.

Second, a focus on consensus voting instead of majority voting has its advantages. The first past the post system has led to instability and conflict across much of Africa. Those who have received a minority of all votes cast nevertheless believe they have a mandate for radical or revolutionary action in religiously and ethnically diverse communities. Consensus voting is time consuming and deliberative, but the fact that it relies on constant communication between disagreeing parties and includes elements of power sharing makes it beneficial for African societies. Finally, institutionalized age grade and gender representation also widen participation. Countries like Rwanda have made great progress in constitutionally institutionalizing gender equality. Since the genocide in 1994, just over 25 per cent of Parliamentary seats are now reserved for women.[2] The law has led to dramatic improvements in terms of the level of female representation in Parliament, with 56 per cent now represented, making Rwanda the leading country in the world for giving voice to women. A similar block reservation of seats for young people would engage and involve their participation in the formal process of leadership and governance. It would provide the sort of apprenticeship system and introduction to governance and power that, at its best, the traditional Igbo village assembly provided.

End notes

1. Census figures in Nigeria are controversial, given the rivalry there is for power between the different ethnic and religious groups in the country. For nearly thirty years between 1963 and 1991, the country was unable to approve its census figures. Different regions accuse others of rigging and inflating figures, as political representation and revenue allocation from the country's oil wealth is linked to the demographic spread. The figures here are taken from the 2007 census. The 2007 census did not measure ethnic or religious affiliations, so the figures are estimates based on the numbers in the five Igbo states and Igbos living beyond these five core states, in neighbouring states and the major cities of the Nigerian federation. There is, therefore, a wide margin of error.
2. http://www.guardian.co.uk/world/2010/may/28/womens-rights-rwanda

References

Achebe, C. 1988. *Hopes and Impediments*. Oxford: Heinemann.
Achebe, C. 2000. *Home & Exile*, Oxford: Oxford University Press.
Economic Commission for Africa 2007. *Relevance of African Traditional Institutions of Governance*, Addis Ababa.
Okafor, O. C. 2000. After Martyrdom: International Law, Sub-state Groups and the Construction of Legitimate Statehood in Africa, *Harvard International Law Journal* 41(2).
Palast, G. 2003. *Best Democracy Money Can Buy*. London: Robinson Publishing.
Uwazie, E. 1991. Modes of Indigenous Disputing and Legal Interactions among the Ibos of Eastern Nigeria, *Journal of Legal Pluralism* 34.
Wambu, O. 2007. Leadership and Followership in an African Village. In O.Wambu (ed.) *Under the Tree of Talking – Leadership for Change in Africa*. London: Counterpoint, British Council.

14
Influences, Tensions and Competing Identities in Indian Business Leaders' Stories

Sharon Turnbull, Tricia Calway and K. R. Sekhar

Introduction

This chapter reports on research into the competing and overlapping leadership narratives found in contemporary Indian business leaders' stories and the implications of these findings for leadership development and knowledge in a global society. The research asked how these Indian leaders have learned to lead, what influences in their lives have shaped their leadership and what influences in Indian society have consciously or unconsciously affected their leadership thinking and practice.

It was clear from this study that Indian leadership is shifting. Western organizational practices have entered the language and practice of modern leaders and entrepreneurs, but the extent to which these either enhance or dehumanize the modern Indian workplace seems to depend on how they are interpreted and implemented. This is a study that has important repercussions and implications for leadership knowledge and leadership development in today's global world.

One of the key research questions posed was whether and how ancient leadership wisdoms are still prevalent in Indian society, whether and how they influence Indian business leaders in India and the United Kingdom, and if so in what way? The research also asked how far western leadership thinking was also evident in the leaders' values and behaviours, as well as how western education and wider global influences blend or compete with the ancient wisdoms in Indian society (whether these be eastern religious influences or secular political, social or cultural influences). Finally we investigated how the leaders accommodate or reject these potentially competing mindsets.

Social values and influences on leadership in Indian organizations – a literature review

There have been various studies of Indian values and their influences on leadership in recent years. Most are based on questionnaire-based surveys, and a number draw on and apply Western leadership theories, particularly transformational leadership to the Indian business context. Sinha and Sinha (1990) identified five social values evident in Indian organizations. These are *affective reciprocity* which means power play in terms of affection and deference; *preference for personal relationships*; *group embeddedness* where members of a group are owned and bound by personalized relationships; *duty and obligation over hedonism* based on the Hindu values of self-control and containing of impulses; and *hierarchical perspective*, illustrated by the hierarchy of the Indian gods. Kumar and Sankaran (2007) point out that *group embeddedness* is normally based on ethnic, cast and religious similarities. They also note that in India, relationships are all-important in the workplace, since work is not normally valued as an end in itself, but is only valued if it is part of a positive personalized relationship. This, they claim is balanced with the *aram* culture which means 'rest and relaxation'.

The hierarchical orientation of Indian society is a recurring theme of these Indian studies, together with the recurrent theme of leaders as gurus or teachers (Kumar & Sankaran, 2007; Rarick & Nickerson, 2008; Sekhar, 2001). The source of the 'leader as teacher' perspective appears to be the ancient text the Bhagavad Gita which advocates a 'raj-rishi' model of leadership where the king (raj) is also a learned one (rishi – a guru, a teacher). Kumar and Sankaran (2007) note that even contemporary Indian boss–subordinate relationships are often enacted as those of teacher–student. Furthermore, this is linked to the Indian preference for a personalized relationship between boss and subordinate which can often influence decision-making. R.C. Sekhar's (2001) survey of 4000 respondents from a cross-section of Indian society ranked the teacher as far ahead of all other professions in societal esteem. Interestingly, he also notes a transition in teacher style in India away from the polemical in favour of a more facilitating and reflective style. This, he suggests, may be more appropriate for the cyber age of knowledge management, and is in line with the ancient tradition of *Gautama Buddha*. The importance of the teacher–student relationship in Indian society is also found in the ancient Indian scriptures, the *Upanishads*:

> O almighty God, you protect both of us (the teacher and the student) together; you bear both of us together, may both earn the

shakti (power of learning) together, may our learning be luminous (impressive); may we never bear ill-will towards each other. (Kumar & Sankaran, 2007)

Sekhar (2001) has argued that the sources of India's ethical and leadership traditions are far broader than the three-way source of 'folkways, ancient Indian wisdom and transnational systems' proposed by Sinha (2000). He points in addition to the influences of 'the varied tribal lore of those living on the peripheries and now joining the melting pot' (p. 360) as well as to the influences of the American, French and Soviet revolutions, which he claims offered egalitarian and democratic inspiration in India. He does, however, acknowledge that despite these complex and varied influences on Indian ethics, the Gita remains strong: 'It is by far the most profound influence among the elite in India' (p. 361), in particular in its emphasis on taking decisions without selfish motives (*nishkama karma*) and in a balanced manner (*sthitaprajna*). Rarick and Nickerson's (2008) reading of the *Gita* manuscript extracts the following leadership qualities: maintaining proper role; being true to one's values; being a good role model; self-sacrifice; being kind and compassionate; acting without pride; forgiving; acting with purity; and acting in the common good.

Two further contrasting ancient literary influences on leadership in India have been identified by Sekhar (2001). The first is Kautilya's *Arthasastra* which proposes a manipulatory ethic for leaders, deemed to be close to the much later ideas of Macchiavelli. The second is Thiruvalluvar's *Kural*, a south Indian classic that propounds an ethic of trust, although it does not go as far as proposing democracy or even transparency.

Even more important than these great classics, however, is the influence of mythology on Indian beliefs and values. The century-old legend of Rama, for example, is cited as one of the most important. The legend is based on compassion and sensitivity, and lies at the root of a compassionate and sensitive leadership style, exemplified by Gandhi and still manifest in contemporary India (Sinha & Sinha, 1990). The Krishna legend offers a more pragmatic leadership style, aimed at achievement even in adverse conditions. Sekhar predicts a revival in this model as competitive forces increase. His thesis overall is that these various leadership styles tend to be combined and balanced by Indian leaders, and that it is the 'self-discipline' and wisdom of the virtuous person depicted in the Gita, combined with the ethos of democracy, that lie at the heart of Indian leadership today.

Singh and Krishnan (2005) studied the unique manifestations of transformational leadership in India, and found that fundamental social values: 'concept of *Maya*, preference for action, potential divinity, and goal of freedom – facilitate the emergence of transformational leadership' (Bass, 1985). The most frequent Indian leadership values in their study (ranked in order) were:

Nurturant (caring, dependable, sacrificing, authoritative, paternal). They posit that the *Karta* (father figure) is one of the earliest and strongest influences on the mind of an Indian. With this leadership model an organization will be viewed as an extended family.

Personal touch (personalized rather than contractual workplace relationships at the workplace, Sinha, 2000). Indians expect informality from every member of an in-group. With this leadership model an open door would be available to the in-group and relationships would extend outside the workplace.

Expertise (possessing great knowledge and experience in many fields). Unique to Indian leaders, they suggest, is the idea of being a 'master of all trades', rather than the western idea of general intelligence.

Simple living, high thinking illustrated by a Gandhian leadership style

In addition, but in smaller numbers, they found: *encouraging and accepting loyalty from followers* (again reflecting personalized relationships), *self-sacrificing behaviour* (representing the simple lifestyle and belief in duty) and *a 'giving' model of motivation* (based on the notion of fulfilling one's duty to society rather than one's individual needs).

Balancing influences of global or Western values on Indian leadership

Singh and Krishnan's (2005) study cited above was based on followers' perspectives of 250 working executives in India. Using dimensions that they deemed were unique to Indian culture, to contrast with those taken from the MLQ that are deemed to be universal, their findings suggested that 56 per cent of the leadership values identified in their study were uniquely Indian, and 44 per cent were 'universal'.

Satyavrata (2004) uses the word 'glocalization' to describe what happens when the waves of globalization 'penetrate the embankments of indigenous tradition and culture' (p. 212). This presents various problems for Indian leaders, who, as Kunnanatt (2007) has suggested are uncertain how to lead a workforce that is often at once high-tech and tradition bound. Kunnanatt's research conclusions from a study in a high-tech bank indicate that authoritarian leadership will no longer work in an educated Indian workforce, and that the follower expectations in this context are now a blend of encouraging, nourishing, empathic and emotionally supportive. This is illustrated in a recent keynote address from the Chairman and Managing Director of the Bank of Baroda in Mumbai, in which he tells the story of the business turnaround of this bank by adopting a 'policy of 'tough love'– balancing compassion with performance' (Satyavrata, 2004, p. 211) which might be seen to embody both Indian and Western leadership values.

The so-called new economy of India is preoccupying many Indian scholars and business leaders, who have posed questions about the impact of globalization, competition, the economy, and information technology on leadership. Gaur (2006) surveyed leaders from what he calls the traditional old economy alongside those from the new digital economy. While the importance given to competencies required by leaders from both groups varied only slightly, with a general upward trend in the importance of competencies, a disturbing finding was a drop from 2nd to 11th place in the ranking of integrity by the new economy leaders. Gaur offers no direct explanation for this, but does point to the recent business scandals in the western world, and warns that Indian leaders should take swift action at organizational, policy and societal levels in order to address this potentially alarming trend.

Kumar and Sankaran (2007) suggest that Indian employees are now embracing so-called global values at the same time as remaining connected to Indian societal values. Sinha and Kanungo's (1997) research concurs. However, in addition, they propose that the Indian workplace may be more able to incorporate a global/local co-existence than other cultures as a result of two sociological factors in India: the first is *context sensitivity*, that is the willingness and ability to adapt an idea or behaviour in context; the second is *a disposition for balancing*, that is avoiding extremes, and integrating or accommodating diverse considerations. Balancing is an idea that features strongly in the Bhagavad Gita (Sekhar).

Our review of the present literature in this field focuses on the findings of a number of mainly Indian scholars relating to Indian social values and their leadership manifestations. It is clear from this small Indian-based literature that societal values play a very important part in shaping leaders and leadership behaviours, but also that Western or so-called global or universal values are also increasingly an influencing factor.

Methodology

The research methodology was inductive and social constructionist in orientation. Semi-structured interviews were designed and conducted in the leaders' workplaces with a view to eliciting the leaders' stories of their leadership journeys, their values and beliefs, as well as their role models and other influences. Seventeen interviews were conducted with business leaders. Twelve of these were in India and five were first-generation British Indian leaders.

At the beginning of the interview, the leaders were asked to consider their biographical timeline, together with events that had influenced their leadership. Questions then proceeded to cover family background, education, professional experiences, and values and behaviours.

The interviews were transcribed and the leaders' stories and narratives coded thematically in order to identify emergent themes. Our analysis of the stories aimed to discover how the leaders perceived their leadership identities, how these had evolved, how these are enacted in practice and whether they implicitly or explicitly draw on specific leadership role models, legends or literatures, either from the west or the east.

We did not adopt any preconceived explanatory frameworks or categories at the interview stage. Having analysed the interview transcripts thematically we observed a number of patterns in the responses of the leaders. As these became clearer, we began to cluster the leaders into 'ideal types' in order to develop an explanatory framework that could help us to understand the differences in beliefs and values we were observing in the data. As a final stage of our research process, we reviewed the themes that had emerged in the literature review onto the findings, asking what supporting evidence we had found for prior theories of Indian leadership, and whether we had discovered any new trends or identities in Indian leadership.

Recognizing that research conducted by two western researchers can only very partially 'get under the surface' of modern Indian society with the complexities of its long history, one of our interviewees became a co-researcher during the sense-making process, and co-authored the chapter.

Findings

Following extensive data analysis, and an iterative discussions between the researchers, we found that a pattern of Indian leadership 'faces' or identities emerged:

The traditional leader

Typically these leaders were heads of family businesses in traditional businesses such as textiles. They were found to display many of the traits identified by the studies described above, in particular the studies by Singh and Krishnan (2005) and Sinha and Sinha (1990). Gandhi, and Rama were the most frequently cited role models by the traditional leaders as providing their guiding principles. On Rama, one leader summarized 'He is a personified image of an ideal man'.

Some of the recurrent themes are illustrated below in the words of the leaders.

Responsibility for family and organizational family

As found by Singh and Krishnan (2005) 'nurturant' leadership was very evident in the language of these leaders. One of the interviewees did not speak English but spoke of his leadership vocation in nurturing terms. His son translated his words about his employees as follows:

> He gave them everything and also took care of their personal lives, you know, provided them with better facilities like at the office or at home, making them aware of the right things, guiding them properly at all the stages. Being a sort of guiding light to them and providing all the facilities that are required and besides a proper salary or a proper monetary benefit, besides that he also gave them personal and moral support also, at all the levels.

Patience and the ability to listen were also presented as virtues by these traditional leaders:

> A leader should be patient, have capacity to listen to others, which is very important, I believe, because without listening to a person you cannot have proper dialogue, proper communication, and you cannot arrive at the right decision.

This illustrates well the concept of the leader as Karta (the father figure), with responsibility first to the family then to the wider family of the organization and finally to the country:

> I started earning adequately to make sure my family lived with reasonable comfort, then the vision came to grow larger and I said we must do something for our country.
> I don't know whether I am right, but what I feel is this, one should create an environment at the workplace as a family environment.

Responsibility for society and future generations

Responsibility for others and acting for the common good is another of the core tenets of the Bhagavad Gita. This was also a value lived and role modelled by Gandhi. This sense of social responsibility appeared very strongly in the behaviour and values of these traditional leaders as discussed below:

> I had the fortune of having uncles who were very socially minded, I mean absolute Gandhian in their approach to business – businesslike, very businesslike – very fair, transparent and equitable. I mean you certainly make your money. You are there to make money so, but you know that, now what comes under this modern management jargon of CSR, you know, Corporate Social Responsibility. I mean he was doing it right from way back, you know, from the Fifties, and all his brothers. Their philosophy was that I have to make enough money to put bread on my family's table; I don't have to have a Rolls Royce to go around in as long as I'm mobile I'm okay...I just feel that every little drop that we do, you know, don't wait for the Government to do this, or so and so to do this...whatever we can do on our own.

Another traditional leader spoke of 'Payback to society, payback to organisation, payback to family'.

Duty to work hard

For the traditional leaders, duty to work hard also appears to be associated with the values of the Gita. Working hard is to act as a role model for others, and to provide for future generations. It is not about material wealth. This is illustrated in the statement below which was very typical of this leadership mindset:

> Results will come with God's blessing and with your hard effort. Because without your work you will not get the blessing of God. The blessing of God will come if you have serious sincerity and you are doing your work, then God's blessing will come.

The legend of Rama presents duty and respect as interconnected, as the interpreter of one traditional leader explains:

> Rama and Sita, how they performed their duties, and it's all about the Hindu mythology. I mean Rama and Sita are a religion to us. So

he follows the character that Rama had – always rightful, respecting his parents, his teachers, his god, you know... So the things that he adopts in his daily business activities, no matter what the situation may be he wants to perform his duties in a very righteous way and a very truthful manner, being honest, taking care of his Mum.

Personalized relationships

A recurring theme in previous research studies is the preference for personal relationships (Sinha, 2000). This was evidenced strongly by the traditional leaders:

I always try to consider people, and I'm a very frank person, whatever's wrong with him I will not say it in sugar coated words, I will always tell him in really frankness, but in confidence, that this is what I feel about you.

For one leader this means being open-minded in order to achieve personal empathy:

Open mind is very important, I believe, and a man is not perfect. Unless we have an open mind, we will not be able to understand the other's perspective.

For another the essence of the good relationships at any level was 'harmony':

We should create confidence and harmony in the family and keep a very good relationship with each and every one, whether they are your close relative or distant relative or friends.

Respect and tolerance

Very much related to the idea of personalized and harmonious relationships is the importance of respect for self and others:

In India we believe in self respect but the respect of others also.

The traditional leaders showed considerable tolerance for those with other beliefs, and indeed one leader was happy to follow both Hindu and Christian teachings:

... that there are different roads and that each road has its own merit, so one has to decide which one you will pick and follow.

Even my children would still go to temple but would still say 'Our Father' before they went to bed sometimes.
Whether the person is a Muslim or a Hindu or a Christian, it doesn't matter.

Humility

The *Bhagavad Gita* expects self-sacrifice; being kind and compassionate; acting without pride; forgiving; acting with purity (Rarick & Nickerson, 2008). This is very explicitly followed in the minds of the traditional leaders:

What I feel is what Lord Krishna says in our *Gita*: 'Your job is to work without any expectations, with all humility, with sincerity and full concentration on your work'. That is your job... And it is bound to come, but that is not your sphere, that is not your field; your field is do your work with all sincerity and never bother about the riches.

The interpreter for one traditional leader states:

He says, 'I don't need any medals for what I'm doing because it's my conscience, I'm doing it with my conscience, so I don't need the recognition'.

Leader as teacher (Raj-rishi) and learner

The importance of teaching and educating followers was found strongly among the traditional leaders:

So we've got to make everyone understand and sit with them, you know, talk to them, explain things in detail so that, you know, they understand.

Without exception, all the leaders interviewed held the view that life is a journey. Learning to lead is also frequently seen as an important element of that journey, particularly for the traditional leaders, but also for the other leaders:

... at different stages of life I define leadership differently.
But I've developed myself also very much because it is a learning process. A person cannot be perfect at the beginning of his career, it's a learning process, and due to learning I have listened to so many

business leaders, I've met them during the course of my business activities, and I've tried to take the best I can take from them.

Role models for learning are also important for many. Family and spiritual role models are dominant for the traditional leaders. The sense of continuous learning is also evident in this leader's words:

> I have learned from my school days, college days and from my organization, from Gandhi, from our Chairman, I've learned with them from my wife, so this is a journey...I still feel I'm not a complete man.

Along with learning, this journey is also seen as a journey of self-improvement, associated with the Hindu notion of Karma, as well as leaving a legacy for the future:

> A person should think, analyse it, ask if I have committed any wrong thing or my decision was wrong, not just to regret it, but to improve, how to correct it, taking lessons from that, and go for that, never think why did this happen to me?
> ... he has always thought of giving a better tomorrow for the coming generations.

The modern traditional leaders

The section above described those who are transparently and consciously influenced by Indian religion, and Hindu legends, as well as Gandhian philosophy. The group that we have labelled the 'modern traditional leaders' displayed many of these values, but as a younger generation there was evidence of changes in their beliefs, and increasingly western influences in their business behaviours and values, together with a new emphasis on professional practice. The role models of these leaders combined those from Hindu mythology with world stage leaders such as Clinton, international film/cricket players and caring political leaders.

From individual leadership responsibility to collective responsibility and accountability

For these leaders the theme of responsibility is as strong as in the traditional leaders, However, in addition, we now see a shift from the concept of leader as 'person' to leadership as 'collective responsibility':

> Okay, leadership for me, when you're talking about leadership this often gives you a misconception that, you know, that if you have

to be a leader, you have to be someone at the top, or you have to be someone in the top of a hierarchy, or you have to be something different from the rest of the crowd. But to me that's not leadership. To me leadership is about taking responsibilities. And, you know, this is something which has been ingrained into me from my childhood days by my parents that you need to take responsibility for your actions and its consequences.

Furthermore, the more western idea of accountability has appeared in the discourse of the modern traditional leaders, alongside the more traditional themes of responsibility for family and organizational family:

So to me leadership is all about accountability and leadership is about responsibility. So you might be taking responsibility for the performance of a whole lot of people, or you could be in a family, you could be taking responsibility for all members of the family. You could be taking important decisions for them. You could be suggesting a lot of things to them to improve their way of life and to improve their overall happiness about things.

From responsibility to society and future generations to practical 'service' and emotional connection

These leaders have the same sense of social responsibility, but offered much more tangible and explicit examples of how they had enacted this in practice. The practical application was more widely embracing than the traditional leaders, and unlike western discourses of service, the language of practical service was infused with strong emotional connectivity with those whom they seek to serve, and genuine evidence of compassion:

One leader describes the moment when he adopted this perspective:

And I started looking at Mother Teresa and Mahatma Gandhi. They are leaders for what they are. It is not about being served but because they serve others. And this was tremendously inspirational for me, and I will never forget this lesson in my life, and if at any point of time if I ask myself do I pass this litmus test, have I stopped being served and have I started serving others.

A medical leader gives a very practical story of service to his patient:

But when a poor patient sits in front of us and says doctor, I can't afford this that and the other, we've so many times said don't worry, that's not your worry, just let's sort you out first, then you pay me whatever you can. And that's a very satisfying thing to do.

From duty to work hard to 'drive' and personal ambition

Drive and ambition were absent from the traditional leaders' discourses, but had become part of the next generation of modern traditional leaders who appeared to blend Indian with western work values. These replaced the discourse of hard work and dedication for its own sake as part of life's journey.

> If you have an ambition for which you've set your targets, then with the drive you may be able to achieve 100% of it, with half the drive you may be able to achieve only 50% of it. With no drive, you will achieve nothing.

Personalized relationships as well as collaboration and partnership

Personalized relationships and respect for others were still very evident in the enterprises in which these leaders were based:

> In the middle of an important task if someone were to come and tell me my child is ill, or my parent needs to be taken, my father needs to be taken to a hospital – I would let that person go. I wouldn't tell him look we are sitting on a very important job, this needs to be completed by evening tonight. I wouldn't do that. I would certainly probably send him with my car and tell him to drop him to the place and take all that responsibility and finish that unfinished task, but it wouldn't be at the cost of the task. But in terms of priority it would be people first and task later.

However, concurrently, a shift from the leader follower paternal model in the quotation above to a more collaborative leadership model was also evident in the modern traditional leaders. The importance of relationships in business remained quite strong, but for these leaders it was couched in a new business language of collaboration and partnerships. One of these leaders' words illustrates this shift:

> Collaborative styles of working are I think rather an important aspect of leadership, to encourage people to work in a collaborative fashion. Team spirit may be a long end of it; I'm talking about partnering. You know, if I say partnering is the universal set, team working could be a subset of that.

From humility to simplicity but also personal achievement

The traditional leaders spoke of working hard but without expectations of reward or recognition. The essence of this idea was still present for the modern traditionals, but their words depicted less of the humility of self-sacrifice as found in the Gita, and more the material simplicity as portrayed by Gandhi:

> I think it's an Indian tradition and belief that happiness lies in simplicity. We're trying to complicate our lives less, try to keep it simple and try to get our happiness out of those small things, simple things.

Sporting metaphors symbolizing aggression and personal achievement were also entering the business language of these leaders, in contrast to the previously strong emphasis on humility:

> So when it comes to nets and their practices, you, as a fast bowler, you know, aggression is always a part of you as a fast bowler...Every time I just imagine a fast bowler, brand new ball, season ball in my hand. Any time I want to do something, I think of myself, suddenly think the ball, the new ball in your hand, and what you can do with that ball to make others believe that you're good.

Leader as teacher and learning life journey – from religious to secular drivers

The desire to teach others was still present for these leaders and often acted as a personal driver for them:

> Of course we all keep learning all the time, but I would also like to give it back to the society, you know, that's the one passion which stands very deeply is to go back to teaching.

The life journey as an important driver of action and values continued to be evident in these more modern traditionals as it was in the traditional leaders themselves, although they were less likely to consciously associate it with religious belief:

> ...when you're at your deathbed, whatever age that may be, the only question you're going to think about is have I done what I should have done, and could I have done anything better than what I have? So at which time if the answers are yes, I have done what I should

have done, and I couldn't have done anything better, then you'll be the most happiest person at that moment.

This also continued to be connected with leaving a legacy: 'I am entrusted with the family's future and can not fail'.

New tensions

Integrity, transparency, honesty

In addition to the transitions noted above, a new language of integrity, honesty and transparency revealed an emerging concern for the modern traditional leaders. While these values may have been implicit in the discourses of the traditional leaders, they were not articulated as such. For this younger generation of modern traditional leaders, however, the need for integrity, transparency and honesty is articulated strongly, perhaps as a result of contemporary shifts in societal values, and their perceptions of increasing corruption.

> We would definitely like to do what we want to do without making any compromises on tenets of honesty and integrity, you know. If you feel that you are going to breach this value at any point of time no matter how wonderful the result you are pursuing but if it is a breach of honesty and integrity I would not like to pursue it even if it means it's the biggest sacrifice that I have to make.

This was the preoccupation of a number of the modern traditional leaders:

> Transparency and honesty and sincerity and those things that I mentioned to you, we want to hold on to those values. We'll never let those values go because otherwise all the achievements of life are wasted.

Hindu values in secular discourses

These leaders in transition tended to be much less explicitly religious than the traditional leaders, but nonetheless the influences of religious values were still shaping their thinking a great deal:

> Religion never really, it never came to my mind.
>   If you do not behave in the right manner, you will not be able to do the right things. So that concept of karma is philosophical, it is not religious, and the concept of dharma, that's why I said these are important

aspects for me, again that's cultural but not religious ... People talk about good corporate governance, having corporate values, that's dharma. Dharma is nothing but a code, the right way to live your life, that is dharma. Hindu dharma prescribes a certain way to live.

The modern leaders

We have labelled this group the 'modern leaders', as these are the typically young entrepreneurs who have set up or grown businesses in a rapidly growing economy. They are strongly influenced by western business language, but have also found themselves operating in a context in which they say corruption appears to have become a norm in some aspects of business and society.

In these leaders many new discourses can be heard that were not present in the previous two groups. While the old discourses are still present in weaker forms, they have to a significant extent been driven out by these new mindsets.

Interestingly the role models for these leaders were similar to those cited by the traditional leaders. However, the reasons given were different:

> Gandhi again is a brilliant example of someone who had a definite sense of purpose.
> Ratan Tata – he has a pure business mind ... he will do everything for business and there is no compromise in what he does.

Drive for success and 'winning the game'

This was an emergent discourse for the modern traditional leaders, but for this group it is an overriding preoccupation. One leader's role model was described as follows:

> He's very positive. He puts it in a positive note, and at the end of the day whatever he talks he talks a win game for all. You know, he will do everything for business, and there's no compromise in what he does.

Profit, productivity and speed

Growth and profit are also seen as preoccupying drivers for these modern leaders:

> You have to bring in profitability in the company, there's no way out. Temporarily you can go here and there but this is the road, very

clear. So you have to take this route, and this is the only route to take a company.

A new focus on measuring success was also evident:

> How we do it is productivity per square feet on a carpet area. What is the productivity we do per square feet in terms of sales – that's how we calculate it.

Whereas human relationships and an eye on future generations gave the traditional leaders a sense of time, and being on a life journey, the modern leaders were focused on speed, and showed evidence of putting themselves and their identities under some of the pressures and personal stresses usually associated with western organizations:

> I'm in a process that I finish one meeting and when I am going in the second meeting I have that other meeting still in my head, so I'm not able to change myself immediately. It's like you celebrate a birthday and all of a sudden you go on to somebody's anniversary and you have to change and say happy anniversary and... How to change this is something which I'm not able to understand. Like... I don't know how those people do that, but you're getting my point, and some days you have to go to ten meetings and you have to get into that mindset and I don't know how to convert myself so fast. That's something which I'm learning still.

A shift from an absolute to a relativist ethical position

The tension experienced by these leaders in deciding how to respond to requests for bribery was evident in all of these modern leaders, some of whom had found themselves taking relativist ethical positions, as a result of a feeling that they had no choice:

> There are certain things which are not ethical you should not do. You do it because it's a must for business. I have taken one principle in my life, and that's how I am now much more clear in what I have to do. I'll tell you the principle. Anything for business in the interests of the company please do it, in India at least, because if you get emotional, if you say this is right and that is wrong, it does not work, you become a failure in India. You cannot make a company in India otherwise. So in the interests of the company do everything; in the interests of the company, not only individual interest.

The same leader went on to explain his perception that there was no choice:

> Because in India if you tell me the law, today you cannot walk on the street, legally you cannot walk but there's no footpath. But as for the law you cannot walk on the street. But if there is no footpath what's the choice? So it's very difficult in India to say this is right and this is wrong.

This position clearly places the modern leaders in tension with the Hindu idea of 'dharma', described by one modern leader as: 'the right way to live your life … so living a principled life, that is dharma', leading them to defend and justify their actions.

Loss of family values – 'a leader of sacrifices'

The previous reliance on personal relationships and paternalistic caring for employees continued in the discourses of these leaders, but was occasionally in tension with their emphasis on people as 'assets'. This meant that: 'In the interests of the company if you have to throw somebody, please throw him, the rest of the company's going to get the benefit', but at the same time this leader had also invested in 'a growth plan for every individual'.

The focus on family values at all levels evident in the previous two groups was also missing from the narratives of the modern leader:

> There's a lot of compromise if you have to make up a business and skill up a business and in a way in a limited time. Yesterday was my son's birthday, he's now I think three years. I'll give you an example. I did not see him yesterday. So I did not see him yesterday at all, and it was his birthday. So I mean by saying that is not only at my level, a lot of senior people and actually I see a lot of sacrifice coming and I'm leading that, let me put it this way. So I'm a leader of sacrifices.

For one leader only his mother had a priority calling on his attention:

> So that's my internal principle that I feel that if my mother wants me for anything so that will be the first priority otherwise it's the company, after that my wife, children and … that is my internal decision.

From teacher to talent manager and human asset developer

Instead of the modern leaders seeing themselves in the role of teacher, their narratives were now using the Western language of human resource development and talent management, which indicates a much more detached and process-driven approach to employees, and one which sees them less as a family and more as human capital:

> I also think that the growth plan for every individual who joins the company is very very important I think, and it has to be in black and white; it cannot be on just the whims and fancies of certain department heads.

One modern leader even calculated his own value as an asset:

> I've had learning that is very different in my life, that whatever you do in your life you have to be towards the asset side of the balance sheet. So you have to be an asset as a brother, as an employee, as a teacher, as whatever... so no matter what the situation is you have to learn how to become an asset in whatever you do, and your value contribution has to count.

The global leaders

The final category identified by the thematic analysis was that of the global leaders, as a group of leaders who had travelled widely, and worked across cultures. They tended to work for large multinational organizations, or had previously done so.

Whereas in the previous three leadership types a societal and values shift had been evident, away from Hindu and Gandhian values towards a more westernized business rhetoric, the global leaders' interviews revealed a re-emergence of some of the earlier values, for example, of empathy and humanity, and a focus on ethics, but this time combined with some personal detachment, and without the clear family bonds that were evident in the traditional leaders.

These leaders possessed an eclectic range of role models including Obama, Kennedy, Bonaparte and Steve Jobs. Gandhi also featured strongly once again.

On Gandhi, one leader remarked:

> He was a consummate politician, he got the job done. He got it done in a very – he essentially left behind social capital on which we are succeeding, you know... I've just completed my 60th birthday and I'm discovering Gandhi all over again.

Communicating with empathy, humanity, fun

A more transformational leadership style is evident in the narratives of the global leaders.

> I communicate, I go to the shop-floor, start talking to people, people can rely on me, and then I talk to, you know. I do some official formal communication sometimes, but it's more in groups, interactive.

These global leaders also considered themselves less hierarchical in their relationships and believed in inspiring others through generating fun:

> When I talk to a junior person, I do not consider him junior, I talk man to man. But in India when you're talking to a junior person he's not talking, his replies are cautious and measured many times, because he's talking to the boss, 'our boss is boss'. So I like to break that.
>
> I tell them always have fun, there's fun in business. So I like to tell stories and sometimes I like to lighten the thing, you know, with a little anecdote here, a little there, to make them relax.

Knowledge and analytical skills

Knowledge was not a theme that had emerged very much in any of the other leadership groups. However, it was felt to be very important to the global leaders, and an integral element of leadership:

> That's very important, because knowledge..., you see people respect you at the end of the day because you have knowledge, you can, on the business side, you can guide them.
>
> But what helps me is my analytical skill or how I approach a problem, and so that is a value.

Integrity and the re-emergence of ethics, moderation and social conscience

The global leaders had clearly learned to adapt Indian philosophies and to blend these with ideas from Western business, in a measured and moderate way, as exemplified below:

> I mean I'm not saying plain living, high thinking, I don't believe in that. If I believed in that, I would have possibly listened to my father.

But reasonable living, reasonable thinking, you know, moderation, I think that's important in the World.

Unlike the modern leaders, some of whom felt that they had little choice, the global leaders we interviewed strongly rejected corruption and ethically relative positions, as illustrated by one of global leaders:

> Integrity is not relative. I mean if you don't cheat someone, you know. You know, I'm talking about that, so it is a basic, very, very basic value.

The global leaders were the group most conscious of the global leadership crisis.

> You know, this guy, Raju, who is now in jail, is somebody all of us my age in business in India know well, we sat on similar committees, and he has built the third largest software company in India employing some 50,000 people. We're trying to figure out what went wrong, what went wrong that he suddenly announced to the World that this company is completely bankrupt and that they claimed $2bn in cash in this company and nothing exists, it's a figment of his own imagination... So something has gone wrong with leadership that we won't know for a few years.... Right now there's a crisis of faith as to what is management, what is, you know, it seems like a big hoax.

Conclusions

The four leadership 'types' identified within the discourses of the Indian leaders were of course not discrete, and their narratives were often a combination of traditional values and modern business language. It is however clear from this study that Indian leadership is shifting. Western organizational practices have entered the language and practice of modern leaders and entrepreneurs, but the extent to which these either enhance or dehumanize the modern Indian workplace seems to depend on how they are interpreted and implemented. The hunger for success, and competitive edge is clearly a growing phenomenon for modern Indian leaders, who have recognized the potential opportunities of the growing Indian economy. However, despite the opportunity for increased wealth creation, many of the leaders have not stopped thinking about giving back to society and taking care of the weaker members of society. It is striking that the global leaders appear now to be taking over the mantle of societal responsibility from the traditional leaders, albeit in a new professionalized form.

For all the Indian leaders interviewed, business and emotion cannot be separated in the way that they perceive it being separated in the West. For many of the leaders increased comfort and material standards are important, but many also call for balance and moderation: 'The West has too much of everything and could be much happier with less.' Religious values still play an important role in Indian leadership today. Although modern leaders articulate their beliefs less frequently than the traditional leaders, the idea of leading a good life still prevails, even when they find themselves making difficult ethical decisions. Whether engaging in bribery or sacking an employee, Indian leaders find these decisions painful.

A long-term focus, the life journey of learning, the importance of investing in education for themselves and their employees and tolerance of diversity continue to underpin Indian leaders' behaviours. At the same time we found a strong will to compete and win, and a growing professionalization of the workplace, evidenced by discourses of human resources and human assets replacing the more familiar family values. Humility is still pervasive. There is little sense of self-importance in any of the four leadership groups. Gandhi's legacy of humility and simplicity are constantly moderating the thrill of the business chase, and the pursuit of wealth. Even those conscious of being caught up in the race to win, are constantly questioning the purpose of their lives, and investing in the learning and knowledge of their people.

There is however certainly a concurrent dilution of traditional values. Leadership as stewardship and organizations as families may be disappearing narratives. The open criticism by the Indian leaders of the lack of such values in Western leadership provides hope that the social capital left by Gandhi is an endemic and enduring aspect of the Indian way of life and continues to inform leadership practice in India, perhaps more than the leaders themselves would acknowledge.

It is recognized that further research is now needed, both to inquire further into some of the findings of this study, as well as to broaden its scope to a wider range of leaders both within and outside India. The implications for other countries, contexts and leadership cultures are also of interest, and replica studies in other developing economies would enrich the current findings.

References

Bass, B. M, 1985. Leadership and Performance. New York: Free Press.

Gaur, A. S. 2006. Changing Demands of Leadership in the New Economy: A Survey of Indian Leaders, *IIMB Management Review* June: 149–58.

Khandelwal, A. K. 2007. Moving HRD from the Periphery to the Centre for Transformation of an Indian Public Sector Bank, Keynote Address 4th Asian Conference of the Academy of HRD, *Human Resources Development International* 10(2): 203–13.

Kumar, M. R. and Sankaran, S. 2007. Indian Culture and the Culture for TQM: A Comparison, *The TQM Magazine* 19(2): 176–88.

Kunnanatt, J. T. 2007. Leadership Orientation of Service Sector Managers in India: An Empirical Study, *Business and Society Review* 112(1): 99–119.

Rarick, C. A. and Nickerson, I. 2008. Expanding Managerial Consciousness: Leadership Advice from the Bhagavad Gita, *Proceedings of the Academy of Organizational Culture, Communications and Conflict, 13 (1) Allied Academies International Conference*: 59–63.

Satyavrata, I. 2004. Globalization and Leadership Development for Transforming Mission in India, *Transformation* 21(4) October: 211–17.

Sekhar, R. C. 2001. Trends in Ethics and Styles of Leadership in India, *13th Annual Conference of European Business Ethics Network* 10(4): 360–3.

Seshadri, D. V. R., Raghavan, A. and Hegde, S. 2007. Business Ethics: The Next Frontier for Globalizing Indian Companies, *Vikalpa* 32(3) July–September: 61–79.

Singh, N. and Krishnan, V. R. 2005. Towards Understanding Transformational Leadership in India: A Grounded Theory Approach, *Vision – The Journal of Business Perspective* 9(2) April–June: 5–17.

Sinha, J. B. P. 2000. Integrative Indigenous Management in India, *Indian Journal of Industrial Relations* 35(4): 439–60.

Sinha, J. B. P. and Kanungo, R. N. 1997. Context Sensitivity and Balancing in Indian Organizational Behaviour, *International Journal of Psychology* 32(2): 93–106.

Sinha, J. B. P. and Sinha, D. 1990. Role of Social Values in Indian Organisations, *International Journal of Psychology* 25(5/6): 705–14.

15
The Competing and Paradoxical Identities in the Narratives of Twenty-First-Century Russian Leaders

Vasilisa Takoeva and Sharon Turnbull

Introduction

This chapter presents findings from research that has explored the competing identities of modern Russian leaders. It aims to identify leaders' values and beliefs, and deconstruct how these have been shaped by their personal experiences and the wider historical (political, social and cultural) context. The analysis is based on the stories of 26 interviewees – fourteen business leaders, eight social activists and four political leaders – obtained between December 2009 and January 2010.

There is a strong connection between a nation's history and culture and its observed leadership. Therefore, one of the key research questions in this study has been what influence the major changes in Russian society (which started almost 20 years ago) and the preceding history have had on its leaders, what identities have emerged from these experiences and how individuals deal with the tensions in their values and beliefs that have resulted from this transition. The purpose of this chapter is to present what is consciously or unconsciously influencing the leaders' thinking and practice, and to draw lessons from Russia about leadership identities in transition in a rapidly changing political and economic world.

Over the last 20 years, leadership and management in Russia have been exposed to a significant shift. Research has consistently shown that Russian culture differs from Western culture (Bollinger, 1994; Fey et al., 1999; Grachev, 2009) and continues to undergo further changes

(Ardichvili & Gasparashvili, 2003). Since its emergence into the capitalist world, Russian society has embraced a world view that directly contradicts what was accepted for over 70 years. Unlike today's Chinese leaders, contemporary Russian leaders do not have a pre-communist point of reference for their business values, and therefore are more likely to adopt Western knowledge and practice (Alexashin & Blenkinsopp, 2005). It is this combination of old 'habits' and newly acquired learning, and the apparent associated inconsistencies in behaviours that makes 'any attempt to decipher Russian business leadership styles an unnerving task' (Kets de Vries et al., 2004, p. xiii).

In the literature review, we have specifically focused on publications in the English language from both Russian and external authors. The first western publications appeared in the early 1990s as an attempt to portray 'the Russian bear' (Puffer, 1994) and observe Russia through the lens of Western theory and experience. At the other end of the scale are endeavours by Russian researchers to present and interpret the reality from within the context. The aim of our research has been to bridge the gap between research carried out by 'insiders' and 'outsiders' and investigate Russian leadership using a qualitative approach in order to deeply explore the identities of the Russian leaders in our study.

Historical background

Russian culture today is a product of its history, and the impact of the 70 years of communist regime is yet to be evaluated fully. During that time, the occasions of interaction between Soviet people and the West were rare, and the Western world struggled to understand their behaviours often seen as a 'bizarre combination of opposing qualities':

> ...cruelty and warm-heartedness; curiosity and dogmatism; anarchism and adherence to a strict social order; laziness and bursts of energy; erratic behaviour and great patience; disorderliness and passion for meticulous planning; caution, aversion to risk, and foolhardiness. (Mikheyev, 1987, p. 493)

Exploring Russian features, Kets de Vries (2001) refers to the 'clinical paradigm' that assumes that behind every irrationality lies a rationale, and brings into focus the Russian national character, the 'habitual ways in which a person deals with external and internal reality' (p. 589). The behavioural and mental patterns observed today in this society are transmitted across generations and deeply rooted in pre-communist history, as well as in the seventy years of socialist education. He argues that, as the result of harsh circumstances of their lives, Russian people possess extreme endurance and stamina and have the tendency to accept suffering silently at present, yet they embroider the past. Suppression of the 'true self', traditionally starting in early childhood through baby swaddling, 'moral upbringing' and strict discipline in the educational institutions (school, universities etc.) and simultaneous permissiveness and overindulgence within families that aimed to balancing the hostility of the outside world, led to creation of further internal conflict and further separation of the *private* and *public* self.

According to de Vries, the Communist propaganda of egalitarianism enforced a collectivist mentality, disrespect for private property, and the need for affiliation to a social group. An atmosphere of distrust and fear during both pre-communist times and later led to strong emphasis on friendship and relationships in business ('personal loyalty is much more important than fair play' (p. 607)), and great care for intimate comrades, with whom Russians are capable of great emotional expressiveness. De Vries suggests that a combination of *Oblomovism* (inclination towards phlegmatic and passive life stance) and passion for 'beauropathology' (control at every level) created the feeling of impotence and lack of power over one's life. At the same time, the necessity to keep processes going developed the skills of interpreting the laws and avoiding prohibitions. The Russian saying 'Everything is allowed that is not forbidden' is a precise representation of this norm.

Similar to the origins of *private* and *public* self as seen by de Vries, Mikheyev (1987) describes the socialisation process in the Soviet Union happening through three channels of influence: 'street', 'school', and 'family'. Each imposed contradictory values, standards and limitations. Therefore when acting, Soviet individuals followed a code corresponding to the situation and person they faced; these are supported today by observations that Russians show 'two sets of ethical standards' (Puffer, 1994, p. 47). Both physical and social environments are assumed to be hostile and dangerous, and therefore the creation of a narrow circle of intimate friends is vital for survival and use of the personal networks for getting things done (see Ledeneva 2008, 2009 for a discussion of the origins and meaning of *blat* in Russia).

Schooling was one of the central channels of political and moral education and thus was regarded as an important part of one's upbringing (Mikheyev, 1987), and there has traditionally been high emphasis and respect for education in Russia. Hopkins (1974) studied the teaching of literature in the schools of the USSR and concluded that the emphasis on these lessons was unmatched elsewhere. While in primary school reading was used to improve children's awareness of language, later on this became a tool of learning about the reality. The soviet writings provided information about the ideals of the time; classics were critically analysed to illustrate the 'struggle of people under the Czars'; and the foreign literature presented the faults of capitalism.

Shift in the economic system

In the 1990s the country fell apart and stepped away from centralized leadership. The sharp transition from a planned economy to an open market provided unexplored investment opportunities for Western business and exposed unprepared people to almost unlimited entrepreneurship possibilities (Kets de Vries et al., 2008). As a result, the directors of Soviet enterprises had to adapt overnight to a new range of roles – 'efficient managers, entrepreneurs, accurate forecasters, legal system monitors, astute negotiators, careful evaluators, accountable leaders, and self-motivators' (Ivancevich et al., 1992, p. 43). Not surprisingly, when in this 1992 study managers were asked what characteristics make a successful leader, the most important factor appeared to be 'knowledge of economics'.

This also required fast changes in individuals' leadership and management styles. Examining four leadership traits known to be efficient in the United States – *leadership motivation, drive, honesty and integrity* and *self-confidence* – Puffer (1994) showed that the period of transition in the early 1990s required changes in all the criteria. Russian managers had to adapt their practices from a highly vertical authoritarian soviet style of micro-management and extreme control to shared decision-making and delegation; from a habit of feeling ashamed by their own ambitions and successes to being proud and outstanding winners; from finding ways to circumvent the strict rules dictated from above to clear and transparent relations. The development of the latter, however, was confronted by many obstacles, including unclear public policy and an unhealthy atmosphere in the business environment (Kets de Vries et al., 2008). This also led to the continued instability in self-confidence, which varied from 'cynicism about their ability to solve problems, to over-promising what they can actually deliver to their business partners and clients' (Puffer, 1994, p. 50).

Over the last twenty years, these changes have caused cultural gaps between generations. Fey et al.,(1999) identified a 'two-work-faces' challenge for managers in Russia: those younger than 30 had not had the negative experiences of the past which affected people over 40, and 'these two groups have very different expectations and concepts of the nature of the company and the context in which it operates' (p. 49). However, having interviewed CEOs across Russia, Ardichvili et al., (1998) found that the age group identifying themselves most frequently with the autocratic leadership style are those between 30 and 40 years old, and not the 'over 40' group that one might expect; none of the participants below the age of 30 preferred that style; and the majority of leaders (56%) claimed they had a 'situational' style, fluctuating between autocratic and democratic styles when needed.

Reports also suggest a dynamic change in women's positions and a distinctive female leadership approach in Russia (Gvozdeva & Gerchikov, 2002). Research has shown that women were 'too equal' under the Soviet Union (Puffer, 1994), and their position has relatively worsened during the times of transition (Metcalfe & Afanassieva, 2005; Izyumov & Razumnova, 2000), mirroring the findings from the GLOBE project (Grachev, 2009).

Organizational culture

The Russians are known for their desire for strong leadership, and balancing it with employee involvement is not an obvious task (Fey, 2008); politically, perhaps a combination of these two is the reason for the existence of a *centralized democracy* (Kets de Vries, 2000). At a deeper level, reasons for preferences for strong leadership could be learned helplessness and identification with aggressors (Kets de Vries, 2000) within the atmosphere of lack of trust (Fey et al., 1999; Engelhard & Nägele, 2003) and volatility of external environment.

Fey and Denison (2003) note that Russians want someone else to make decisions for them and are also keen to blame someone else for their failures. In this environment, two factors that have the highest influence of organizational effectiveness are adaptability and involvement (Fey & Denison, 2003). In turn, effective involvement and psychological empowerment are dependent on trustworthiness of their leaders (Barton & Barton, 2010), especially with the strong emphasis in Russia on personal relations. Fey et al. (1999) note that team-working is natural for Russians, who value friendship, social contacts and equality at work, and since they value peers' opinions higher than their manager's views, even lazy Russians are likely to work harder if their peers do.

This combination of contradictory observations is summarized by the results of the GLOBE studies (Grachev, 2009):

> ...the attributes that Russians believe contribute to effective organisational leadership display a rather mediocre profile that is far from outstanding, value-based, charismatic behaviour; instead it is extremely pragmatic and quite professional. This explains the societal acceptance of assigned rather than elected leaders at different levels of the social hierarchy and the level of obedience in economic life. (p. 10)

Leadership identities

The methodology of our study was designed to capture the multiple competing identities exhibited and experienced by the leaders we interviewed, and to understand how these identities are enacted in their leadership. In recent years, there has been growing attention to studying leadership and leadership development from an identity perspective, and to analysing leadership as a relational interaction between 'leader' and 'follower' (Luhrmann & Ederl, 2007; DeRue & Ashford, 2010). Luhrmann and Ederl (2007) suggest that one has to differentiate between the situated identity *as* a leader and the general identity *of* the leader: the latter is constructed and refined through years of social relations and becomes a relatively stable part of one's self-system, the former is constructed and activated in a specific situation, for a particular audience.

Day et al. (2009, p. 298) define identity as 'the culmination of an individual's personal attributes, values, knowledge, experiences, and self-perceptions'. Markus and Wurf (1987) argue that some self-conceptions are core and salient and are better elaborated and therefore affect behaviour more powerfully than peripheral and less well-elaborated self-conceptions. Therefore, a working identity consists of a combination of core conceptions that are more or less stable and peripheral conceptions that are developed to respond to the context. Despite the fact that there is evidence of a positive relationship between the number of identities available to a person and their mental health, the question of what happens when these are incompatible remains open (Markus & Wurf, 1987). Shaw (2010) suggests that separation between the existent and the narrative identities happens through separation of the narrator from the narrative, and therefore, it is possible for different life stories to exist simultaneously.

A leader identity can be seen as 'how one thinks of oneself as a leader; the subcomponent of one's identity or self-concept related to being a leader' (Day et al., 2009, p. 302). Scholars propose that a leadership identity is developed at three levels: individual, relational and collective (Day & Harrison, 2007; DeRue & Ashford, 2010). While individual self-concept is based on one's perceptions of particular experiences or personality traits associated with leaders or leadership and differentiate the person from others, the interpersonal aspect is based on recognized relationships with other people that they would identify with followership. Finally, at the collective level, an individual identifies themselves with a particular group or organization.

Korotov (2008) describes the challenges of accelerated leadership development in Russia and notes the need for leaders to develop a leadership identity and reinvent self, which includes doing new things, setting up new social networks and re-establishing the new self through a new story.

Methodology

Our research methodology was inductive and based on narrative inquiry. We conducted 26 interviews, comprising: 14 business leaders, 8 social activists and 4 political leaders. These were deliberately conducted prior to conducting the literature review. The design of the semi-structured interviews was focused around the 'biographical time line' of each respondent (i.e. the key moments in their lives that they felt had influenced their leadership) and in particular were focused on the influence of their personal experiences (e.g. family, school, sports, education, employment, politics, society) on their leadership thinking and behaviours (Shamir et al., 2005; Kempster, 2009).

All the interviews were carried out in Russian and recorded for further analysis. Even though some of the interviewees spoke fluent English, this decision was made to enable understanding of leadership language in its context (see Schedlitzki, Chapter 2 of this volume). As often happens in Eastern Europe (Hollinshead & Michailova 2001), when Russian business environment borrows words from the Western context, their interpretation might be different from the 'original' Western concepts (Kets de Vries, 2000; Khapova & Korotov, 2007; Holden et al., 2008). Understanding of differences in languages and deep cultural awareness were found to be crucial both for the Russian educational context (Gilbert & Cartwrite, 2008) and business (Engelhard & Nägele, 2003; Camiah & Hollinshead, 2003). We aimed to capture the specifics relating to the Russian language used to describe leadership and its relationship to culture (Schedlitzki, this volume).

The interviews were transcribed and translated by the Russian researcher, and the analysis was conducted jointly by her and a British researcher. This combination of an insider and an outsider was exceptionally beneficial, as on the one hand, the Russian researcher brought knowledge of the culture, understanding of language and ability to interpret language expressions and logic transitions; on the other hand, the British researcher was in a position to notice and question things that were normal and assumed for the insider. In these discussions, the narratives were coded thematically in order to identify emerging themes.

We did not adopt any preconceived explanatory frameworks or categories at the interview stage, and following a similar methodology to our study of Indian leadership (Turnbull et al., Chapter 14 this volume), we aimed to investigate patterns in the leaders' stories, developed our themes and finally we reviewed the themes in relation to the existing literature.

Most of the leaders were based in Moscow; however, some participants come from other cities in Russia (e.g. St-Petersburg, Grozny, Togliatti, Yekaterinburg etc.). They were aged from 24 to 56, and had various educational and professional backgrounds. Thirteen interviews took place face-to-face in Moscow, and 13 were carried out on Skype due to geographical dispersion of the participants. Most of the participants had changed their career several times.

Identities of Russian leaders

As our analysis and sense-making progressed we noted a number of recurring themes in the narratives of the leaders. In their stories and metaphors, definitions and language we found five 'ideal types' of Russian leadership. These leadership identities were not discrete and most of the leaders exhibited many of these, depending on the situation and context. On occasion these identities created tensions for the leaders.

Leader as builder (Figure 15.1)

In my understanding leadership is an ability to shape the picture of the future; that is, to shape, to see the picture of the future and to organise people around in order to build this picture; and to be able to build this picture. *(Young Political Leader)*

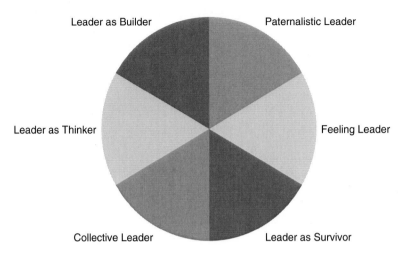

Figure 15.1   Leader as builder

A recurring theme in the leaders' stories was the need to create or build an entity that would last into the future, and a sense of responsibility to create, or 'build' something to enhance the world:

> You have to leave something after you in this world. You can build with your hands, you can build with your head, you can build in a group of people or on your own, but you have to leave something in this world. Simple living of 80 years 'consuming' good – this is not [bringing] value, even if you do it better than the others. Because the first value is spending your potential and knowledge to the humanity. *(Senior Business Leader)*

> Earning money is a very pleasant and useful activity, but it should not be in the first place. If in the first place is earning money – he is a bad leader; this is a mere imitation. In the first place should be building something. Something he wants to build, this should be ... And it does not matter, whether you would be a leader above the laws or a leader of society. You have to understand what you want to build. *(Senior Business Leader)*

This need to create a legacy is likely to be rooted in the discourse adopted during the Soviet era, when the whole nation lived their lives in order to 'Build Communism'. Mikheyev (1987) regards the 'The Moral Code of a Builder of Communism' to be one of those conflicting Super Codes ('set of the highest and most general principles of societal conduct prescribed usually by religious doctrines', p. 501) that influenced young Russians in the process of their socialization.

The Leader as Builder thinks about the long-term impact of their leadership, and needs a sense of purpose in their activity. The Communist discourse about a bright future but hard present is today regarded as mere mockery and therefore people do not talk about it explicitly. However, it appears that this focus on social well-being still remains in the consciousness of many Russian leaders:

> Principles are...well, first of all they are based on the consequent realisation, and therefore, on the long-term-ness of all this. Because if we keep thinking only about tomorrow and do not think about consequences in the future, then...we will have a [wrong] long-term result. *(Young Political Leader)*

> The leaders in life – in politics, in business, spiritual ones – are those leaders who stay leaders for long period of time, and then really enter history. *(Senior Business Leader)*

One of the historical figures who was mentioned several times in the interviews as an example of good leadership is Peter I (the Great). When asked for the reasons, the participants pointed out *the results* of his activity and his ability to realize his goals:

> So, firstly, this is *courageous imagination*, and secondly, *impeccable realisation. (Senior Business Leader)*

> This was the person who grieved for Russia, who could, who wanted, *who did a lot. (Senior Social Leader)*

As discussed above, Russian people prefer strong leadership, and most often, strong leadership is associated with a combination of care and cruelty for the people, as the latter might be needed in order to achieve the ultimately 'caring' goal. Our research found an inherent expectation that leaders must achieve goals irrespective of the means.

> The goal must be realised, the task that I face. This is one of the major conditions, the goal must be achieved *(Senior Political Leader)*

And a leader who cannot achieve the goals is not a leader, but rather a…. windbag. *(Senior Business Leader)*

A number of the leaders suggested that this identity was created by the environment of a developing market, where people faced 'an empty field' in most areas of economics and society and had to build their business from scratch:

> I think a motivating factor was us moving to a different city, and the necessity to build something from scratch was objective. Building your everyday life from scratch, building your company from scratch, building your business from scratch – at that time that was absent in the country. *(Senior Business Leader)*

> I think that childhood and, partially, youth spent in the USSR, they influenced a lot people of my age and older. Because when you have practically nothing and then you have the choice 'To have nothing or to have more than nothing' – then I suppose people… people who were born in the USSR are more focused and firm of purpose than those born even in Russia. *(Young Business Leader)*

Leader as survivor

> Most likely, the essence of leadership is to bring something new in and stand up for this new, because it is important to defend it. *(Young Business Leader)*

For many of the leaders interviewed, leadership means survival and adaptation, looking for new solutions to problems, and using their creativity and flexibility to do so. The *survivor* identity of Russian leaders focuses them on becoming resilient and is often accompanied with toughness in their decisions and actions:

> That stress resistance, the theory of survival… Let's say, they [Russian leaders] get up much quicker after being hit. Let's put it this way: my 'ultimate stress limit' is often somewhat higher than most of the [foreign] acquaintances I work with. (*Young Business Leader*)

> We, Russians, generally speaking, are quite stress-resistant. We are considerably better suited for managing difficult unforeseen situations. And also we can solve them… when we are being pushed to the river… and then a Russian becomes super-efficient, "super-resilient". That is, you can hit him with your leg on his head, but he will not

care about it and will still stand up. He becomes very creative, his 'inventiveness' goes over the top. But unfortunately in order to make Russians behave in this way, you have to push them to the river. And if they are not pushed against a river, they will be lying on an oven for 33 years and do nothing *[reference to a Russian folklore story]*. *(Young Business Leader)*

Drawing on multiple illustrative examples from the history, Kets de Vries (2001) states that 'in spite of (or perhaps because of) the harsh circumstances under which the Russians have lived, predominantly on vast, empty plains or on the Siberian taiga, Russians are a people of enormous endurance and stamina' (p. 595). An assumption of hostility of both social and physical environment has meant that one of the basic attitudes in the Soviet mentality is the perception of life as an incessant struggle for survival (Mikheyev, 1987).

The leaders we interviewed considered that the ability to survive, look for solutions and continue one's existence during hardship and times of trouble would not be possible without creativity, flexibility and the ability to adapt quickly to the situations.

The quality of creativity is not developed anywhere else as strongly as in Russian leaders, and orientation /navigation within a hard situation too. The reason for this is that in a situation of full frustration, people had to do something, to survive, to remain people and to achieve something in their lives. We have a very extreme style of leadership that develops skills of risk management way better than in Europe or in America. *(Young Social Leader)*

They [Western leaders] lack, using one word, 'mother wit' – practical common sense, that is, an ability to find an unusual and non-standard solution where normally they [foreigners] use template, like, there is a definition of a problem – and that's how you should act. And they do not always understand that sometimes you might act a bit differently. *(Young Business Leader)*

Well, here you have to mention the word *manoeuvring*, because it does not always happen that you go straight the way you thought something. Well, of course, it might happen as well. So, be constantly ready, be always ready to change in all possible ways and solutions ... *(Senior Business Leader)*

A possible echo of this habit of *manoeuvring* with a view to achieve a goal comes out in the form of a reported relativistic attitude towards morality and acceptance of double standards towards enemies and friends (Mikheyev, 1987). The interviewees spoke about 'the rules of the game' and a necessity to establish them daily as they work:

> At first, in every team you have to establish rules, right? At first, we have to understand how we do things; we agree on the rules. This is the starting moment. *(Senior Business Leader)*

> The rules of the game. Let's call them 'rules of the game'. They are established there [in the West]. That is, there you have to understand that the rules of the game are clear. A Russian leader, from my point of view, is not a profession and even not a gift, but rather tightrope walking. That is, in addition to making a certain path to become something significant in the West, here you face continuously changing rules of the game. And these are on the edge of art. *(Senior Business Leader)*

As a result of the constantly changing environment, Russian leaders have to take and retain control over situations and be prepared to act tough and quickly if it is required so:

> Next, this is tough control of the process, any process. If you loosen and do it on trust, you lose the threads of management and then be prepared that, this might lead to a big set-up [from outside]. There has to be control, analysis and control of any situation. Simply, there must be a habit of constantly keeping yourself in up-to-date state. *(Senior Business Leader)*

> To a certain extent you might argue over the matter of Russian leaders. But what you cannot deny about Putin – his decisiveness and goal-orientation; because I simply do not see in leaders that toughness and goal-orientation, decisiveness and consistency in many Western. *(Senior Business Leader)*

> There is no coercion or compulsion, but the higher person rises [in the hierarchy], the tougher are the moral-ethical problems that he solves, at least here. *(Senior Business Leader)*

Leader as thinker

> I would say, the closest [synonym to the word 'leader'] would be 'a teacher'... [And in business] surely a teacher too! *(Senior Business Leader)*

The third identity of the Russian leaders we interviewed emphasizes education, mental outlook, intellectual and analytical capabilities and ability to make quick and justified decisions. The quote above represents this interpretation of a leader's function: a leader is someone who knows what to do and shows this to others. The other interpretation of the word 'Uchitel' (teacher) is 'the Master' (as in religious studies); additionally, this can be used as one of the words for spiritual leaders, and in recent years, gurus. There are two dimensions to this identity as constructed by the leaders we interviewed: one, the leader has to be intellectually gifted and able to think in systems and solve complex problems; two, a leader has to have a certain level of cultural awareness, knowledge of literature, music and the like and general wisdoms of the world.

Strong emphasis on education in Russian society and having adequate training and experience was a recurring theme in all the interviews we analysed. This theme sometimes also emerged in responses to the question, 'What is good leadership?':

> By the way, I liked Putin when he was the President... Why do I like him? Because having a good degree, and even in the KGB school where he studied, there still were very good professors. And I think that he received a good education. At the same time it also seems to me that one of his main merits is that he lived in Germany for quite a long time. I don't know for how long, five years? Maybe even more. And the person simply saw... Although I was there, in Eastern Germany – this is almost the Soviet Union by 50%. But he saw other people, a different society, another culture and at least speaks other languages. It seems to me that it is very important for a leader, both for a leader and for a formal manager, any formal manager: the one of a country, of a company, of a kindergarten – for environment. *(Young Business Leader)*

> Well, an uneducated leader is some kind of nonsense for me, unless we speak about some bandit groups or street gangs, then an uneducated leader is nothing. Well, I cannot even imagine this, it's like... I do not know, 'un-buttery butter'. *(Young Social Leader)*

First of all, they must have good education, a good mental outlook. Without education one cannot have mental outlook. *(Senior Business Leader)*

The leaders we interviewed regarded expertise and knowledge as a necessary prerequisite for the followers' perception of them as leaders, but they suggested that this should always be combined with hard work and displayed through a record of successfully accomplished projects:

A leader is first of all a huge 'ploughman', who works very much himself and is striving to be very competent... You are a leader not because you speak loudly, not because you are tall, you are big – look at me, I am a complete opposite. If you are young, beautiful, you studied in Harvard, and have all those certificates on the wall... No. A leader, first of all, has to know what he has to do and how to do this. *(Senior Business Leader)*

The central theme for the leader as thinker identity is their ability to analyse the situation, using their intellect and giving great attention to details around them. One of the possible explanations for such deep respect for education might be found in the Soviet mentality. Mikheyev (1987) suggests that in order to be prepared to act outside one's safety zone, Russian leaders have to possess a wide set of instruments. This is mirrored in interviewees' discussion of the qualities of a good leader, the value of exact sciences and the importance of investigating a problem and relevance of knowledge to assess a current situation:

Undoubtedly, the second [quality of good leadership] is, and most likely it came to me from the technical university – and in general technical university fortunately disciplines your brain, and it's absolutely clear that you can never solve a problem correctly if its definition is wrong. If problem definition is correct, sooner or later, with bigger or smaller difficulties, with mistakes, but you will solve it. *(Senior Business Leader)*

I knew that knowledge for knowledge does not result in any effect. Knowledge has to be applied to something, based on some experience. *(Young Political Leader)*

I think in general, that 90% of people should first finish a technical university, and only then go and work as painters or film directors, they do it better then. *(Senior Business Leader)*

Moreover, education was often seen as the necessary or even sufficient quality needed for the success of Russia as a country in the future:

> What leaders [Russia will need in the future to succeed]? Clever normal people. *(Senior Business Leader)*

> They [future Russian leaders] have to gain education here in Russia and gain corresponding second education abroad. They have to have professional experience here in Russia and there, abroad. *(Young Political Leader)*

Inevitably, this long-standing intellectual emphasis of the leadership function had an impact on the practices managers adopt. Above we mentioned the tendency of Russian people to beat the system, and carry out subtle strategies rather that open battles. Similarly, in a number of interviews, description of leadership and management processes and decision-making were presented as a manipulation or a game:

> Manipulation is guessing the desires of the masses, of those who you work with *(Senior Business Leader)*

> Churchill [is an example of good leader]. He could calculate in advance, he was able to use even his enemies. Let's say, he could be friends even with his enemies. That's why he is a genius manager, a genius politician, a brilliant diplomat. *(Young Political Leader)*

Alongside intellectual technical abilities of problem solving, it was deemed important for the thinking leader identity to have common-sense knowledge, be aware of day-to-day wisdoms, and have an open mind and a broad cultural outlook. For example, a necessary prerequisite of a good leader having a good breeding and wide erudition, being aware of culture:

> [He is a good leader because] he has good education, because he has good breeding, because he is informal...because, let's say he has a broad / unblinkered mind, if you can say so. *(Young Political Leader)*

The feeling leader

> I think that Leadership is attitude of a person towards oneself. First, he has to respect himself. Second, believe in his own powers and be

sure in himself... And he needs to think in a positive way... *(Young Business Leader)*

The feeling leader is responsible for the internal harmony of the followers and their emotional welfare, as well as their higher values and fit within general life. This identity appears to be linked to the 'private' self, which appears at the moment of separation of 'safe' family life and the unpredictable unreliable life outside one's home. As Kets de Vries (2001) notes, 'prone to extravagant mood swings, they can be extremely cold, controlled and even rude in a public setting, but they exude great warmth among friends' (p. 608). Although this is a nation of stoics, a lot of them are also romantics, and 'they have an intuitive understanding of the human heart and the tragic sense of human life' (p. 609); but this emotional introspection might lead them to impulsiveness or even self-destruction. The other feature illustrated in this quote is the unstoppable optimism of Russian leaders, belief in a bright future, which, however, might swing into crushing pessimism.

This concept of Russian soul (*dusha*), a term denoting warmth and emotional openness of people, was repeated frequently when the interviewees expressed their views on the culture and mentality and strength of the nation:

The Russian soul can never be regulated. *(Senior Business Leader)*

And another thing – Russians is a nation which is, however paradoxically this would sound, 'soulful'. I suppose, one can learn from us this warmth. *(Young Business Leader)*

I think, there are several things that are in nature of Russian people but not in nature of the outside world. This is some sort of sensuality. Not this cold Anglo-Saxon weighted hypocrisy, but sensitivity... In some way, some sort of 'craziness'. I don't know what is a right Russian word for this... Emotion... Openness, absence of anxiety about possible mistakes that they make. Acceptability of making mistakes. Infatuation... Not for business, for humanity. *(Senior Business Leader)*

Relating one's activity with their values, beliefs and sense of purpose means looking for own path, much associated with the Eastern approach to life. It also means maintaining inner balance and calmness, listening to one's own heart and intuition in making decisions, and trusting them:

There is the difference between western-oriented and eastern-oriented models; because I cannot recall a point in my past that would have influence. The thing is that eastern history is cyclical in general, and every point is connected to a whole lot of others. That is, any event that happened in my life, either in my personal side, some sort of love anxieties or some career anxieties, they are still perceived by me as a part of a general plan or some integrated scheme. *(Young Social Leader)*

Another recurring theme in several interviewees' reflections over their lives was that taking a leadership position or finding themselves in that role was to a certain extent a surprise or something defined by their destiny or higher purpose. This much supports both the view expressed by Kets de Vries (2001) about Russians' perception of their lives being subject to great forces out of their control, and more Eastern-oriented understanding of life, purpose and destiny.

Still it's hard to hold back your nature's character [and not act like a leader] *(Senior Political Leader)*

So it happens in my life that I have never achieved anything, never asked for anything. But if suddenly I even think of asking something – once I asked my CEO when the project would be over. So, if I ever ask for anything, this means that I will never receive it. *(Senior Business Leader)*

The Feeling Leader identity is largely shaped by family, the warmth and indulgence that children would receive there as opposed to the strict outside world (Kets de Vries, 2001). In fact, as the quote below illustrates, for most of our participants, earlier family stories were vital for their views, their understanding of leadership and the future choices they would make:

For me the history of our family, our clan is very important. There were people in our family who I would consider to be leaders, who set an example for me. Leaders, managers, and in different positions, with different tasks, facing different choices, and I heard discussions about these questions, heard about the challenges that they faced, and of course I would start thinking. I heard about decisions that were made and how this was discussed. *(Young Business Leader)*

Keeping inner control and gripping emotional self were seen as an important skill for the Feeling Leader identity. From some of the interviewees' stories it became clear that they saw self-awareness as the key to survival in a hostile environment:

> This is a very important to understand your place in this world. You must not belittle your own significance. This happens either this is from foolishness, or from slyness. And neither of them are right. But at the same time, it's not efficient to exaggerate your significance either, because sooner or later this is bound to lead to "full failure". *(Senior Business Leader)*

> There should be no euphoria in your soul. The minute you start celebrating, you can expect the first set-up / 'road racket' behind the corner. There are a lot of managers who you know, have just left the coast... 'Yes, guys, this is cool!' *(Senior Business Leader)*

The collective leader

> [Leadership is] an ability to feel the future or an ability to feel what has already happened; and an ability to catch the course of things and an ability to follow this course and to help, to show this course to other people, not turning this into a huge thing and not focusing people's attention on yourself. *(Young Social Leader)*

This identity is centred around fairness, justice and humility or equality, and is mirrored by Mikheyev's (1987) conclusion on one of the features of the Soviet mentality, that is, 'perception of social justice as an equal distribution of both happiness and suffering' (p. 519).

> I am always on equal terms with them [followers. If there are some works being carried in our village, I am not standing apart and giving managerial instructions, but I take a shovel myself and work together with the group. That is, leader is a person who is ready to lead and mobilise an individual or a group of people to some achievement or solution of a problem, with his own personal example and own actions. *(Young Social Leader)*

> And funnily enough, there should be some humility, although there is also a fine line between ambition and humility. That is, you create not for yourself, but for the others. And this is the value – to satisfy yourself and your ambitions. *(Senior Business Leader)*

The leaders often spoke about themselves and their perceptions of their leadership in ways that appeared to be humble and self-effacing, often denying that they were leaders at all:

> I have never considered myself as a leader. I have deemed myself a person who just really does something for good. *(Senior Social Leader)*

> The problem is that at the end of the day I do not consider myself a leader, because I am not the 'first face'. I am rather a service, that is, maybe of rather good quality, but service. If you look at leadership here, I have a big 'kollektiv', with all the branches that report to me personally as the head of financial division, I would estimate it to be five thousand people across Russia. *(Senior Business Leader)*

> Broadly speaking, I have some leadership characteristics, and this was clear from the very childhood when I used to lead all those neighbourhood games. In addition, I was captain of the combined regional volleyball team. But I would not identify myself as a leader. *(Senior Business Leader)*

> You simply 'plough' *[=work hard]* like a horse, and naturally, make the job interesting for the other people so that they would be willing to work next to you. If you suggest / inspire this in them, then you might consider yourself... Not consider yourself a leader. *(Senior Business Leader)*

In the narratives of the interviewees, one of the reasons for the influence of the Collective identity, this sense of a 'collective us' was significant, and seemed to be of importance. The two quotes below represent the possible origins of these feelings in the leaders' consciousness; one focuses on survival; the other portrays the influence of the Soviet times on Russian people:

> I think that in Russia we have this feeling that we are all together with you, that leaders say 'We are together'. Even if you consider the New Year speech of Medvedev, of course this is funny from one side, but on the other – normal, that he says that we are Russians going through

a hard period, holding the bar, that we are together... And this has always been there, and I think that this is cool. *(Young Social Leader)*

If you take into account the 80 years long period of soviet history and maybe even before, then the term... in general, differentiation between yourself and others was not welcome. And since everyone was equal and we were building communism, in which you are a part of big history (one), you do not stand out (two), you are humble, you are giving away all your potential powers / efforts for construction of the future – then there was no phenomenon of leader. *(Senior Business Leader)*

The paternalistic and authoritative leader

A leader is a person who others follow. I think this way. A person who has something to show to the others. Who can somehow inspire, carry people along. *(Young Social Leader)*

Unlike the Collective Leader identity, the Paternalistic Leader identity sets the leader apart from their *kollektiv*. This is a constant paradox in the narratives of the leaders. The leaders' stories show two sides of paternalism, caring on the one hand, yet sometimes also the cruel and strong leadership that Russian people desire (Kets de Vries, 2001) and a tendency to domination and search for respect, not love or sympathy (Mikheyev, 1987). On the one hand, this identity makes leaders set themselves apart, act in a superior manner, patronizing, and tough towards their followers; on the other, it makes them take responsibility for the employees, care for them and protect them from the outside world.

A distinctive element of this identity is charisma, a good sense of humour and a positive influence on other people.

Personal charm is important, and it is very important to be fully absorbed with the process and be able to infect with this 'drive' the people around him. *(Young Social Leader)*

He was able to lead people after him from scratch, jump on a barricade, shout in a very inspiring way and move forwards. And through interaction with him, I understood how important personal charisma is, one's conviction in their own words, absolute conviction about themselves, yes, how confidence influences people. *(Young Business Leader)*

The Paternalistic Leader identity is also concerned with followers' personal development and emotional and mental welfare:

> This is not simple exploitation of people, but you understand that this is future of this company. That's why you share with them; you permit them empathy and allow that they might become better than you are. *(Senior Business Leader)*

Having a position of authority and trust of their followers, leads the Paternalistic Leader identity to feel responsible for people and the result.

> I understood that now I have a feeling of responsibility that I should not let down all the people, and this was a strong motivational factor. *(Young Social Leader)*

According to the GLOBE studies' findings, Russia scored very high on the *power distance* scale of behaviour and this despite a significantly lower score on the 'should be scale'. Grachev (2009) sees this as a response to Russia's struggle to balance order in society with democracy. This sense of separation of a leader in their superior position from the followers, according to their narratives, came from their individual experiences:

> You can never allow yourself boorishness towards your subordinates – on the one hand. But on the other, buddy-buddy manners are not welcome either. *(Senior Business Leader)*

> You cannot make friends with subordinates, this is almost unreal, and otherwise it's very hard to ask afterwards ... This is almost impossible, you have to understand it from the very beginning. *(Senior Business Leader)*

Juggling identities – the 'chameleon' leader

In this research we have found that this multifaceted set of identities is present, often simultaneously, in the narratives of every individual we interviewed. Mikheyev (1987) has reported that Russians adapt their behaviour to the person they face in the context they find themselves in almost immediately; and we found evidence that Russian leaders appeared to be constantly juggling these identities even within a single sentence. An example of such shifting identities is illustrated in the following interview extract:

A priori Russians treat each other with suspicion. That is, *a priori no one smiles, 'by default' the attitude towards you is negative.*	*Surviving*
	Feeling
But the moment a person proves he does not deserve that negative attitude, *he is immediately being accepted in the club.*	*Collective*
	Feeling
There is immediate fraternisation, all that human-love-good etc. Because this is not emotional openness I guess, but rather after you pass a starting test, a Russian will give all of him away. He gives a lot, and not like Thai people do, who are just very 'friendly' and that's why they are 'nice'. They are 'friendly' simply in their life. And there are Europeans who always have a certain barrier.	*Surviving*
They will never let you into their inner world. And Russians will. And that's that...heartfelt generosity. We, Russians, we do not feel sorry for ourselves.	
(Young Business Leader)	

Discussion and conclusions

The research has identified six leader identities which appear to co-exist in the behaviours of all the leaders we interviewed and were exhibited both simultaneously and in contradiction in the leaders' narratives according to the context and situation. These are leader as builder, leader as survivor, leader as thinker, the feeling leader, the collective leader, the paternalistic/ authoritative leader. When combined we see a chameleon leader who exhibits these simultaneously often in the same sentence.

Reflecting on leadership identities in Russia against the backdrop of the country's emergence as a BRIC country and therefore as a fast developing economy, and on the leaders' identities as shaped by that context we also found a number of key factors that may have implications for future research into leadership in emerging economies and transitional economies.

1. The Russian leaders have a strong vision of the future they want to create, and work towards achievement of their results both short-term and long-term.
2. Creativity, flexibility and adaptability are seen as essential for organizational sustainability; toughness and control as important for its survival.

3. Deep education and broad cultural knowledge is seen to enable the leaders to operate within their own zone of responsibility, but also to make judgements outside their expertise, especially when they have to act in an unexpected environment.

4. Inner moral values are the reference points that allow the leaders to stay 'authentic' in making their decisions. However, changing the broad guidelines or rules of the game according to the changing context while keeping these values intact is seen as a skill needed for turbulent times.

5. A sense of collectivism and equality can be a motivating factor in certain work environments, especially if the organization is built on fair and just principles. Devotion and self-sacrifice of the leader is seen as essential for a bright future for Russia.

6. While an authoritative / superior position of a leader is something to be used with caution, the other side of this in the Russian context is the care and protection of their followers.

7. Finally, it is the ability to balance and combine these apparently competing identities, almost simultaneously, according to the changing demands of the context that makes Russian leaders stand out.

The multiple, conflicting but often simultaneous Russian leaders' identities that we have found in our research support many of the longstanding findings on the Russian mentality as discussed in the literature sections above. However, the depth and texture of our findings, offered through the lenses and narratives of the leaders we interviewed, provide a rich picture of the complexity and contradictions that Russian leaders today experience in their daily lives and roles, thus adding to previous findings. Our research offers a colourful illustration of the 'menu' of identities from which Russian leaders choose (consciously or unconsciously), and how these often competing identities influence their behaviour and decisions.

Many of the leaders started their careers prior to the 1990s, and these leaders were able to offer insights into the dramatic shift in their thinking and practice that took place as a result of the remarkable shifts that they lived through in the political, social and economic climate of Russia, during and after the Soviet era. Most of the leaders saw their personal values as remaining constant, being given to them by their parents (Mikheyev, 1987), while acknowledging at the same time that the external guidelines and rules of the game had changed dramatically.

A number of implications for leadership 'identity' research might also be drawn from this study. In the West, the dominant narrative is of a single 'authentic self', with other identities being viewed as inauthentic or simply acting. Leaders consequently often seek self-awareness above all else, and see the quest for their inner core or fixed self as an overarching goal of leadership development. However, in the thinking of these Russian leaders we have found a much more fluid notion of identity, as behaviourally driven and contextually shifting, tailored ephemerally to a context. This mirrors Mikheyev's (1987) explanation of light, grey and dark areas of one's knowledge of the world.

This research also makes a methodological contribution. The two researchers adopted insider (Russian researcher) and outsider (UK researcher) lenses as a way to deepen our analysis. We were keen to learn what surprised each of us in our dual readings of each interview and to discuss and learn from our different perceptions. We are not aware of a similar approach to the coding of qualitative interviews in leadership research. This was also invaluable when working with the language of the leaders, especially when interpretation involved both literal translation and explanation of the connotations and nuances of this language. This has previously been shown to be a source of frustration in a Russian-foreign working environment (Camiah & Hollinshead, 2003). We were able to turn this frustration to a methodological advantage.

Our findings suggest a great deal of scope for further research. An ethnographic study of Russian leaders, investigating how these conflicting and competing identities play out in practice, and how each is triggered by context or situation would be a valuable extension to our research. The leader–follower relationships in Russia have been explored in this study solely from the leaders' perspectives. Further research into the relational aspects of Russian leadership would benefit from seeking the followers' perspectives.

We are also curious to know whether some of these identities might be found in other transitional or fast emerging economies, thus replica studies in other BRIC countries would be very valuable for global leadership research. Generational and gender differences were also noted in this study, although not explored in depth. Consequently, further research into the gendered and cross-generational leadership identities in Russia and other fast developing economies would also be beneficial. The relationship between leadership identities, and the political, social and economic contexts in which the leadership is situated has been explored very little to date. The findings of this research suggest that there is scope and need for more research in this area since it has a great deal to contribute to the western-centric literature on global leadership.

References

Alexashin, Y. and Blenkinsopp, J. 2005. Changes in Russian Managerial Values: A Test of the Convergence Hypothesis?, *International Journal of Human Resource Management* 16(3): 427–44.

Ardichvili, A. and Gasparashvili, A. 2003. Russian and Georgian Entrepreneurs and Non-entrepreneurs: A Study of Value Differences, *Organization Studies* 24(1): 29–46.

Ardichvili, A., Cardozo, R. and Gasparishvili, A. 1998. Leadership Styles and Management Practices of Russian Entrepreneurs: Implications for Transferability of Western HRD Interventions, *Human Resource Development Quarterly* 9(2): 145–55.

Barton, H. and Barton, L. C. 2010. Trust and Psychological Empowerment in the Russian Work Context, *Paper presented at BAM conference 2010*.

Bollinger, D. 1994. The Four Cornerstones and Three Pillars in the 'House of Russian' Management System, *The Journal of Management Development* 13(2): 49–54.

Camiah, N. and Hollinshead, G. 2003. Assessing the Potential for Effective Cross-cultural Working Between 'New' Russian Managers and Western Expatriates, *Journal of World Business* 38(3): 245–61.

Day, D. V. and Harrison, M. M. 2007. A Multilevel, Identity-based Approach to Leadership Development, *Human Resource Management Review* 17: 360–73.

Day, D. V., Harrison, M. M. and Stanley, S. M. 2009. *An Integrative Approach to Leader Development: Connecting Adult Development, Identity, and Expertise.* New York: Psychology Press.

DeRue, D. S. and Ashford S. J. 2010. Who Will Lead and Who Will Follow? A Social Process of Leadership Identity Construction in Organizations, *Academy of Management Review* 35(4): 627–47.

Engelhard, J. and Nägele, J. 2003. Organizational Learning in Subsidiaries of Multinational Companies in Russia, *Journal of World Business* 38(3): 262–77.

Fey, C. 2008. Overcoming a Leader's Greatest Challenge: Involving Employees in Firms in Russia, *Organizational Dynamics* 37(3): 254–65.

Fey, C. and Denison, D. R. 2003. Organizational Culture and Effectiveness: Can American Theory Be Applied in Russia?, *Organization Science* 14(6): 686–706.

Fey, C., Nordahl, C. and Zätterström, H. 1999. Organizational Culture in Russia: The Secret to Success, *Business horizons* 42(6):47–55.

Gilbert, K. and Cartwright, S. 2008. Cross-cultural Consultancy Initiatives to Develop Russian Managers: An Analysis of Five Western Aid-funded Programs, *Academy of Management Learning & Education* 7(4): 504–17.

Grachev, M. 2009. Russia, Culture, and Leadership. Cross-cultural Comparisons of Managerial Values and Practices, *Problems of Post-Communism* 56(1): 3–11.

Gvozdeva, E. S. and Gerchikov, V. I. 2002. Sketches for a Portrait of Women Managers, *Russian Social Science Review* 43(4): 72–85.

Holden, N., Kuznetsov, A. and Whitelock, J. 2008. Russia's Struggle with the Language of Marketing in the Communist and Post-communist Eras, *Business History* 50(4): 474–88.

Hollinshead, G. and Michailova, S. 2001. Blockbusters or Bridge-builders? The Role of Western Trainers in Developing New Entrepreneurialism in Eastern Europe, *Management Learning* 32(4): 419–36.

Hopkins, E. 1974. Literature in the Schools of the Soviet Union, *Comparative Education* 10(1): 25–34.

Ivancevich, J. M., DeFrank, R. S. and Gregory, P. R 1992. The Soviet Enterprise Director: An Important Resource Before and After the Coup, *Academy of Management Executive* 6(1): 42–55.

Izyumov, A. and Razumnova, I. 2000. Women Entrepreneurs in Russia: Learning to Survive the Market, *Journal of Developmental Entrepreneurship* 5(1): 1–19.

Kempster, S. 2009 *How Managers Have Learnt to Lead. Exploring the Development of Leadership Practice.* London: Palgrave Macmillan.

Kets de Vries, M. 2000. A Journey into the 'Wild East': Leadership Style and Organizational Practices in Russia, *Organizational Dynamics* 28(4): 67–81.

Kets de Vries, M. 2001. The Anarchist Within: Clinical Reflections on Russian Character and Leadership Style, *Human Relations* 54(5): 585–627.

Kets de Vries, M. Shekshnya, S. Korotov, K. and Florent-Treacy, E. 2004. *The New Russian Business Leaders.* Cheltenham: Edward Elgar.

Kets de Vries, M., Korotov, K. and Shekshnya, S. 2008. Russia: A Work in Progress. Transcending the Fifth 'Time of Troubles', *Organizational Dynamics* 37(3): 211–20.

Khapova, S. and Korotov, K. 2007. Dynamics of Western Career Attributes in the Russian Context, *Career Development International* 12(1): 68–85.

Korotov, K. 2008. Citius, Altius, Fortius: Challenges of Accelerated Development of Leadership Talent in the Russian Context, *Organizational Dynamics* 37(3): 277–87.

Ledeneva, A. 2008. *Blat* and *Guanxi*: Informal Practices in Russia and China, *Comparative Studies in Society and History* 50(1):118–44.

Ledeneva, A. 2009. From Russia with *Blat*: Can Informal Networks Help Modernize Russia?, *Social Research* 76(1): 257–88.

Luhrmann, T. and Ederl, P. 2007. Leadership and Identity Construction: Reframing the Leader–Follower Interaction from an Identity Theory Perspective, *Leadership* 3(1): 115–27.

Markus. H. and Wurf, E. 1987. The Dynamic Self-concept: A Social Psychological Perspective. *Annual Review of Psychology* 38: 299–337.

Metcalfe, B. D. and Afanassieva, M. 2005. The Woman Question? Gender and Management in the Russian Federation, *Women in Management Review* 20(6): 429–45.

Mikheyev, D. 1987. The Soviet Mentality, *Political Psychology* 8(4): 491–523.

Puffer, S. 1994. Understanding the Bear: A Portrait of Russian Business Leaders, *Academy of Management Executive* 8(1): 41–54.

Shamir, B., Dayan-Horesh, H. and Adler, D. 2005. Leading by Biography: Towards a Life-story Approach to the Study of Leadership, *Leadership* 1(1): 13–29.

Shaw, J. 2010. Papering the Cracks with Discourse: The Narrative Identity of the Authentic Leader, *Leadership* 6(1): 89–108.

Index